Praise for Goddesses of the Americas

Lydia Ruyle's goddess banners are a joy to behold! In Goddesses of the Americas, image, symbols, description and place of origin the Americas tell us about each goddess. It is a full-color experience that can be savored. At the very end of there is a photograph of Lydia in a hallway at the Parliament of the World's Religions, standing between her goddess-banners that line both sides of the hall. Walking that hallway was like going through the pages of this book, an affirmation of the sacred feminine as embodied and experienced.

– **Jean Shinoda Bolen, MD** author of *Goddesses in Everywoman*. Jeanbolen.com

I have been with Lydia Ruyle in a number of countries and I have experienced her powerful Goddess banners flying in many of them: their very presence always brings me into sacred space. For many years, Lydia's banners have provided inspiration for me and for thousands of other people, all over the world. The banners create spiritual community in a unique and beautiful way. This gorgeous and informative new book of Lydia's banners of the Americas is a gift to all who honor the Goddesses of many cultures, in their multiplicity of forms.

– **Miriam Robbins Dexter, Ph.D.**, author of *Whence the Goddesses: A Source Book; Sacred Display: Divine and Magical Female Figures of Eurasia* (with Victor Mair); and co-editor of *Foremothers of the Women's Spirituality Movement: Elders and Visionaries* (with Vicki Noble).

In this beautiful book, sophisticated artwork and valuable information come together to bring back to life the submerged essence of the divine feminine in the American continent.

– **Malgorzata Oleszkiewicz-Peralba**, University of Texas at San Antonio, author of *The Black Madonna in Latin America and Europe: Tradition and Transformation*, and *Fierce Feminine Divinities of Eurasia and Latin America: Baba Yaga, Kali, Pombagira, and Santa Muerte*

The great gift of Lydia Ruyle is that she manifested in space, in physical locations around the world, the consciousness of the Divine in female form. She brought into present time the breadth and potency and passion of this great She by painting the icons of diverse cultures, so She could be seen and remembered.

– **Max Dashu**, founder, Suppressed Histories Archives, author of *Witches and Pagans: Women in European Folk Religion*. www.suppressedhistories.net

Here is the Goddess seen through the collective imaginaries of the peoples of North and South America. The spirits of populations decimated or radically changed the last 500 years of colonization speak to us now in the present day through these archetypal images. As the Goddess returns we are witness to Her infinite and beautiful diversity. Lydia Ruyle's new book makes it possible for everyone to participate in a spiritual festival of colors and cultures. Long may Her banners wave!

– **Genevieve Vaughn**, author of *The Gift in the Heart of Language: The Maternal Source of Meaning*, and *Women and the Gift Economy: A Radically Different Worldview is Possible.*

Lydia Ruyle's wonderful Goddess GIRLS have flown at the Glastonbury Goddess Conference every year since 1998. With their glowing colours and evocative iconic imagery they have lined the walls of the Assembly Rooms, hung from the Town Hall Temple ceiling and in the Courtyard of the Glastonbury Experience. Every year we have carried them in procession through the town of Glastonbury and the landscape of Avalon, singing in praise of Goddess and Her many faces.
Many people have awakened to the multitude of ancient Goddess images from all around world through Lydia's pioneering Goddess Icon banners. We are deeply grateful to Lydia for all she has shared with us so generously over so many years. We love you, Lydia.

– **Kathy Jones**, author of *Priestess of Avalon: Priestess of the Goddess.*
www.goddessconference.com

Artist and mother, Goddess researcher and teacher, Lydia Ruyle exemplifies the generous spirit and clear purpose of women who have dedicated their creativity to the re-emergence of the Divine Feminine. In Goddesses of the Americas, her brilliant and celebratory banners are framed by her true intent. Lydia is here to change the world, and she does this through her art. With contemporary materials, she depicts a multitude of ancient Sacred Female Beings. By doing so, she brings their enduring presences into our lives. She invites us to learn how to honor our own sacred femininity and to honor the enormous diversity of the old cultures who first created these images. Her work shines a bright light on the evidence that we can flourish in loving relationship with ourselves, each other and the Earth. Her commitment to beauty encourages us to reclaim what is sacred in ourselves and in life. The banners are joyful, expressive, abstract, pictorial, colorful, playful, serious and fierce. She lets us in on the secret: the Divine Feminine has a thousand faces. To be among them is to enter a ceremony of remembering what has been forgotten in order to restore balance to the broken world. I am so happy that this gorgeous book will bring her Goddess banners to an even wider audience. Thank you, Lydia, and Goddess Ink, for bringing this gift to us. It is needed now more than ever.

– **Ann Filemyr**, author of *Love Enough and The Healer's Diary*

This is a treasure of a book that beautifully and richly catalogues an astounding and impressive body of work which has travelled the world and been seen and appreciated by thousands of people.

– **Cristina Biaggi**, author of *Habitations of the Goddess, In the Footsteps of the Goddess* and *The Rule of Mars, Readings on the Origin, History and Impact of Patriarchy.*

What a blessing this book is! As I opened the pages and began my first "peek" I knew I would want to return very quickly for a deep appreciation; I have not been disappointed. This book is crammed full of information I had never read before. The full colour pictures of the banners are a gift as are the pictures of Lydia as she travelled to gather this cornucopia of information and beauty. As a High Priestess, training other women to be Priestesses of the Global Goddess, this book will be an important resource when we study the Goddess in the Americas. Thank you Lydia, your legacy will live on and on and on.

– **Anique Radiant Heart**, Priestess of the Global Goddess,
Founder of the Temple of the Global Goddess Maitland, Sacred Singer Songwriter,
Creatrix of 7 internationally acclaimed CDs of sacred music to celebrate and honour the Goddess.
www.goddess.net.au.

Goddesses of the Americas

Spirit Banners of the Divine Feminine

LYDIA RUYLE

Dedication
For Bob, Lydia, David, Stephen, Margaret, Robin, Mae, Katherine, Bridger, Alexandra, Leeden and Remington with all my love.

Printed in the United States of America
ISBN: 978-0-9969617-1-4

Published by

Goddess Ink
www.goddess-ink.com

Goddesses of the Americas:
Spirit Banners of the Divine Feminine
by Lydia Ruyle
www.lydiaruyle.com

Goddesses of the Americas

Spirit Banners of the Divine Feminine

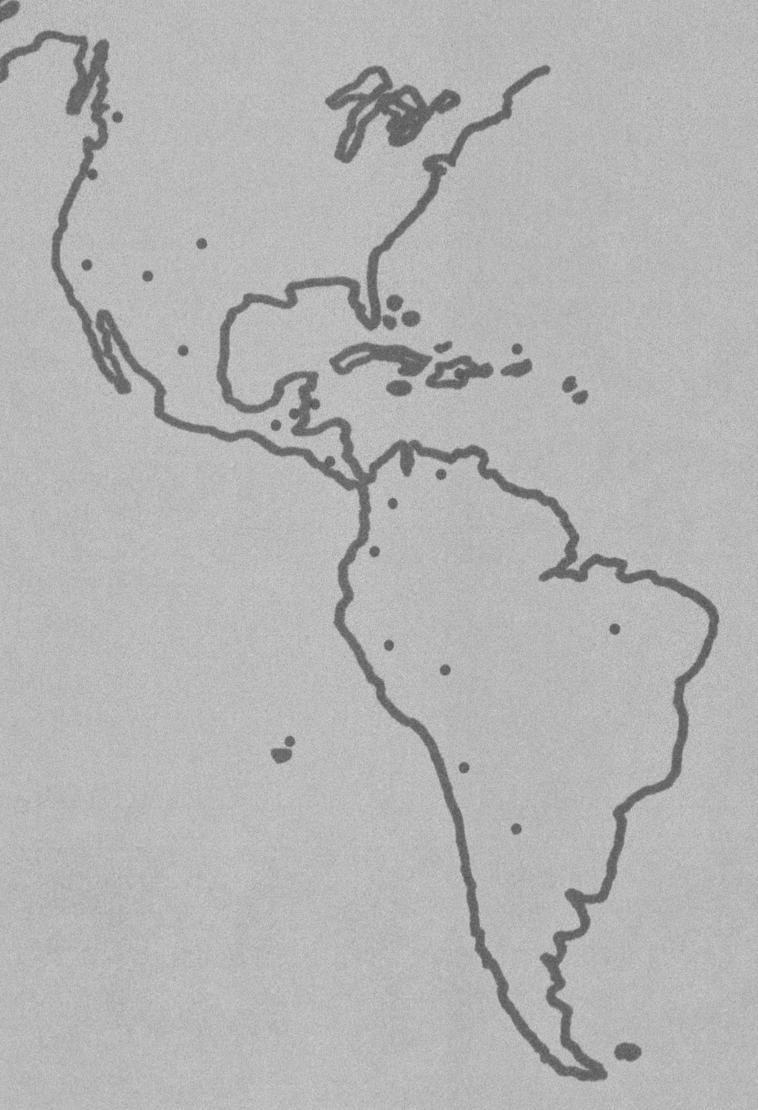

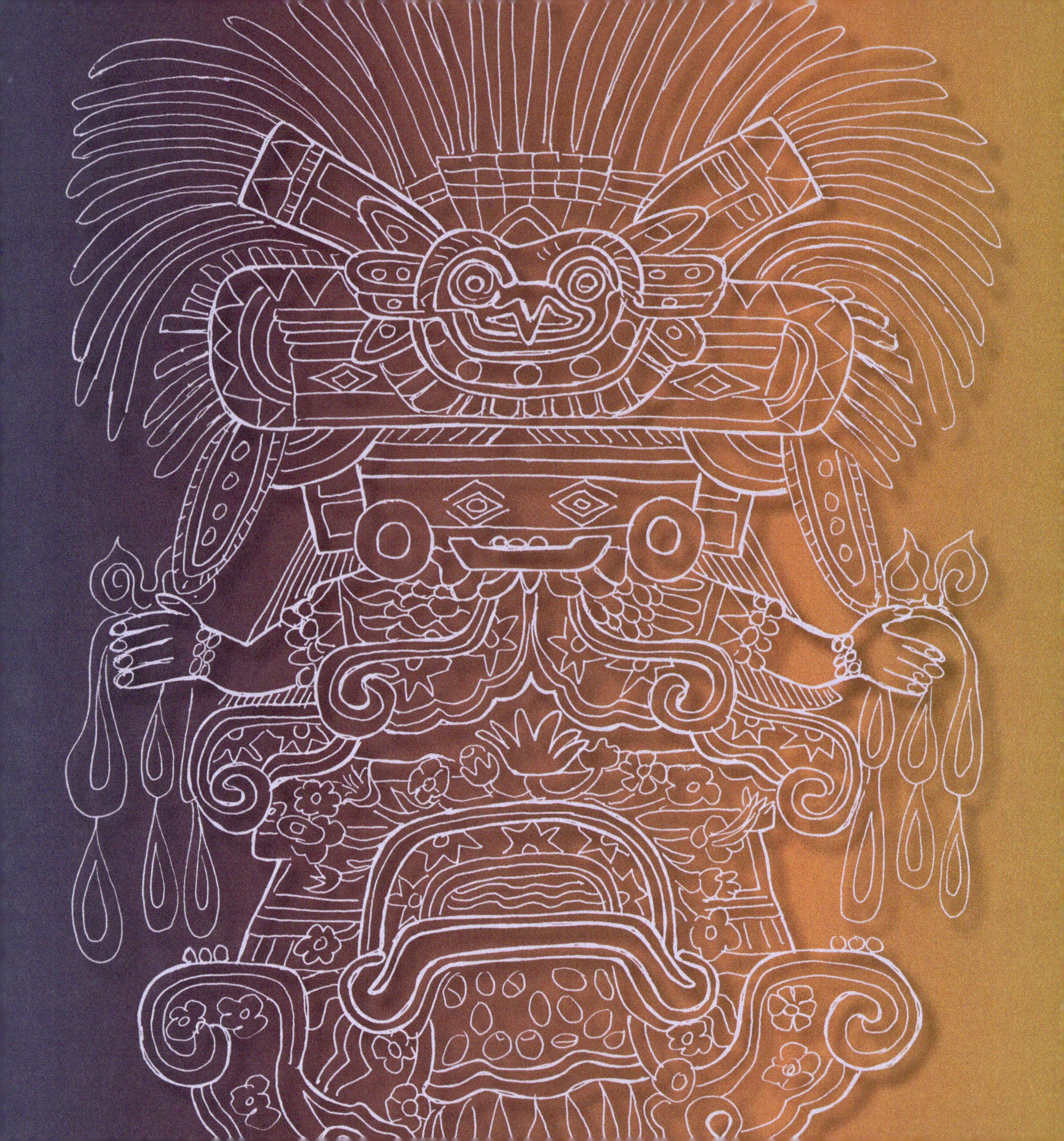

Introduction

Art and the Ancient Mothers call me on a journey. I am an eighty-year-old artist and scholar pursuing goddess research for decades with my mind, body and spirit. I make icons, each image created and revered at some time in human history. Since 1995, the icons have become goddess spirit banners, sacred images of the divine feminine from the many cultures of the world.

How did I find the Goddess? She called me and I listened. She told me to see, touch, learn, laugh, cry and share with art, stories and sacred places of Mother Earth. She continues to support my work. I do my part by eating well, exercising and "keepin' on, keepin' on." Two major bodies of art, crop circle banners and goddess icon spirit banners, have manifested since I was sixty.

Over thirty years ago, I began collecting images of women from art history, which I taught at the University of Northern Colorado, to use in my art. In March 1987, an art exhibition at the Loveland Museum and Gallery in Loveland, Colorado called "Better Homes & Goddesses" was my first display of Goddess icons, born for National Women's History Month.

In 1993, I invited other women to travel to sacred places with goddess tours in England, Wales and Cornwall. Since then, over 300 women have joined me in Britain, Turkey, France, Germany, Greece, Italy, Sicily, Malta, the Czech Republic, Russia, México, Peru, Hawai'i and the southwestern US. On the journeys, we sing, dance, play and learn about the Goddess from very special wise women and each other. The journeys are soul journeys. They are about finding the divine feminine within each of us, and in the culture of each pilgrimage.

I made the first goddess banners in the series for an exhibition in 1995 at the Celsus Library in Ephesus, Turkey, where they flew and spread their energies throughout the month of July. Since then, the banner collection has grown from eighteen to 300. I have used them to empower, teach and share their stories at sacred sites in Australia, New Zealand, China, Cambodia, Japan, South Korea, France, Germany, Hungary, Romania, Bulgaria, Greece, Malta, Finland, England, Iceland, Italy, Belgium, Czech Republic, Poland, Switzerland, México, Canada, Peru, Costa Rica, Brazil, Argentina, Colombia, Russia, Turkey, Ghana, South Africa, India, Nepal, Tibet, Bhutan, Hawai'i and the US.

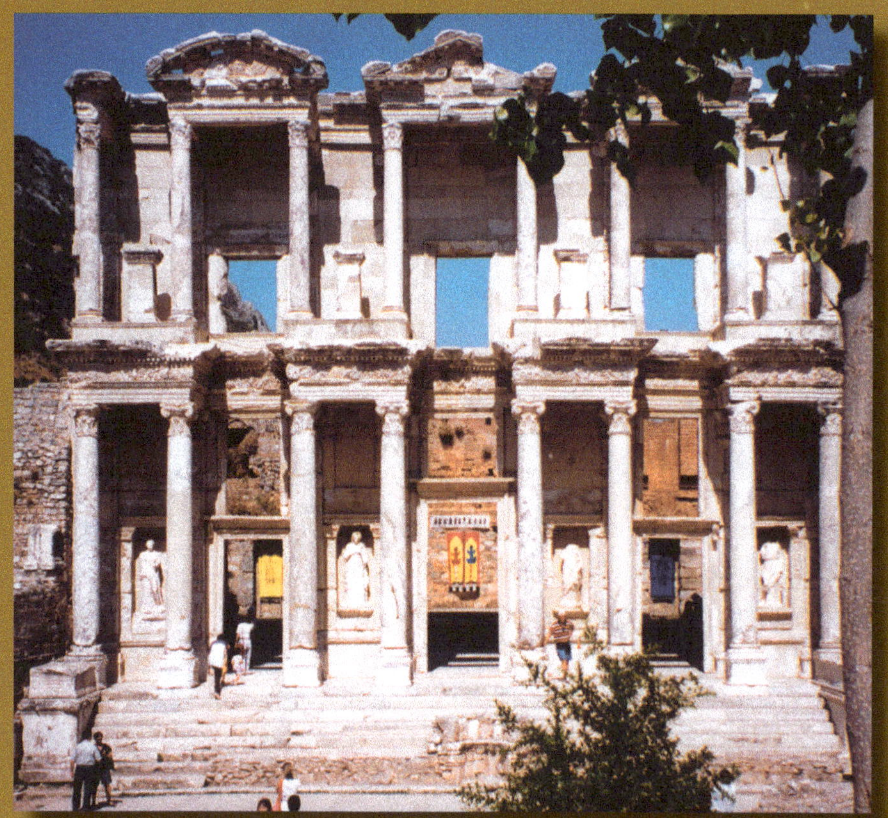

Banners at Celsus Library

The goddess banners transform space and time, making it possible to communicate one-on-one with the divine feminine in her infinite manifestations. Hanging in the Celsus Library, they re-membered the Goddess, stirring the energies and sending them out into the world. They also absorb the energies from each sacred place they visit and share that energy as they travel.

The banner designs reflect the cultural image-making traditions of time and place in the world and in art history. They are portable, lightweight and can be shipped easily. Made of rip-stop nylon, the colors are bright and strong. Most are 36-inches wide by 72-inches long; two are circular like wind socks. They may be hung with light coming through them or on a wall with light reflected from them. They can also hang from poles and be carried in processions. At Machu Picchu, we anchored them with tent stakes.

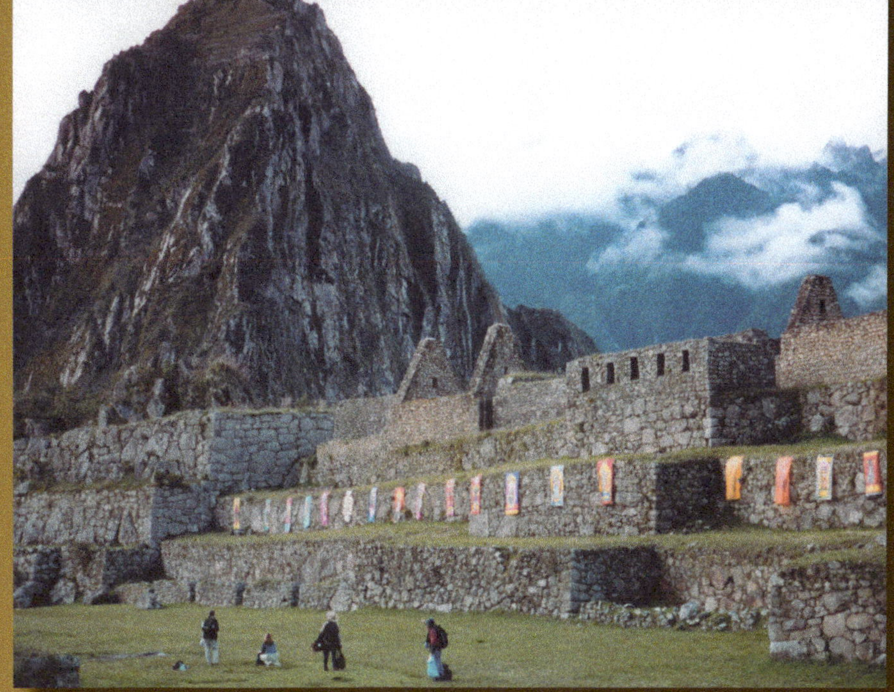

Banners at Machu Picchu

How do I choose the images? They literally find me. When I am invited to an exhibition, I research the images of the feminine divine in a culture and then create banners of these images. My artistic eye sees the visual and spiritual connections.

The first step in creating a banner is to draw the image. Next, I blow it up and have it transferred to rip-stop nylon. Then I design the background. Louise Keirnes, my vexillographer (a person who fabricates flags professionally) then sews the figure and the background, creating a banner. (Louise has sewn all my goddess banners since 1995; she is 87.) Finally, I paint the image using acrylic fabric paints. Recently, I've been using paints that reflect light to enhance the image.

My favorite banner is whichever one I am working on currently. She has my full creative attention and energy. The creative process is like the birth process: inspiration, gestation, effort, manifestation and then letting go and letting be.

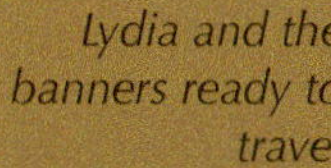

Lydia and the banners ready to travel

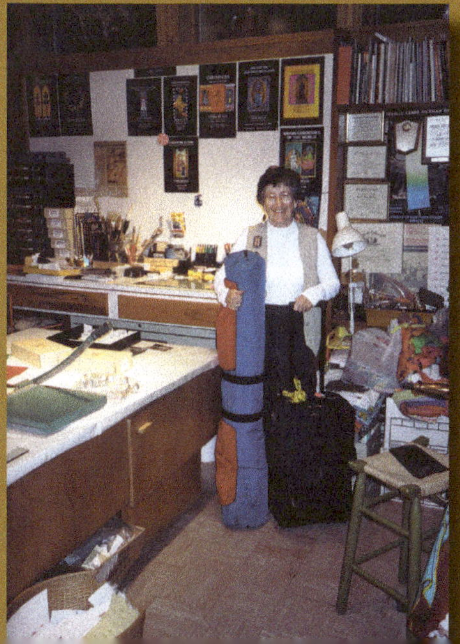

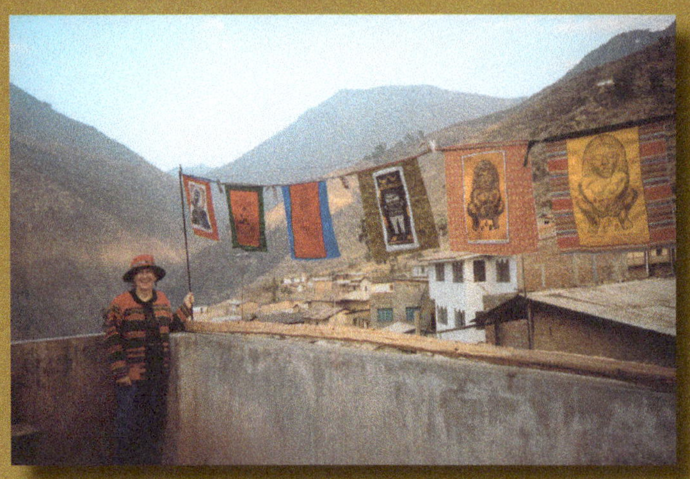

Lydia with Prayer flags at San Pedro de Casta

I create some banners quickly; with others, the process takes years. I create and paint the banners in my home studio, which is made of rammed earth. I literally live and create in Mother Earth on my grandparents' land in Greeley, Colorado, where I am surrounded by art and images of the feminine divine. I also create on my travels. Some of my early banners were painted in a small kitchen on a golf course, and others in studios in Italy and Chicago.

"The girls," as I sometimes call the banners, are multi-million-mile travelers with infinite stories and detours. They hang in conferences, libraries, galleries, kindergartens, art centers, universities, town halls, a golf club, a women's prison, a musical production and, once, at a funeral celebration. Goddess prayer flags, which are eighteen-inches square, are smaller versions of the banners. I leave them at sacred sites to empower the divine feminine herstories and images.

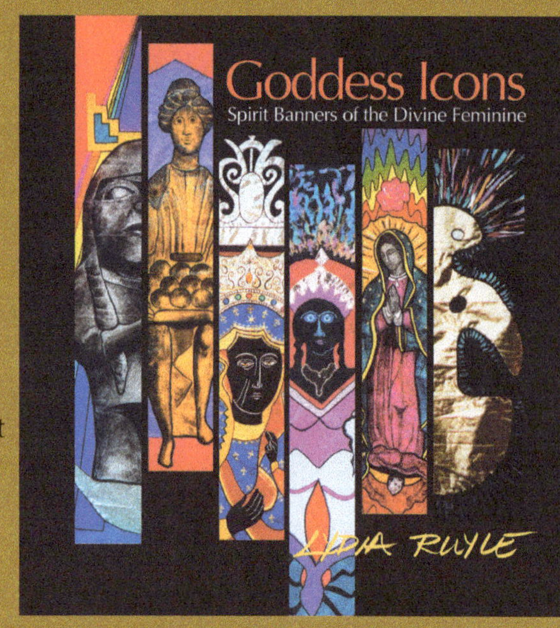

My book, *Goddess Icons: Spirit Banners of the Divine Feminine*, grew out of the many exhibition catalogues I created and photocopied. Now PDFs on my magical Mac record my images and the internet makes it possible for the girls to be in approximately twenty exhibitions around the globe each year. Keeping track of them is a full-time job.

Finding the creative spirit within changes the paradigm without. The great advances of humankind have occurred through creativity and imagination. The creative is the place where no one else has been. You get there by exploring, working hard, taking risks and not quite knowing what you're doing; what you

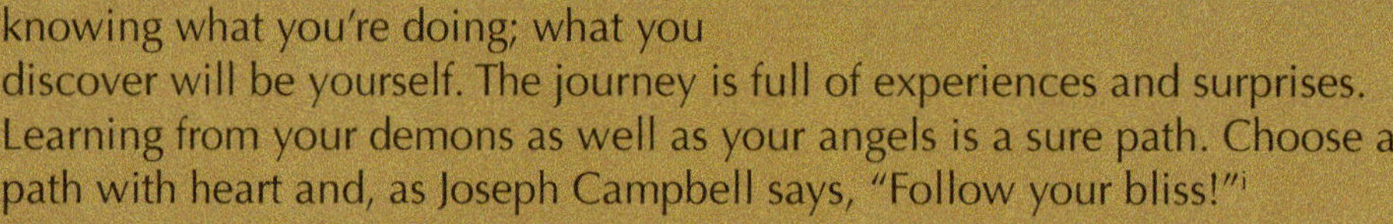

discover will be yourself. The journey is full of experiences and surprises. Learning from your demons as well as your angels is a sure path. Choose a path with heart and, as Joseph Campbell says, "Follow your bliss!"[i]

I believe we are here to learn . . .

I believe we are here to learn and that education is our best hope for the human race and the planet. Human experience, whether written, spoken or recorded in artifacts, art and architecture, links human beings in time and space. Education is how we pass humankind's accumulated knowledge on to future generations. Knowledge develops the foundation for human ethics and values. In our technological world, it is important for us to learn from and understand history; in studying history / herstory, we discover ourselves.

I also believe we are spiritual beings on a human path to learn wisdom and compassion through the choices we make each day, and we are in charge of those choices. Along the way may we laugh, sing, dance and paint, walk in love and beauty, trust the knowledge that comes through the body, speak the truth about conflict and pain, practice generosity, take only what we need and think about the consequences of our actions for the next seven generations.

"You must be the change you wish to see in the world," said Mahatma Gandhi. It's good advice, which I've followed for eight decades with persistence, practice, patience and hard work.

The Ancient Mothers called me to weave a web to bring about a greater consciousness of the divine in each human and in nature, the oneness of all. In my teaching, travels and exhibitions, I meet thousands of people interested in the divine feminine. I call it the Goddess with a Billion Names, Faces and Places.

Terms Used in this Book

Matriglyphs: This is my own term designating female rock art images.

Petroglyphs: These are images created in stone by means of carving or "pecking" the outer stone surface away and exposing the deeper stone surface beneath. Most stone surfaces in the southwest US are covered by a thin layer, called a patina or "desert varnish." This patina is created naturally by the rock's exposure to the elements. Prehistoric people would chisel or peck away this thin, dark outer layer and expose the original stone surface to create petroglyph images. The tools used were simple hand-held hammer stones, stone chisels—often just a small, round river cobble.

Pictographs: These are images painted on a stone surface. Few pictographs survive the ravages of time, most in caves and under rock ledges, where they are protected from the elements. Painted colors include blues made from ground turquoise, reds from iron oxides, white from kaolin, yellow from limonite and blacks or grays from charcoal. Prehistoric people would grind these naturally occurring pigments into a fine powder and then mix them with water, saliva, urine or blood to paint on the stone surface. It is probable that many carved and pecked petroglyphs were originally enhanced with paints, which have now faded. We know this because cup stones, which are small depressions for grinding colored pigments, are often discovered in petroglyph areas.

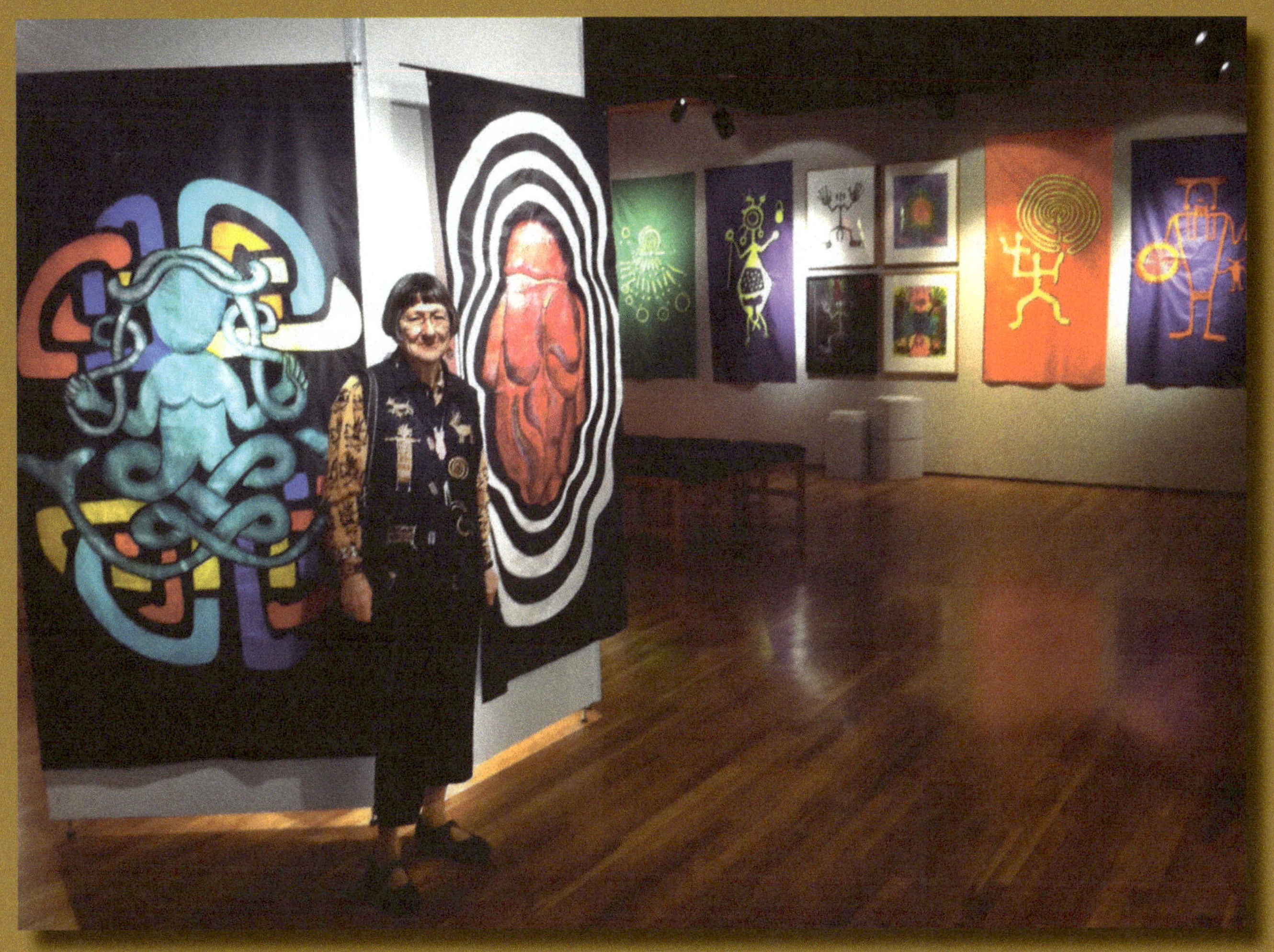

Banner Exhibit, Mariani Gallery, University of Northern Colorado, 2012

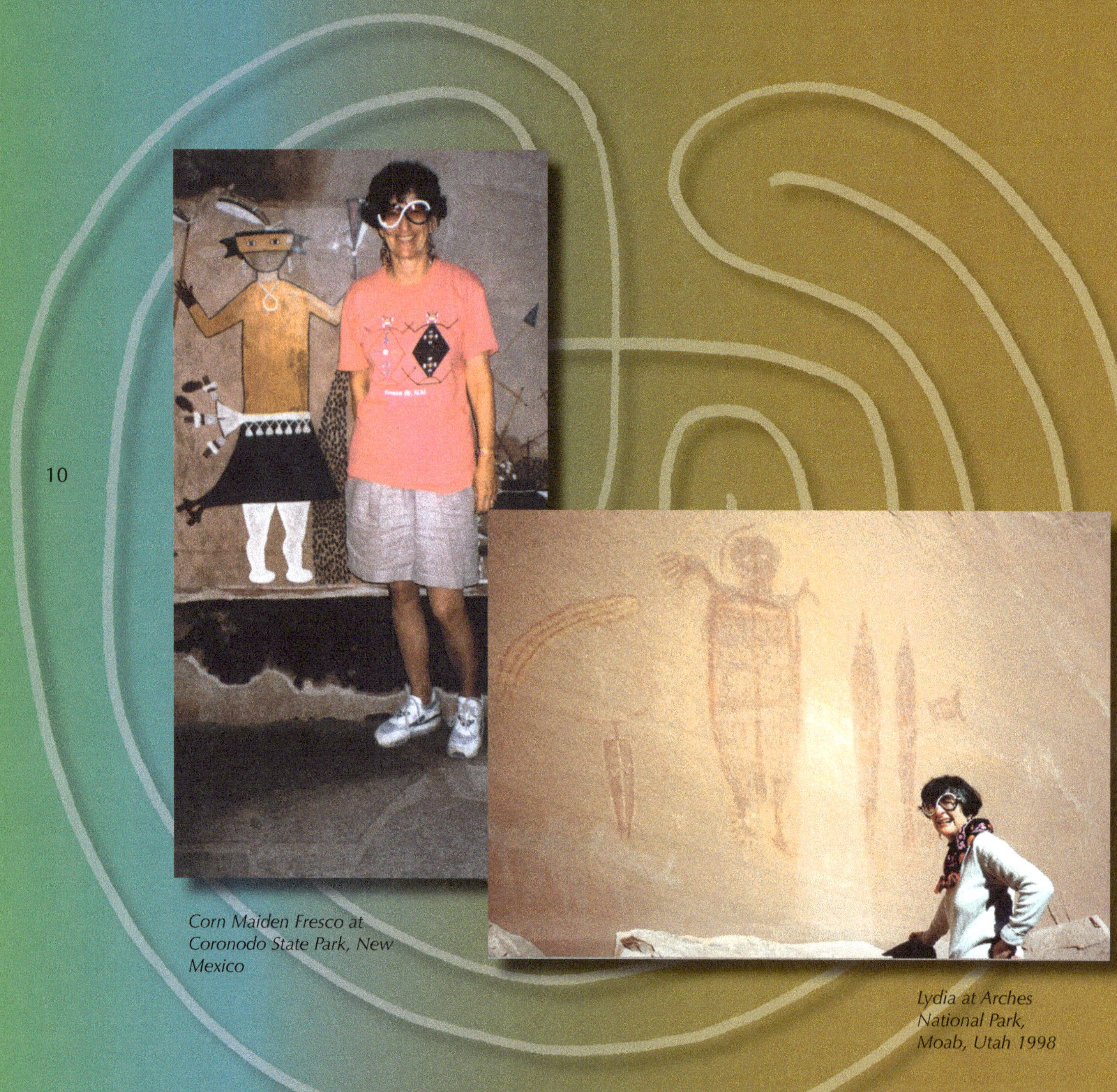

Corn Maiden Fresco at Coronodo State Park, New Mexico

Lydia at Arches National Park, Moab, Utah 1998

North America

In the beginning, Tsechenako, Thought Woman, finished everything, thoughts, and the names of all things. She finished also all the languages. And then our mothers, Uretsete and Naotsete, said they would make names and they would make thoughts. Thus they said, Thus they did.

–Keresan Pueblo saying[ii]

In the Art Center at Ghost Ranch, New Mexico, the light is shining through Crow Mother and the Navajo Twins. Virgin Guadalupe sends her rose essence into the room, the Black Madonna from Chartres blesses the space, Corn Mother offers corn, Spider Grandmother gifts us with her presence. Lydia's banners, waving in the breeze, sanctify the space, changing it from an art classroom into a holy temple. Once I can be with the banners, I feel peaceful and enter into the holy ground which we had prepared.

–Susan Elizabeth Hale, singer, sound healer, author[iii]

North America

Europeans coming to North America had their own framework, their own visual tradition, which bore no resemblance to the art of the Native Americans. Often they were blinded by their own cultural preconceptions and they projected their own world onto that of North America.

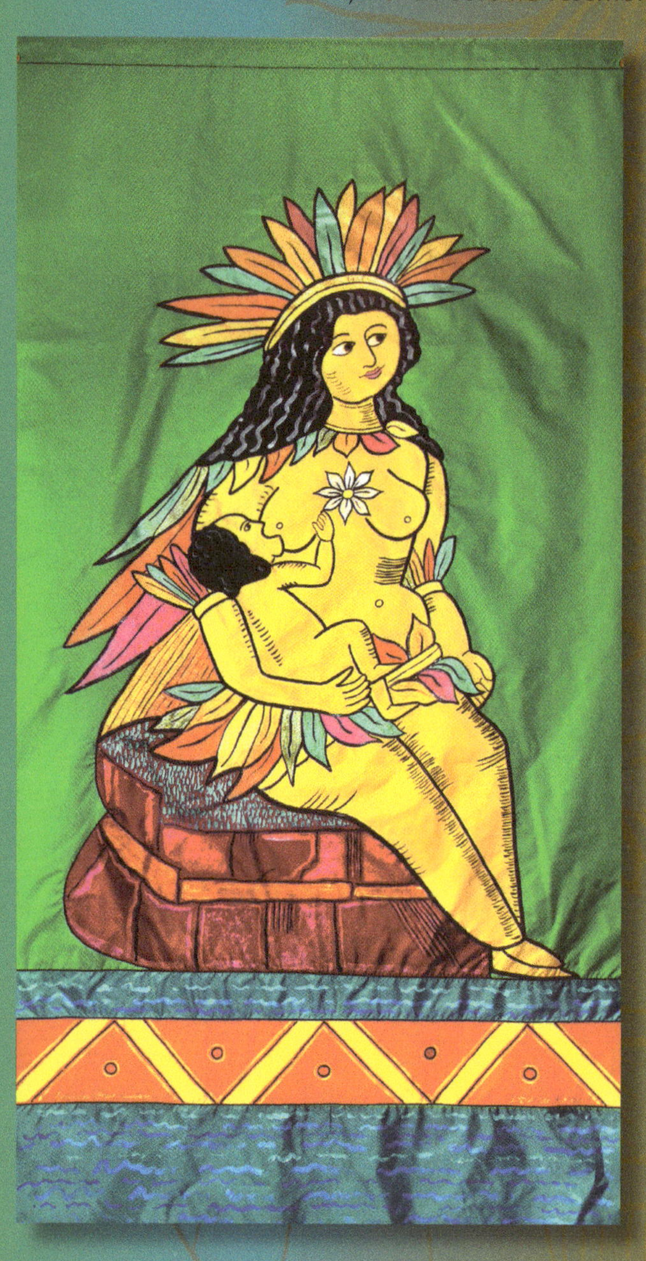

America's great goddess, as envisioned by these early explorers, was a dark-skinned, full-bodied woman wearing a feathered headdress and a skirt of tobacco leaves. When the cultures of Europe met the cultures of the Americas in 1492, she came to symbolize the First Lady of the Americas and the western hemisphere. The First Nations east of the Mississippi River and in the Caribbean were often matrilineal societies in which the clan mothers possessed political power and cultural freedom. They were traders, farmers, artisans and healers. The "Indian princess," as envisioned by the Europeans, is an amalgamation of the European concept of liberty and the goddess Minerva.

I have always loved woodcuts; they are considered to be the earliest print technique. Here is a banner I created based upon an early German woodcut depicting their interpretation of Native Americans, but clearly fused with their European preconceptions and visual tradition.

America's Great Goddess

Source: Woodcut. German. 1505 CE

This ceramic sculpture, which now resides in the Detroit Institute of the Arts, was made by one of the cultures that inhabited the middle of the US and was found in Arkansas. I call her Our Grandmother, Old Woman Who Never Dies; she is the mother of all beings. The lines around the mouth of the kneeling figure emphasize the importance of her words. Her heart energy flows from her center. The copper flowering ornament at the top of the banner originates from a First Nation in what is now Ohio. The spider shell *gorget* (a collar or ornament for the throat) at the center bottom is from Tennessee. The vulva figures on the right and left are derived from Missouri petroglyphs.

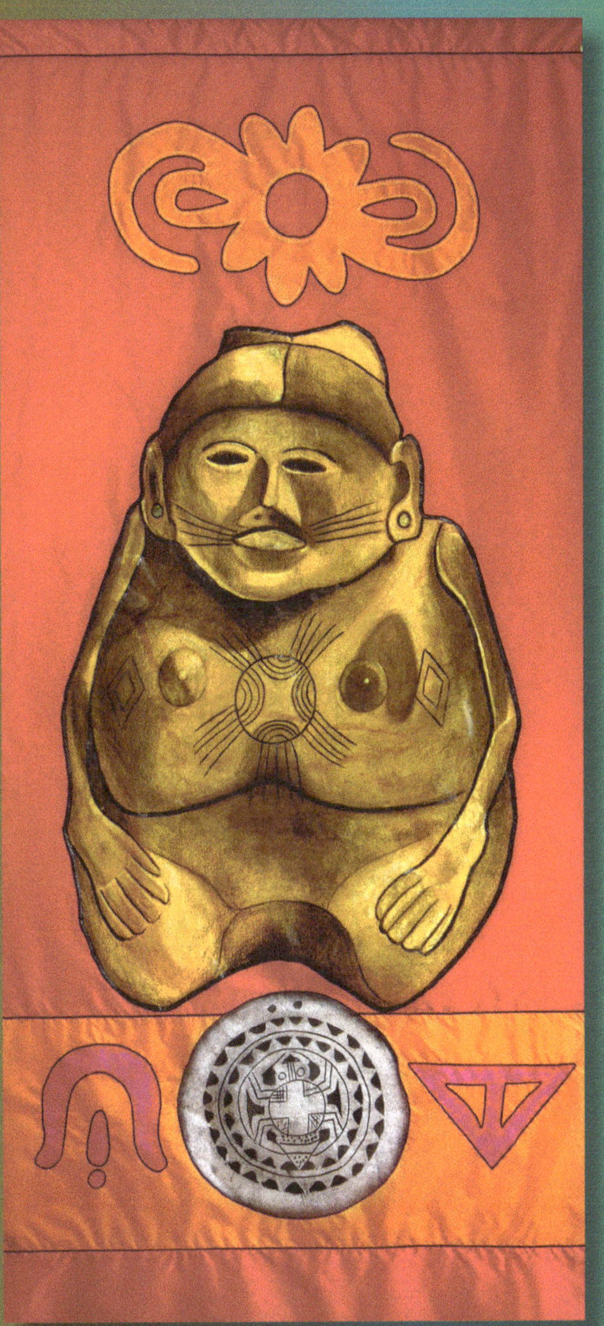

Our Grandmother Old Woman Who Never Dies

Source: Ceramic sculpture. 1350–1500 CE. Arkansas
The Detroit Institute of the Arts
Top: Copper ornament. 1–400 CE. Ohio
Peabody Museum. Harvard
Bottom / center: Engraved shell gorget. c. 1400 CE
Tennessee. State Museum. Nashville
Bottom right / left: Petroglyphs. n.d. Missouri

North America | Southwest

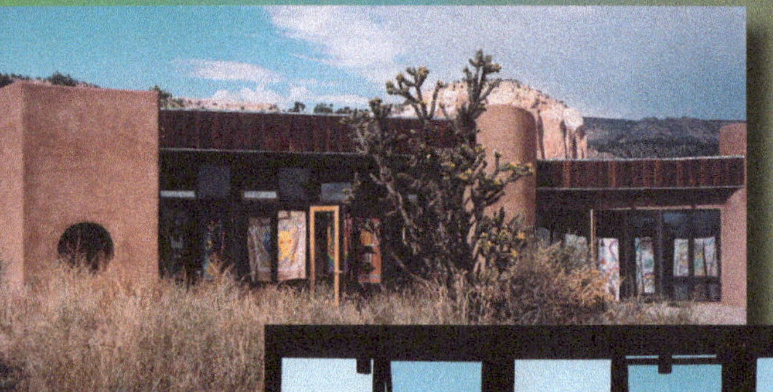

The Southwest banners were first exhibited at Ghost Ranch Art Center in Abiqui, New Mexico in 1997. Every time I have visited, I have felt the sacred feminine energy of the land. Georgia O'Keeffe, one of my artist foremothers, lived and worked there. Small prayer flags of Grandmother Spider Woman and Guadalupe hang today on the shrine at Ground Zero in New York City offering their healing energy.

The sacred feminine creatrix has many names in the southwestern US: Grandmother Spider Woman, Changing Woman, First Mother Moon, Rainbow Woman, Thought Woman, Hard Substances Woman, Crow Mother and Iariko.[iv] Images in rock art and clay were telling her story for thousands of years before the European settlers arrived, including my ancestors. I found her in the landscape, clay, frescoes, kachinas, sand painting, fetishes, rock art and myth.

Upper left: exterior, Ghost Ranch Art Center, Abiqui, New Mexico
Lower left: interior Ghost Ranch Art Center
Right: Prayer Flags at Ground Zero Shrine, St. Paul's New York City, 2001

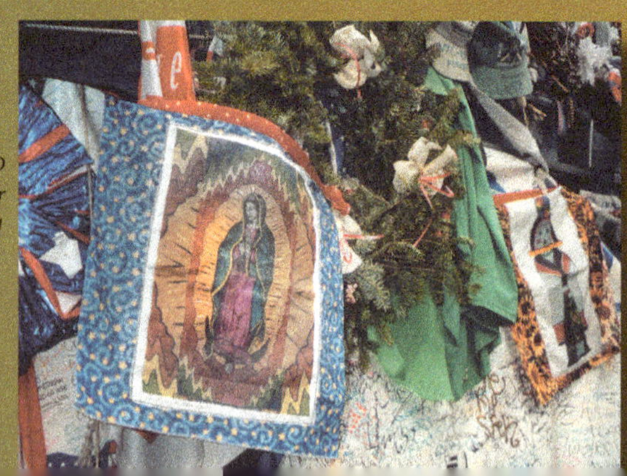

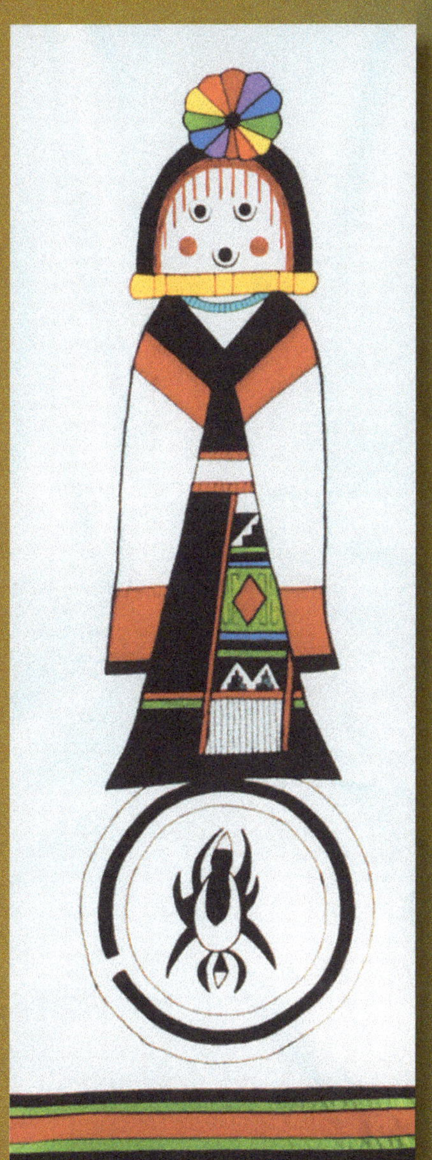

Grandmother Spider Woman weaves and nourishes life. She takes four colors of earth, mixes them with her saliva and shapes four pairs of thoughts. After spinning her cloak of creative wisdom, which she is wearing, she covers the thoughts and sings four pairs of humans into being. She then watches over them for the rest of time. Grandmother Spider Woman rock is the altar at Canyon de Chelly, the Navajo holy ground and outdoor cathedral at Chinle, Arizona. Grandmother Spider Woman loves visitors.

Grandmother Spider Woman

Photo: Canyon de Chelly, Arizona

Corn Maiden calls forth the mysteries of life arising from death, the plant from the seed, the relationships between the underworld of burial (burying the seed) with the world of light and rain. She is about the secret of sustenance connecting the below with the above, the sunlight and the rainclouds. From her vessel, she waters the earth, the pueblo community and the corn tree of life. Corn Maiden stands above a *sipapu* in a fresco in a *kiva* at Coronado State Park in New Mexico. (In Hopi culture, *sipapu* refers to a small hole in the floor of a kiva, a room used by the Pueblans for religious rituals.) Corn Maiden is surrounded with images of the mysteries of growing food. Corn maidens are found also in Zuni stone fetishes and Hopi *katsinas,* a type of doll representing rainmaking messengers. On the mesa to the east of the Zuni pueblo, which is called Dowa Yolanne, meaning "our mother," corn maidens nurture and protect the Zuni pueblo.

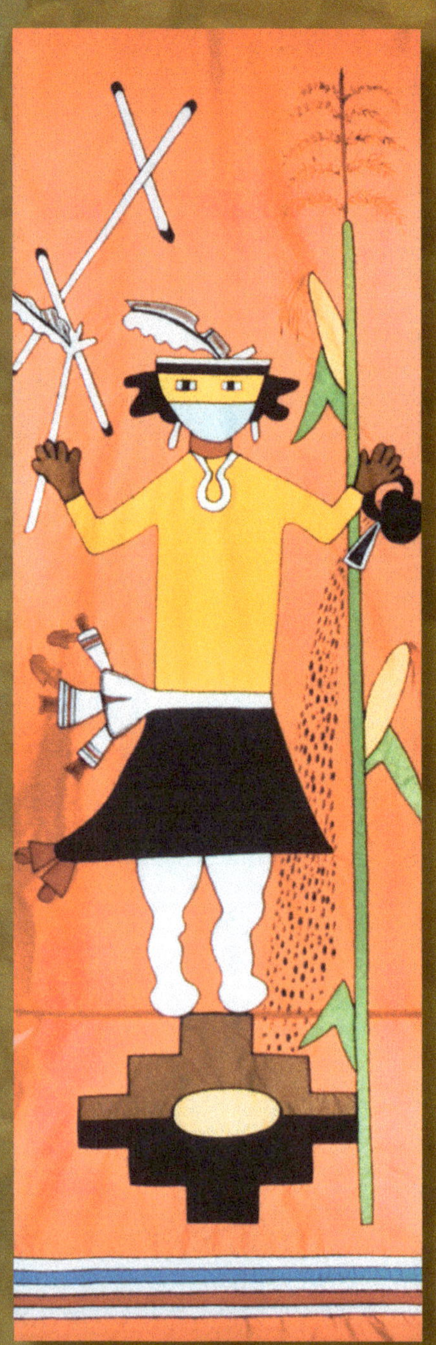

Corn Maiden

Source: Wall fresco
Kiva
Coronado State Park
Bernalillo, New Mexico

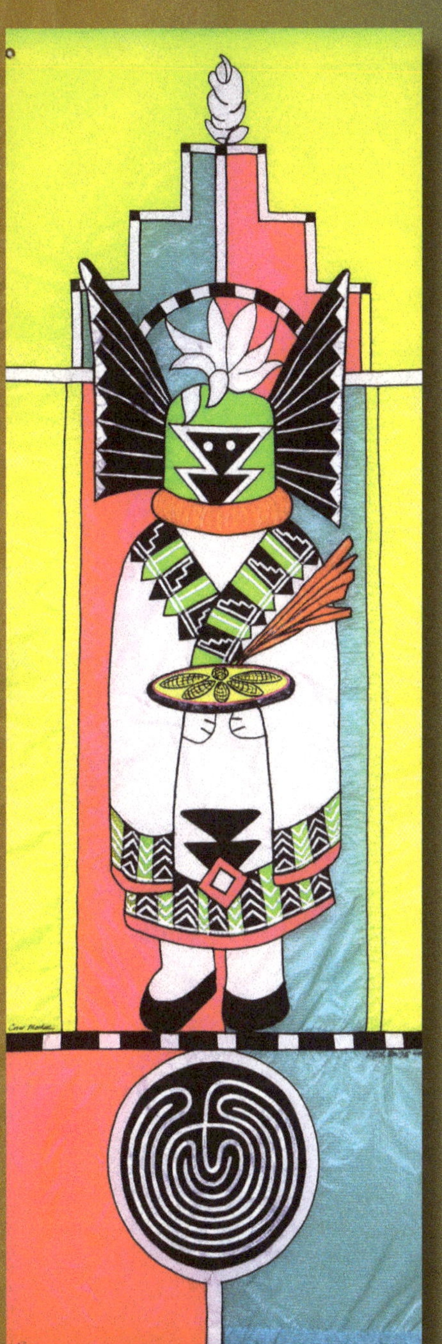

Crow Mother is the mother of all the *katsinas* who are spirits of the Hopi universe. The Hopi, whose name means "peace," believe all beings in the universe carry energy. They are one of the oldest living pueblo cultures and reside on three mesas in northern Arizona. Crow Mother appears during the *powamu*, or "bean dance." She offers corn to sustain life, and branches, or switches, for discipline and protection. The labyrinth she stands upon symbolizes the intricate human journey. Black crows are attracted to humans and love the corn humans grow.

Crow Mother

Source: Katsina. Painted wood
Hopi. Museum of Northern Arizona. Flagstaff

North America | Southwest

Mother Earth and Father Sky in sacred marriage birth the worlds together, creating all. The sun, moon and stars are in Father Sky's ample belly. The sacred plants grow from Mother Earth's vulva. Both hold growing stalks of sacred corn in their right hands. The pair is surrounded by Rainbow Woman, who brings essential water as they walk the beauty way.

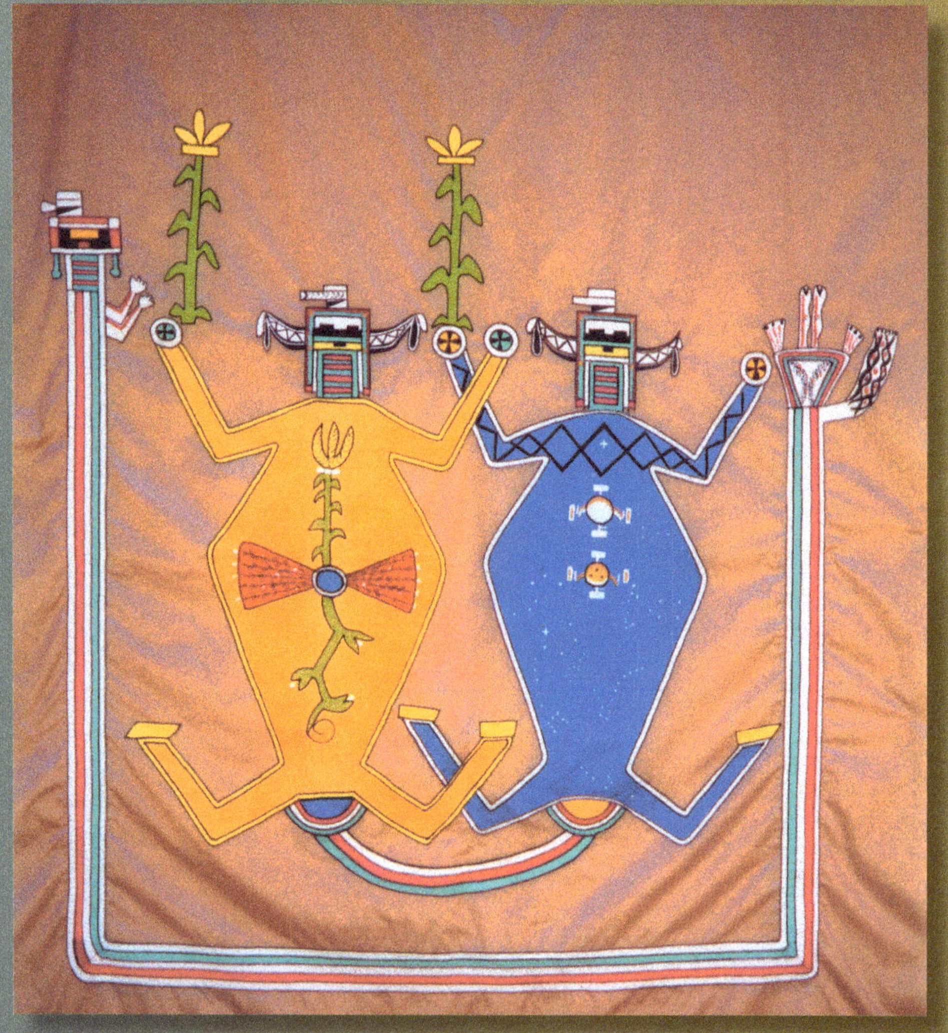

Mother Earth Father Sky

Source: Sand painting. Navajo

The Fremont Goddess fervently protects her tribe. Tears of compassion flow from her eyes. She is trapezoidal in shape and wears necklaces, a belt and a skirt. Her pubic triangle connects her to the *sheela-na-gigs* of other world cultures, which depict the cycles of birth, death and regeneration. The horned snake with breasts, below, is from rock art discovered in Arizona.

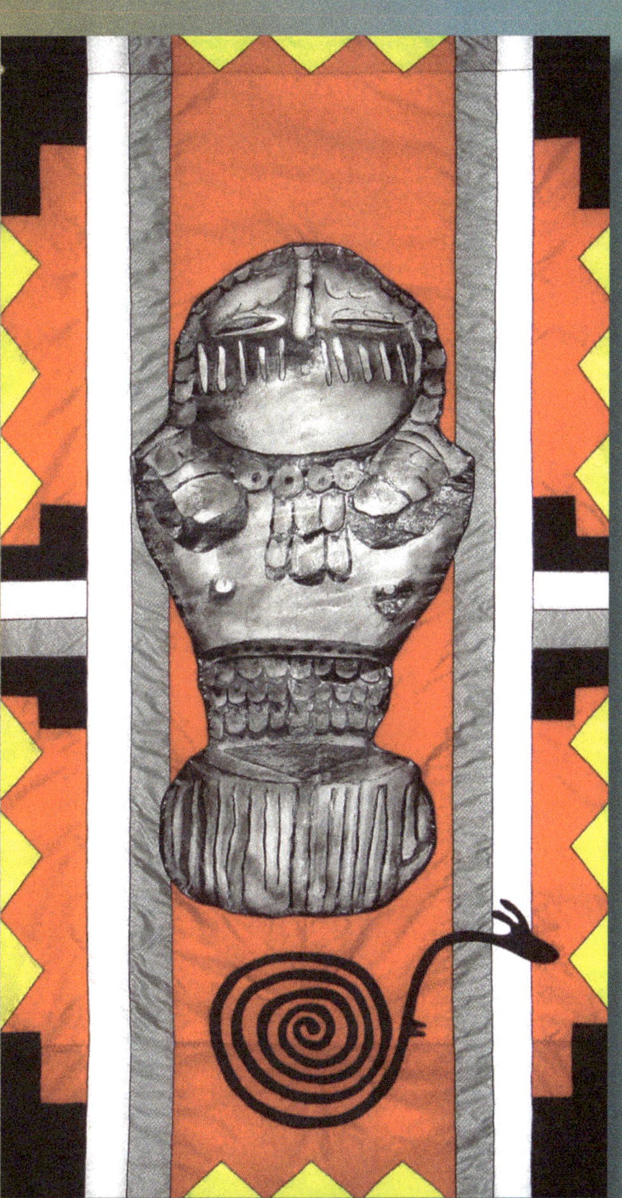

Fremont Goddess

Source: Clay sculpture. 900–1000 CE
Prehistoric Museum of Eastern Utah. Price, Utah
Background: Clay vessels. Snake Valley, Wasatch Plateau
Bottom: Rock art. Nine Mile Canyon, Utah

Hocker Matriglyph "Hocker" is a term used by scholars and archaeologists to describe native peoples' rock art images of females in a position of sacred display. The shapes on both sides of her head are hair coils. The emphasis on the labia suggests a complex meaning of initiation or transition and links Hocker to sacred display figures from around the world. The hands are those of the artist from a monoprint she created in 1994.

Hocker Matriglyph

Source: Rock art Image Female Figure. n.d. Canyon de Chelly, Canyon del Muerto. Arizona in Alex Patterson's A Field Guide to Rock Art Symbols of the Greater Southwest Johnson Books: Boulder, Colorado.1992

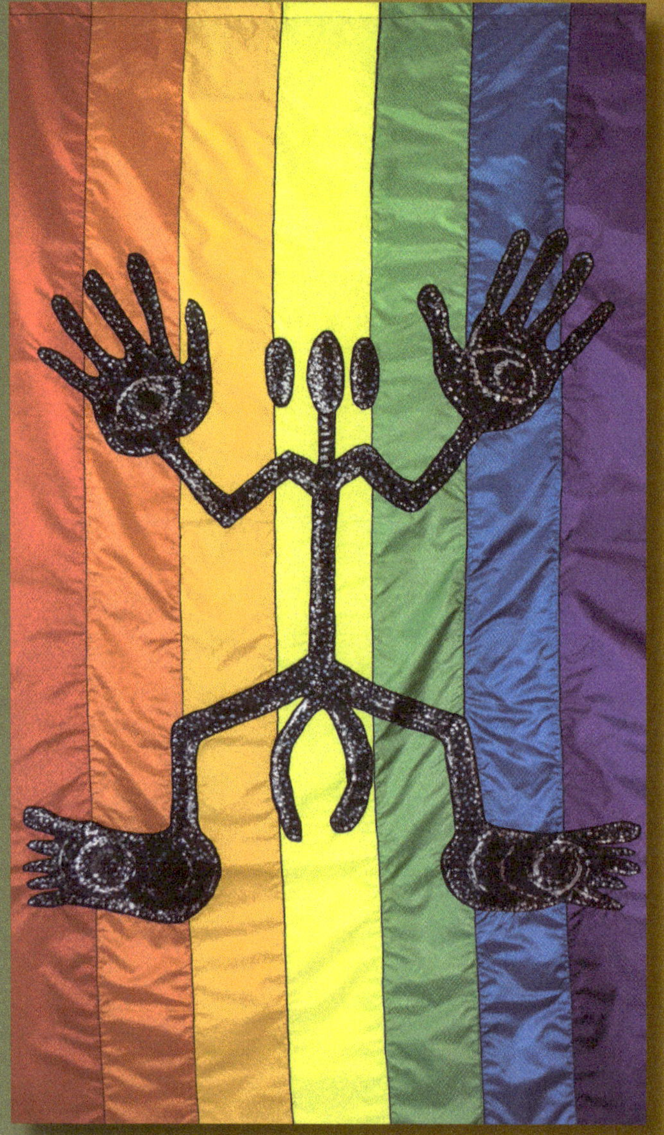

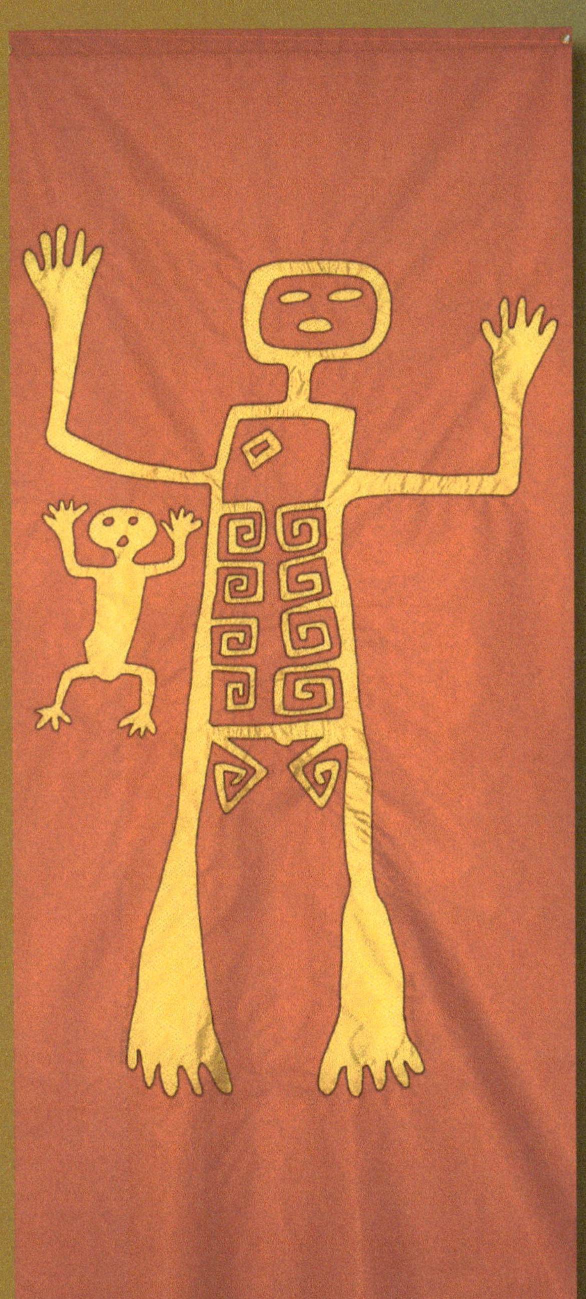

I call this figure, incised in the rock of the Little Colorado River, The Great Goddess Matriglyph. She expresses the sacredness of life. The spirals adorning her indicate her supernatural power and status, as do her feet and her great upraised hands. The figure under her upraised arm is protected. The spirals in her pubic area connect her to the *sheela-na-gigs* of birth, death and regeneration around the world.

Water is the most precious substance in the desert landscape of the southwest US. All life depends on a source of water. The Little Colorado River flows into the Colorado River, named thus by the early Spanish explorers because of the high content of red soil in the water (*colorado* is Spanish for "colored," referring to the red color). It was aptly named for the color of life, as it has flowed for millions of years and symbolizes the sacred substances of earth, water and blood.

The Great Goddess Matriglyph

Source: Rock art. Little Colorado River, Arizona

North America | Southwest

This image, which I call Great Mother Matriglyph, stands firmly on a rock art panel in Dinosaur National Monument in northeastern Utah. Her right arm holds a labyrinth with multiple rays of energy. The Great Mother connects to a small figure on her left side, the arm holding what could possibly be a whorl of yarn to symbolize the threads of life.

Great Mother Matriglyph

Source: Petroglyph rock art. c. 500–1350 CE Unita Style. McKee Springs, Utah

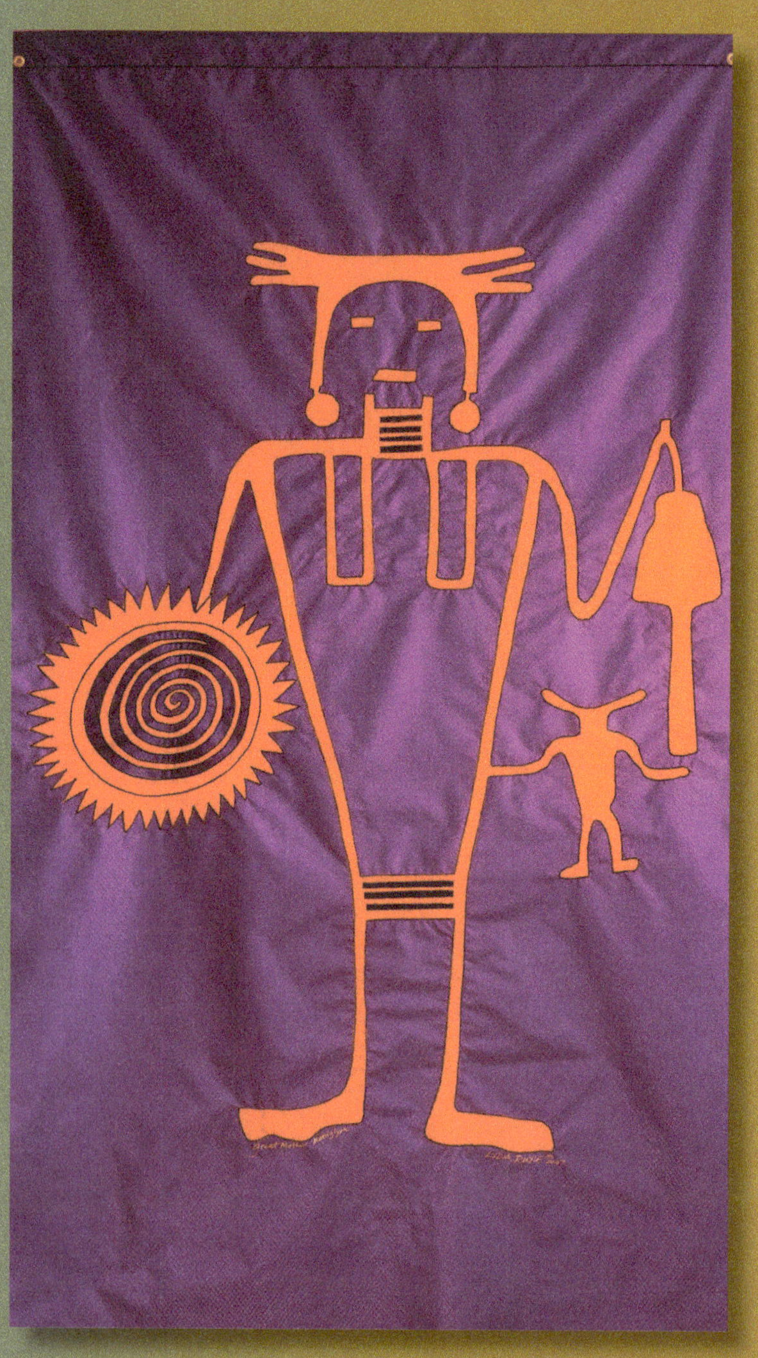

This row of extraordinarily square-shouldered figures pecked onto a rock art panel stands above the San Juan River in Utah. I based my concept of the San Juan Matriglyph on these larger-than-life characters, each of which has a small figure within a larger one; this could represent an actual pregnancy or a spiritual one. A line of water connects the matriglyph to a horned animal, symbolizing the importance of water in the southwestern desert. The horns might also represent the fertile crescent of the waxing moon.

The arcs above her head, necklaces and earrings indicate her shamanic spiritual power, as do her large hands and feet. In the rock art of the southwest, I see the female genitalia emphasizing the labia and clitoris; the labia are especially visible in the figurines referred to as *hockers*.

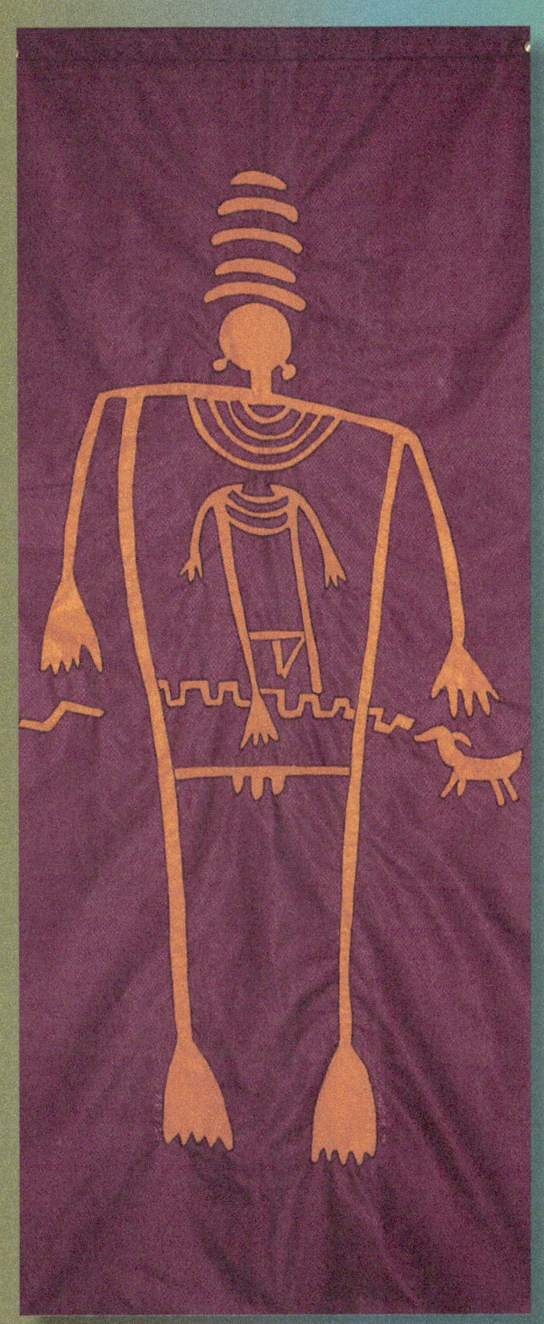

San Juan Matriglyph

Source: Rock art, San Juan anthropomorphic style
San Juan basketmaker
Early pueblo culture of central Colorado plateau, c. 1–900 CE
Butler, Wash. San Juan River, Utah
Possibly includes hocker image

Soyok Wuhti, from the Hopi culture, is also known as Monster Woman. She appears during the Powamu ceremony dressed in black with long, straggling hair, staring eyes and a wide, fanged mouth. She carries a blood-smeared knife and a long, jangling crook to threaten naughty children. She speaks in a long, wailing, dismal hoot of "Soyoko'-u-u-u" from which her name is derived.

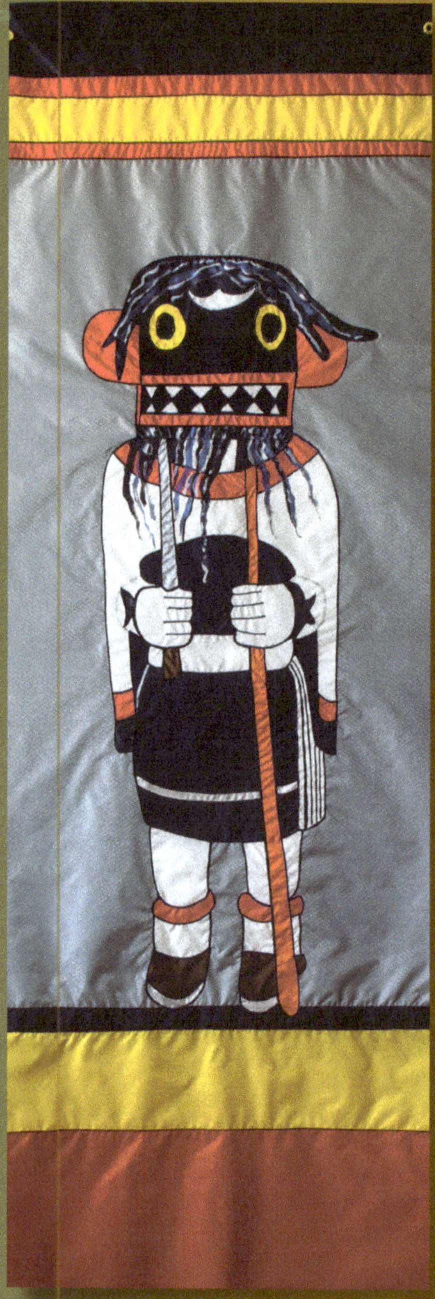

Soyok

Source: James Kootshongsie (1916–1996), better known as Jimmie Koots Soyuk Wuhti Katsina

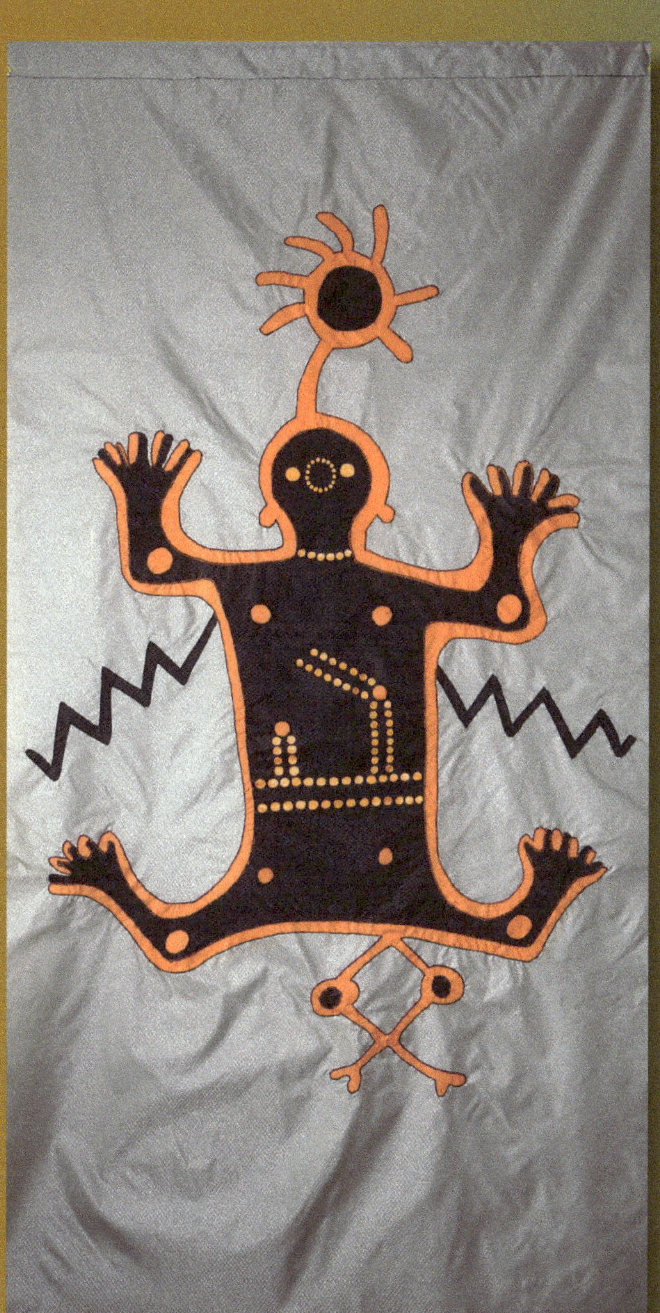

Chumash Matriglyph, with arms stretched above, is a pictograph painted in a cave hidden from sight in the remote mountains above Santa Barbara, California. A whirling sun energy bursts from her head and zigzags come from her breasts and heart. She could represent a shaman. Chumash pictograph sites are usually found near permanent water, a spring or running stream.

Chumash Matriglyph

Source: Rock art, n.d.
Cuyama Chumash culture. California
Drawing from The Rock Art Paintings of the Chumash, Campbell Grant.[v]
Photo: Chumash and Yokuts Yonig-Megalith painted rock. Carrizo Plain National Monument California

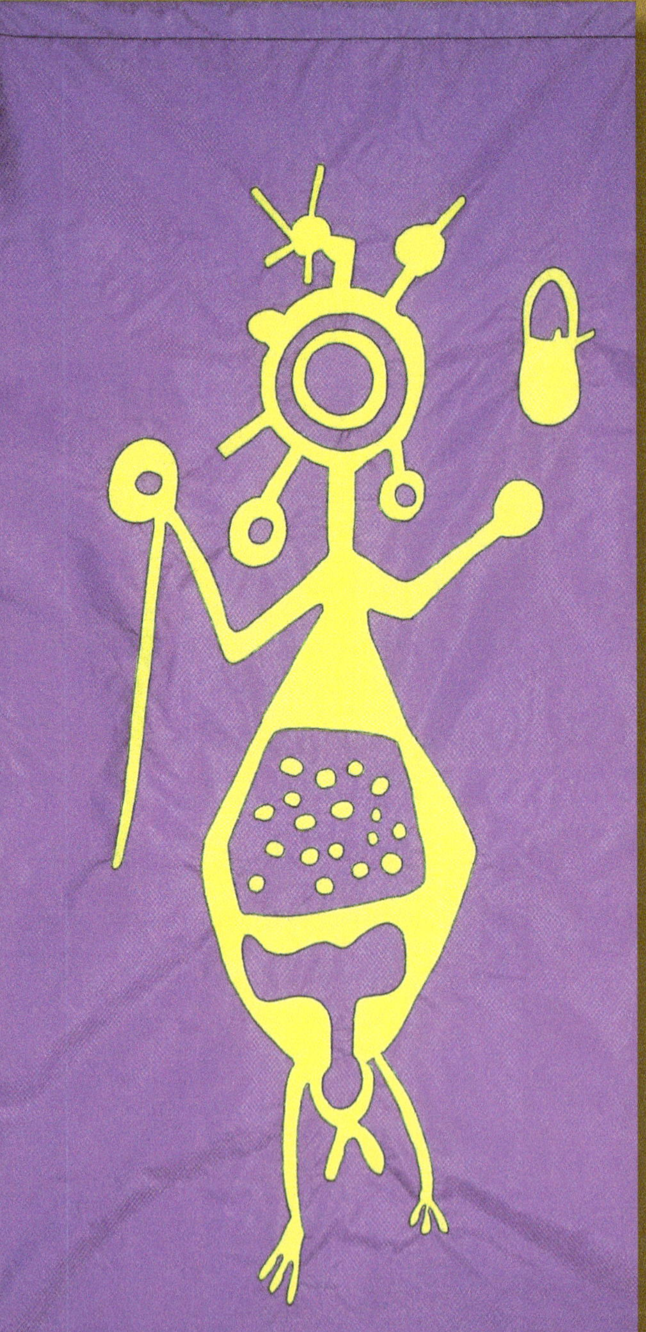

The Coso Mountain Range in California has the largest known collection of petroglyphs in North America. They are on a protected site on the United States Naval Weapons Air Base, China Lake. One particularly stunning petroglyph is a rare female rock art figure; most shamans of this area were male. She is pear-shaped and has many seeds in her belly or womb area as well as exaggerated pendant labia. I call her Shamanika to emphasize her female lineage. She carries her medicine bag on her left side, and earrings dangle from her head. You can visit the petroglyphs at the Maturango Museum in Ridgecrest California.

Coso Shamanika

Source: Rock art. n.d. Big Petroglyph Canyon Coso Range, Naval Weapons Air Station China Lake, California

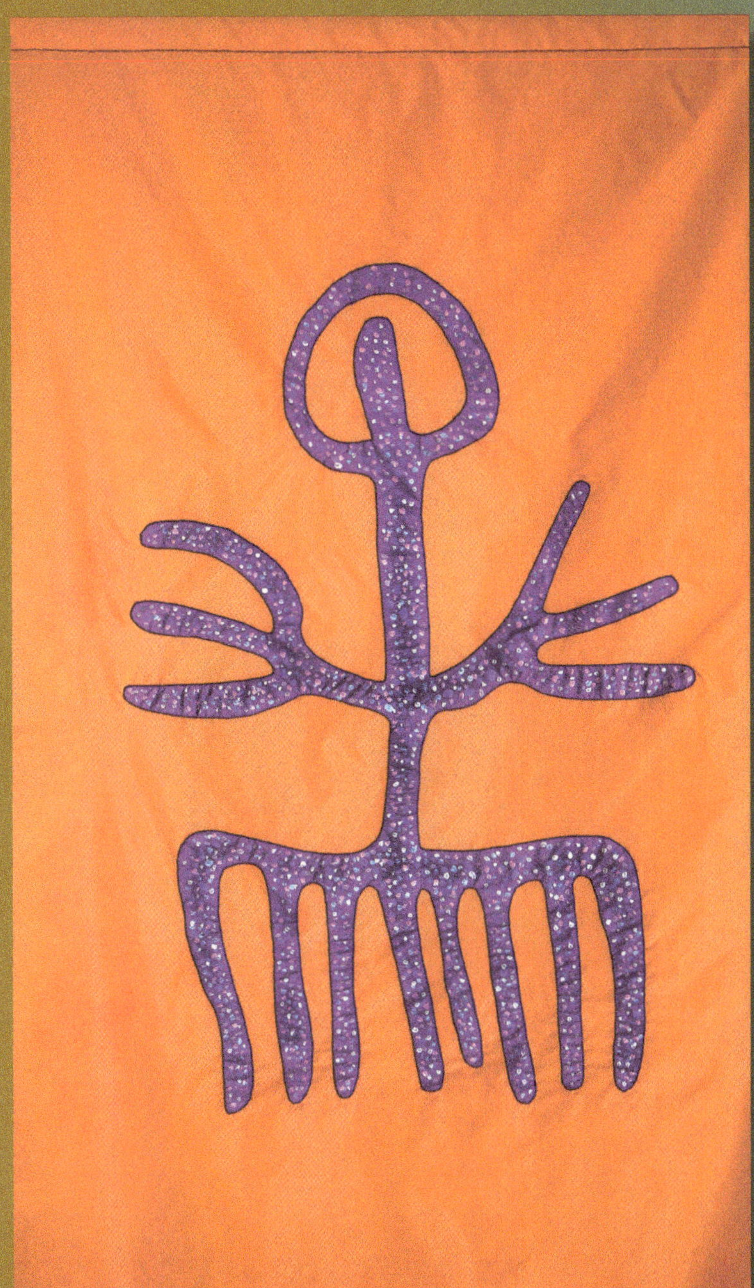

In a petroglyph pecked into an outcropped rock formation in the southern California Mojave desert is a female image that I call Mojave Yoni Dancer. She has a vulva-like head, and her arms extend upward to embrace the shamanic energies of the spirit world. Her dancing skirt calls for rain, life-giving water, which is essential for survival in the desert.

Mojave Yoni Dancer

Source: Rock Art. n.d.
Mojave Desert, California

North America | Northwest

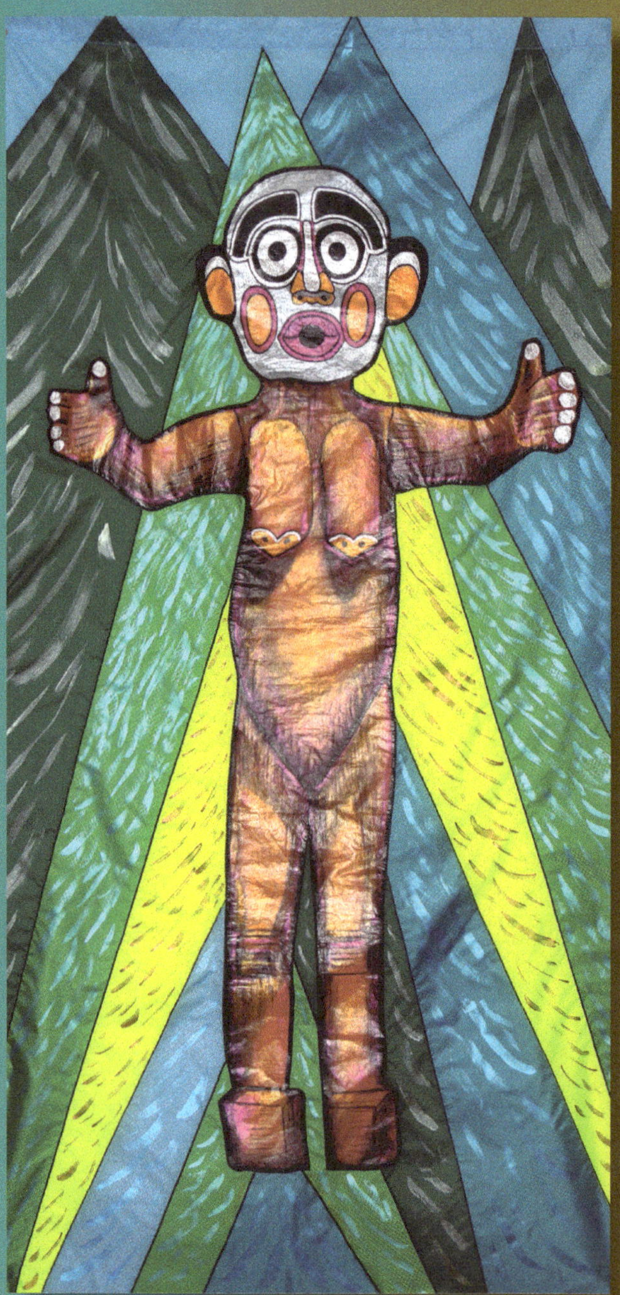

D'Sonoqua is a fierce ogress ancestress from the mythology of the Kwakiutl (Kwakwaka'wakw) tribe, who dwell deep in the primeval forests along the coasts of North America's Pacific northwest, in what is now known as British Columbia, Canada. Her head and trunk are carved of red cedar and her breasts are two eagle heads. Her arms extend forward to embrace those who look upon her. Her red pursed lips give off the call "Hu!," the sound of the blowing wind. D'Sonoqua is venerated as a bringer of wealth, but is also greatly feared by children, because she is known to steal and carry them home in her basket to eat.

D'Sonoqua

Source: Carved cedar totem. c. 1910–15
From Edward S. Curtis photo of Dzonokwa with Outstretched Arms
Kwakiutl Native Peoples, British Columbia

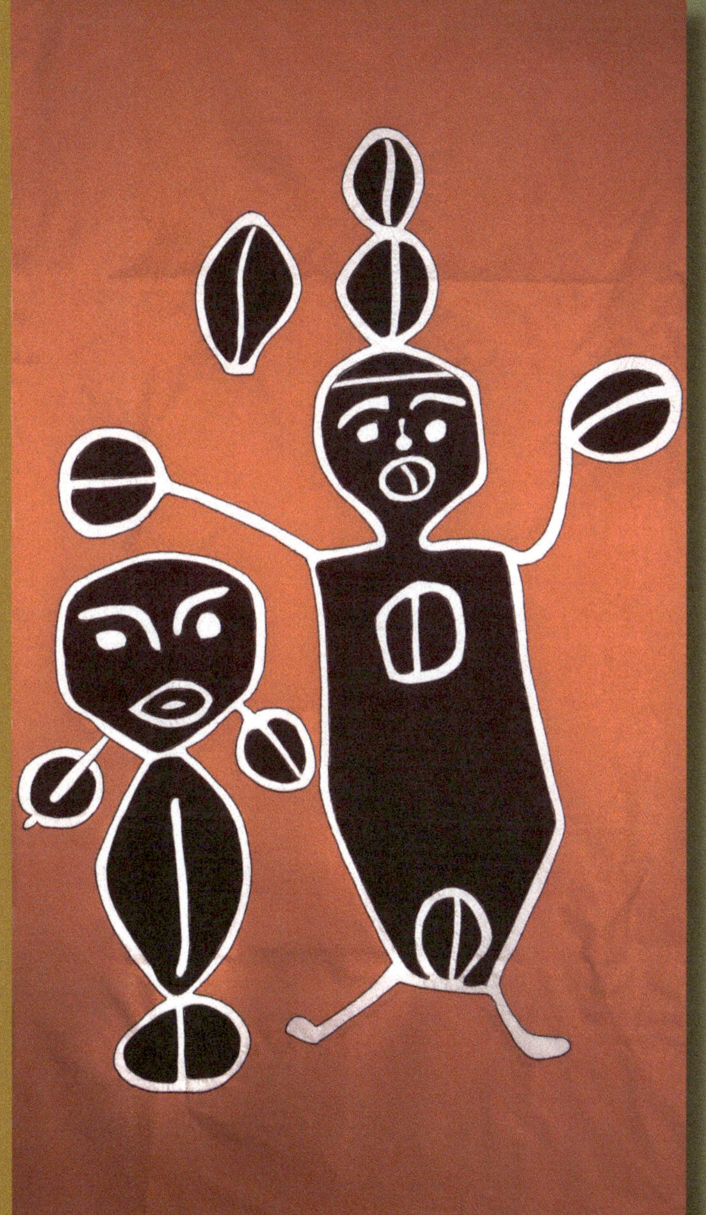

Here are female images pecked into rock next to a formation that resembles a vulva on a sheer cliff near Ozette, an old Makah Native American whaling village at Cape Alava on the Olympic Peninsula of Washington. I call them the Makah Vulva Women, and I envision them singing and wearing multiple female vulva symbols as headdresses, hands, hearts, wombs and earrings. The site honors procreation of all life.

Makah Vulva Women

Source: Petroglyph rock art, n.d.
Ozette, Cape Alva, Washington

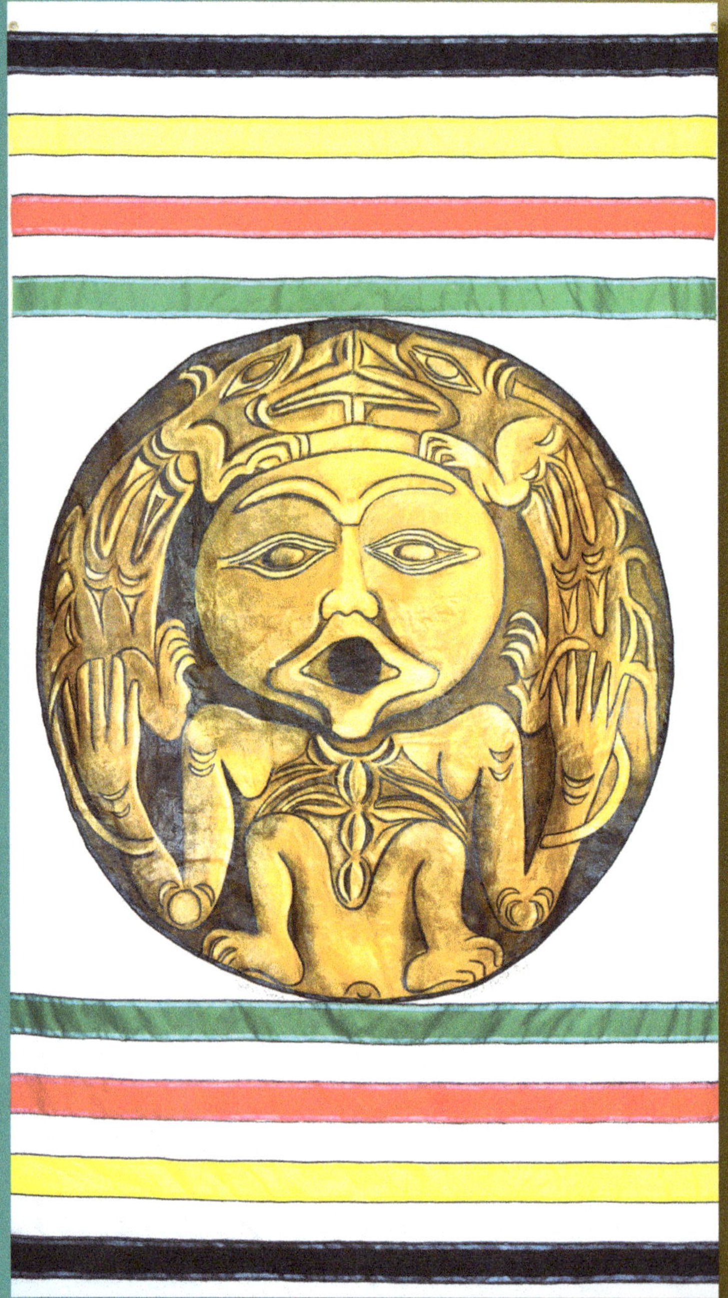

Spindle whorls, used in weaving, were a classic art form for women in Native American cultures. When I saw this spindle whorl, I named her the Salish Sheela. She is a spinner of life and death on a spindle whorl carved from maple. Two fierce creatures on either side of her head defend and protect her. Most early First Nations people, including the Coast Salish, made objects that were both functional and decorative, carving images onto wood and bone. Salish Sheela may represent the sun and has similarities to sacred display figures around the globe.

Salish Sheela

Source: Carved maple spindle whorl
19th century Coast Salish[vi]
Background: Traditional Pendleton blanket pattern
Collection of the artist

Sedna, the Ocean Goddess in the mythology of the Inuit people, is both feared and loved. She is the guardian of all sea creatures and provides food for her people. The people send prayers to Sedna asking for her protection and guidance in finding food and escaping the dangers of frozen waters.

Sedna

Source: Inuit stonecut print. 1961
Unknown artist

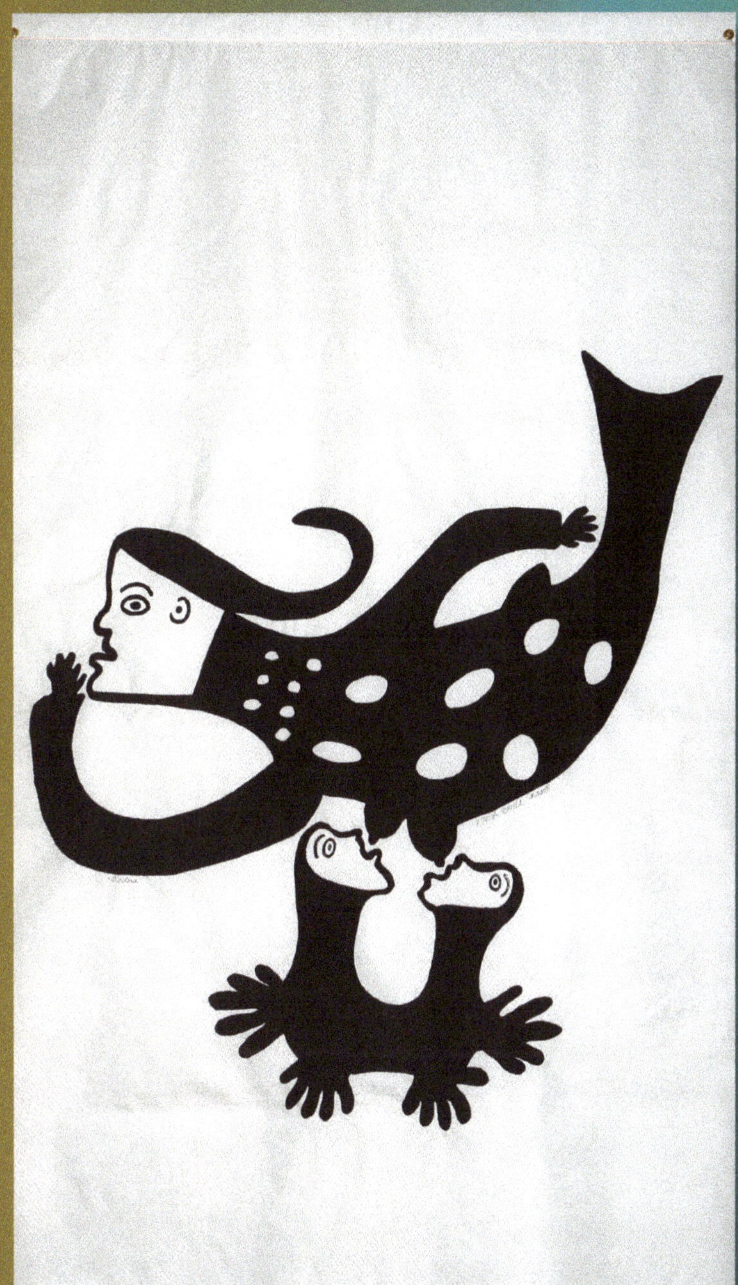

In the mythology of the Chinook peoples, Tsagaglalal is also referred to as "she who watches." Carved on a red sandstone cliff overlooking the Columbia River in Washington State, she is perhaps the most famous petroglyph in the northwest US. A legend describes Tsagaglalal as a woman chief watching over her people.

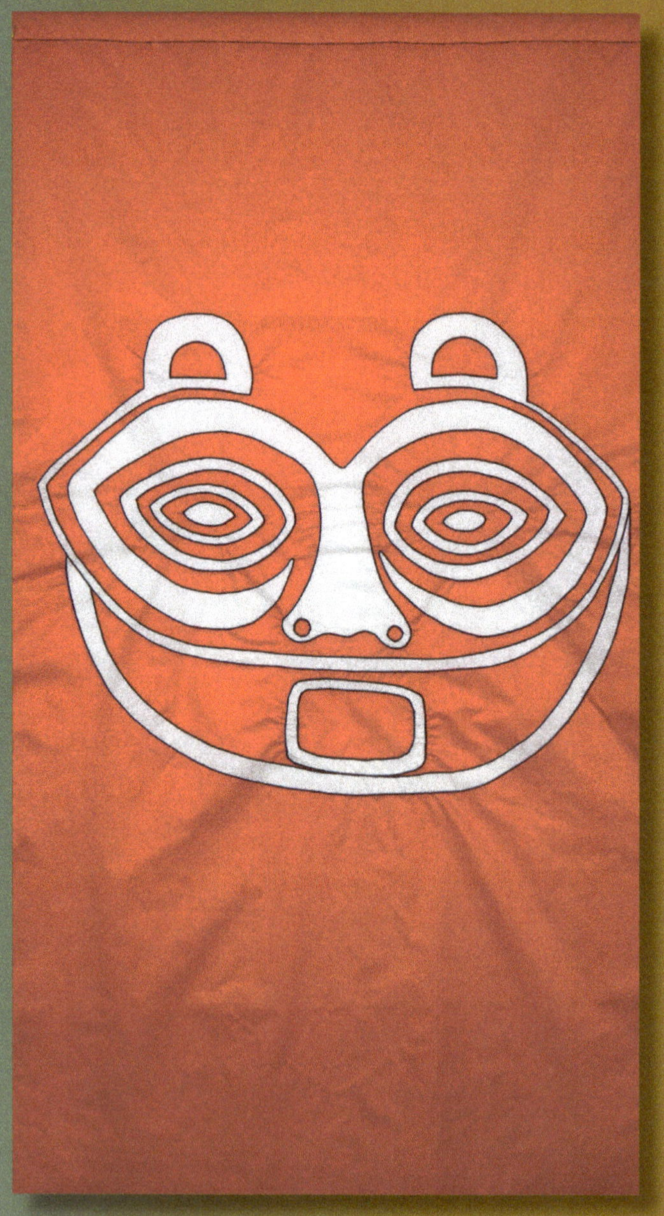

Tsagaglalal

Source: Petroglyph. n.d.
Columbia River, Horse Thief State Park
Washington

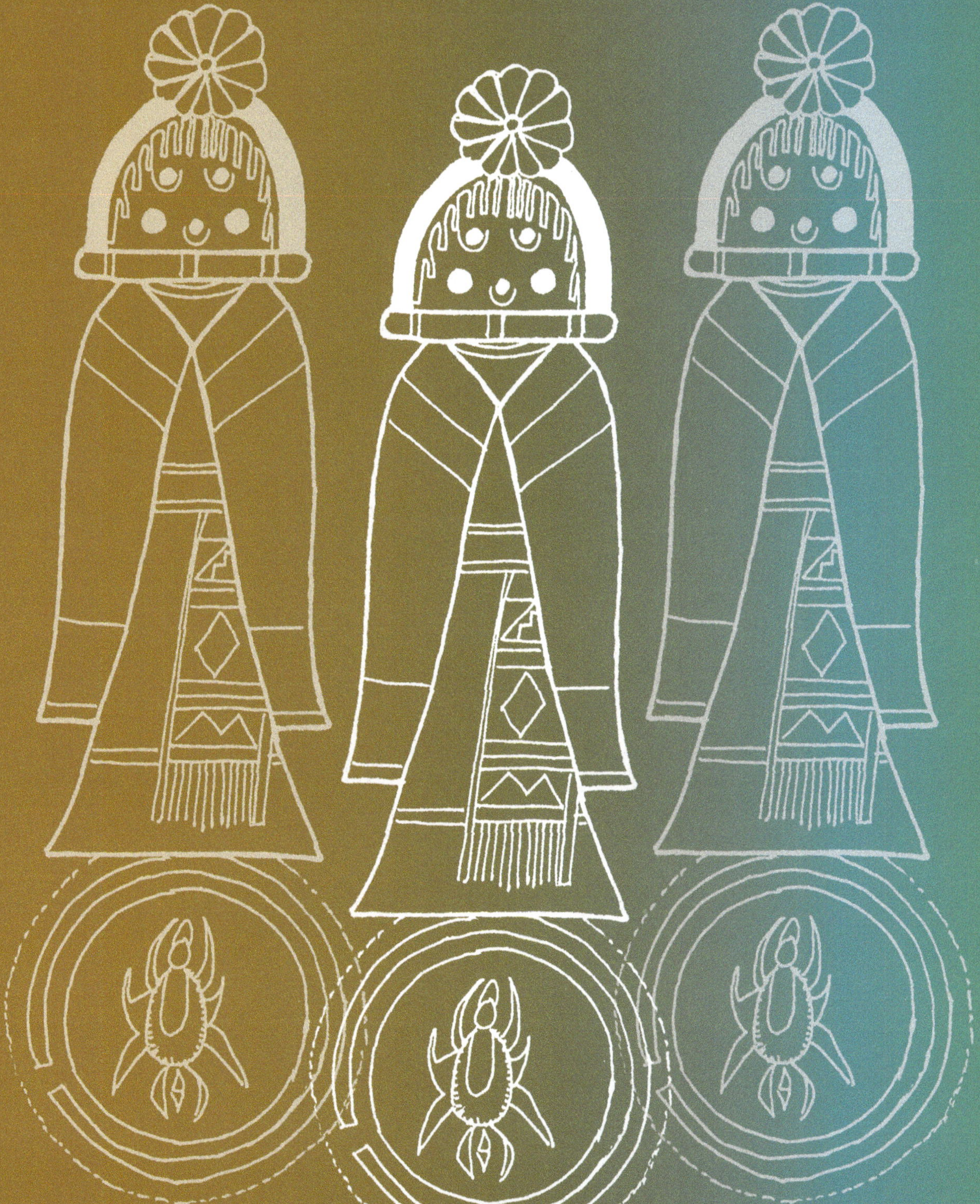

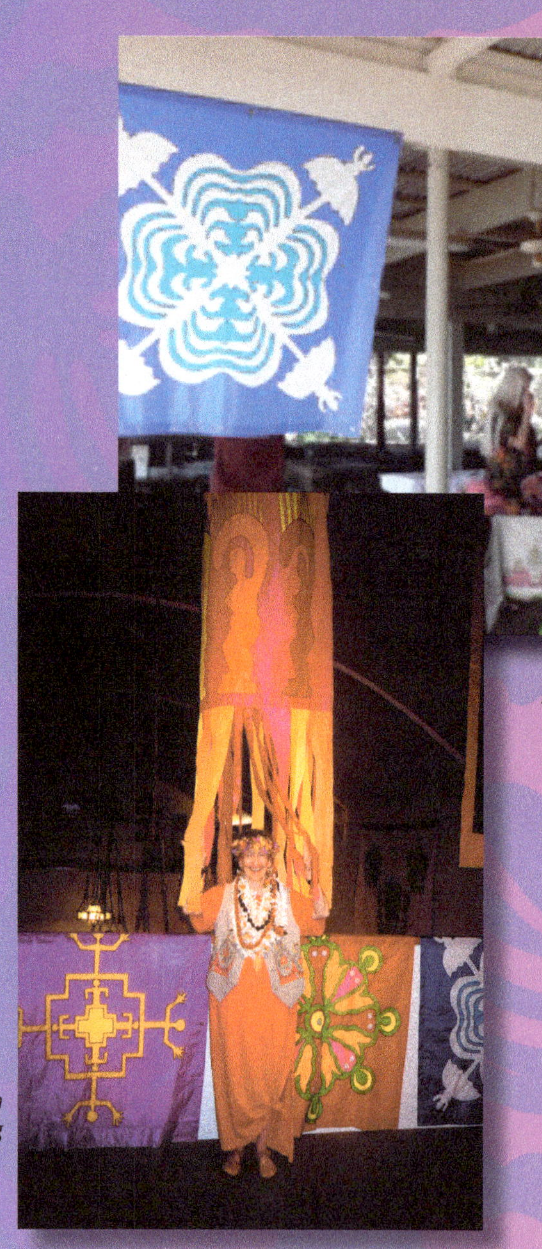

Jo Do Buddihist Mission,
Lahaina

Kauai Museum
exhibition opening

The Islands of Hawai'i

Lydia's goddess banners hung in a huge open room at Kalani Honua where we met to teach and share the ancient tradition of Hawaiian Huna healing and spirituality. Dancing into the room (one always dances when one is with Lydia) and experiencing these gorgeous works of art flying so grandly profoundly touches the soul. I am awestruck by the size and beauty and energy they convey. I think of the places they have flown and the places they are yet to fly and feel a part of the continuum of the unfolding grace and power of the goddess as she unfolds herself in these special times. They enhance and inspire the teaching experience and it is a thrill to be with them. Aloha nui loa.

–Laura Kealoha Yardley, The Heart of Huna[vii]

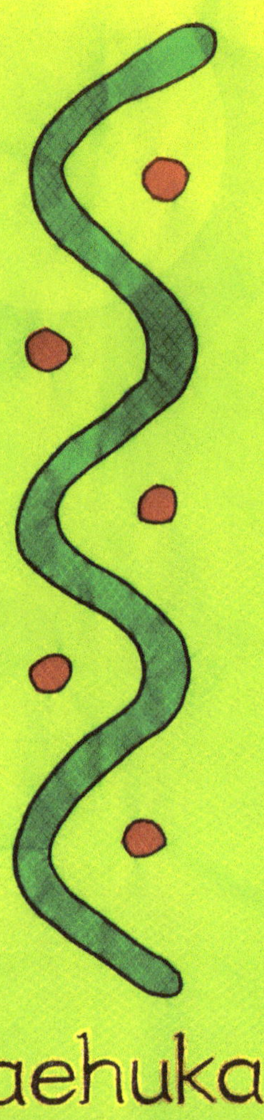

This is a mini-banner made at the request of Apela Colorado to mark the grave of Alice Shaw, a woman with links to a priestess of Kamehameha, the last ruler of the Hawaiian Islands. The serpentine path with dots represents Kihawahine walking along.

The Islands of Hawai'i

The volcanic landscape of Hawai'i is rich in natural formations, which change constantly with the vigorous environment. Red lava is the blood of the earth and transforms into black obsidian sand as it reaches the cool water. *Pohaku* stones are *mana*, meaning they are believed to embody sacred energy; in *pohaku*, spiritual and physical worlds meet. *Tikis* are piles of stones that connect to the spirit world. Human-made petroglyphs mark the hardened lava in sacred places and serve as a record of their existence. *Heiaus* are sacred energy places made of lava stones. *Kahunas* and priestesses are the wisdom keepers of the sacred *heiau* sites, or "places of worship," today.

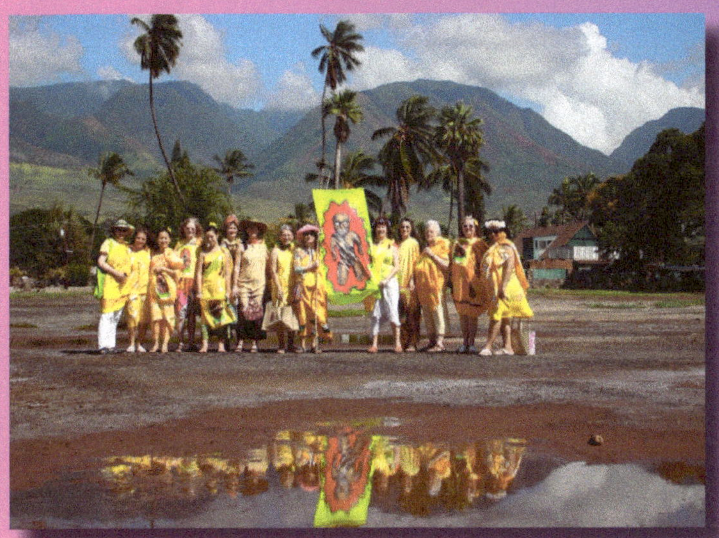

Maui Goddess Retreat with Kihawahine Banner

The islands have a long tradition, presided over by the goddess Kapo, of making patterned cloth with tapa fibers. This rich tradition was transformed into quilt-making after the arrival of New England settlers to the islands in the early 1800s. My banners reflect the pattern-making traditions of both cultures. In these banners, I have incorporated feminine images from petroglyphs, quilts, flowers, art and sculpture. To create the designs, I first draw the image and then fold the paper into sections and cut out the image. Four, six or eight figures emerge in a mandala, depending on the number of folds.

Kalani Honua (harmony of heaven and earth), a nonprofit retreat center on the big island of Hawai'i, exhibited the Hawai'i banners in 1997; in 2001, they were displayed again, this time at the Kauai Museum in Lihue. When I visited the Kauai Women's Correctional Facility to share goddess stories with the inmates, I took small prayer flags of the banners with me. In Lahaina on Maui in 2011, the banners flew at JoDo Buddhist Mission and for a kahuna-led ceremony to bless the goddess Kihawahine at Moku'ula. They continue to fly at the JoDo Mission during retreats with Dr. Apela Colorado, founder of the Worldwide Indigenous Science Network.

The Islands of Hawai'i

Aumakua, a family deity who is often a deified ancestor, must be honored with respect, responsibility and ritual, because every human stands on the shoulders of her ancestors; all are connected. The circle of elders teaches that humans must choose their actions by considering the consequences for the next seven generations.

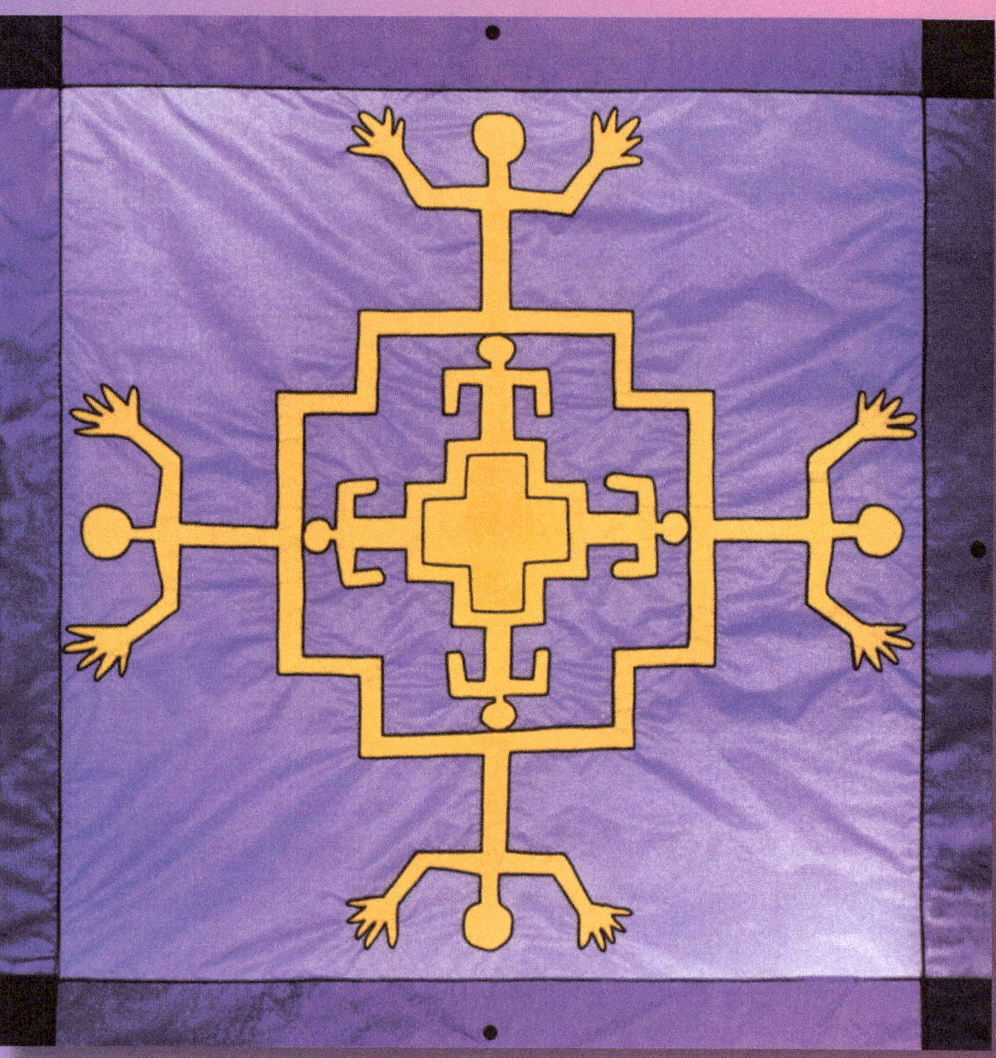

Amakua Ancestor

Source: Marks on lava, Puako petroglyph site, Hawai' i

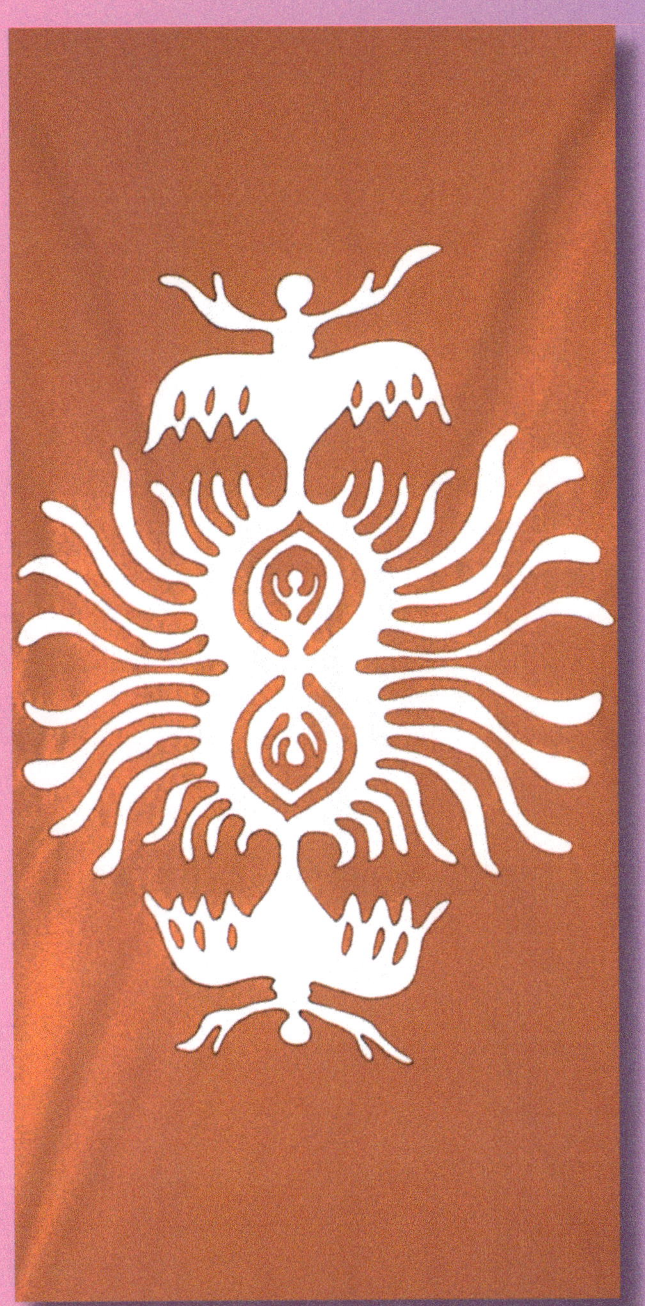

Hiiaka and Pele dance as goddesses of the above and below. They are sisters, daughters of Haumea, the great mother. Hiiaka was born from an egg incubated in Pele's armpit as she traveled from Tahiti. After her birth, Pele nurtured and raised her sister and they had many adventures together. On the banner, the sisters are depicted in the act of creation as they dance the hula.

Hiiaka and Pele

Source: Crown of India quilt pattern, 1973
Academy of Arts and Mission Houses Museum
Honolulu; and Stella M. Jones
Hawai'ian quilts
Daughters of Hawai'i
Honolulu

Hina is the goddess of the moon. A *piko*, or "place of emergence," is drawn in volcanic rock after the birth of a child as a way to join the marks and spirits of the ancestors. Hina emerges gradually from darkness; she returns to darkness every 28 days to emerge into fullness again. Her journey is celebrated as feminine birth by many cultures around the world.

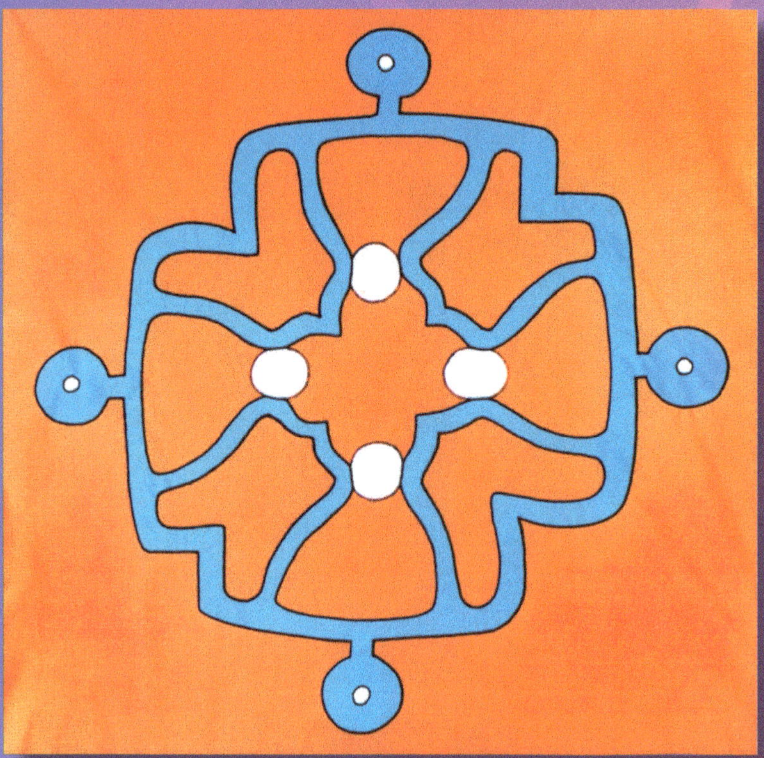

Hina

Source: Marks on lava, Anaehoomalu petroglyph site South Kohala, Hawai'i

Kahuna Aumakua is a fierce protectress of the sacred wisdom knowledge of *huna*, the healing tradition of the islands. *Kahuna* are called by the spirits and engage in fasting, prayer and meditation as part of their training and healing practices. Aumakua's eyes are shining pearl shells, which symbolize her sacred vision. Human hair grows from her mighty head and her vulva conveys her power of creation, connecting her to other healing traditions around the world.

Kahuna Aumakua

Source: Wood sculpture with shell and human hair
c. 1780
Private collection, London

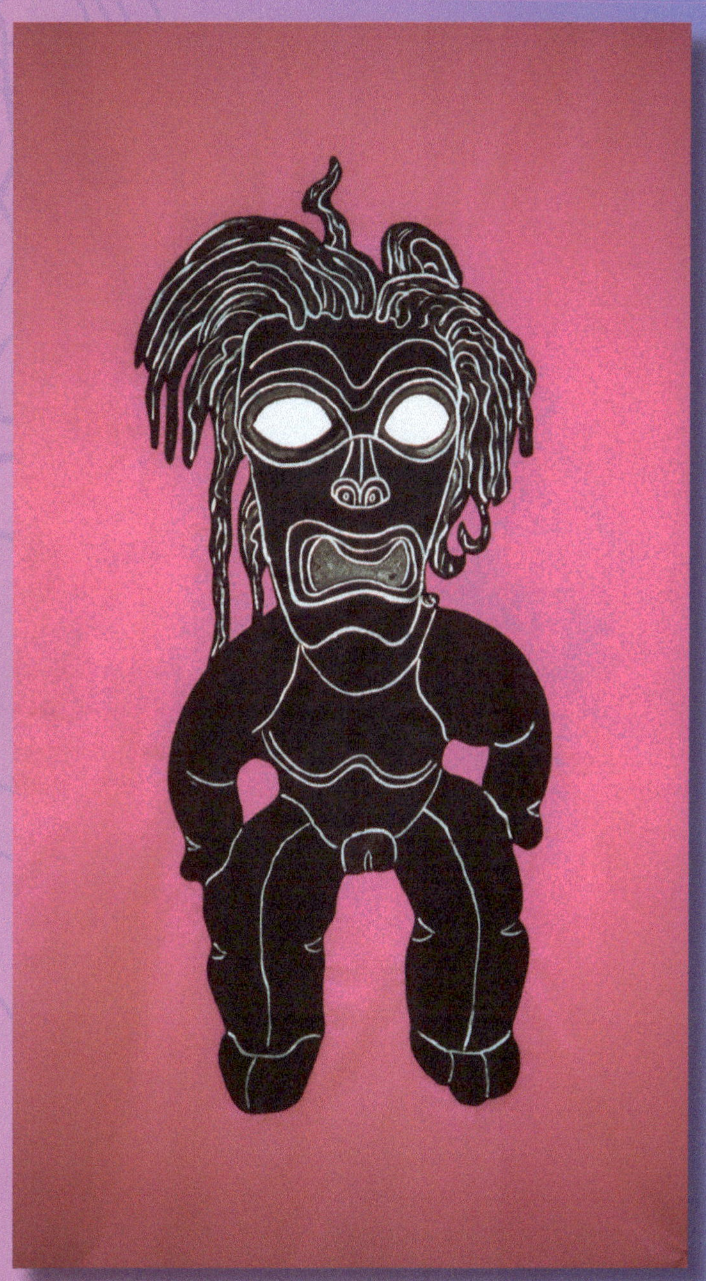

Kapo is a clever goddess who lifts her skirt and shows her genitalia in order to save her sister Pele from the clutches of the pursuing pig god, Kamapua'a. Kapo left a *pali pohaku*, or "volcanic mark"—in this case, a *kohelepelepe*, which means "flying vagina"—east of Honolulu. Other traditions, like Baubo of Greece, Isis of Egypt and Uzume of Japan, celebrate stories of goddesses displaying their pubic source of power.

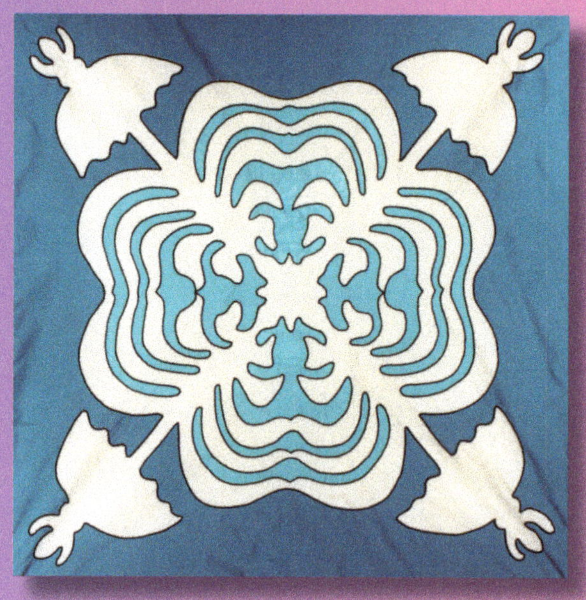

Kapo

Source: Crowns and kahilis quilt, 1890
Parker family, Hawai'i;
and Stella M. Jones, 1973
Hawai'ian Quilts, Daughters of Hawai'i
Honolulu

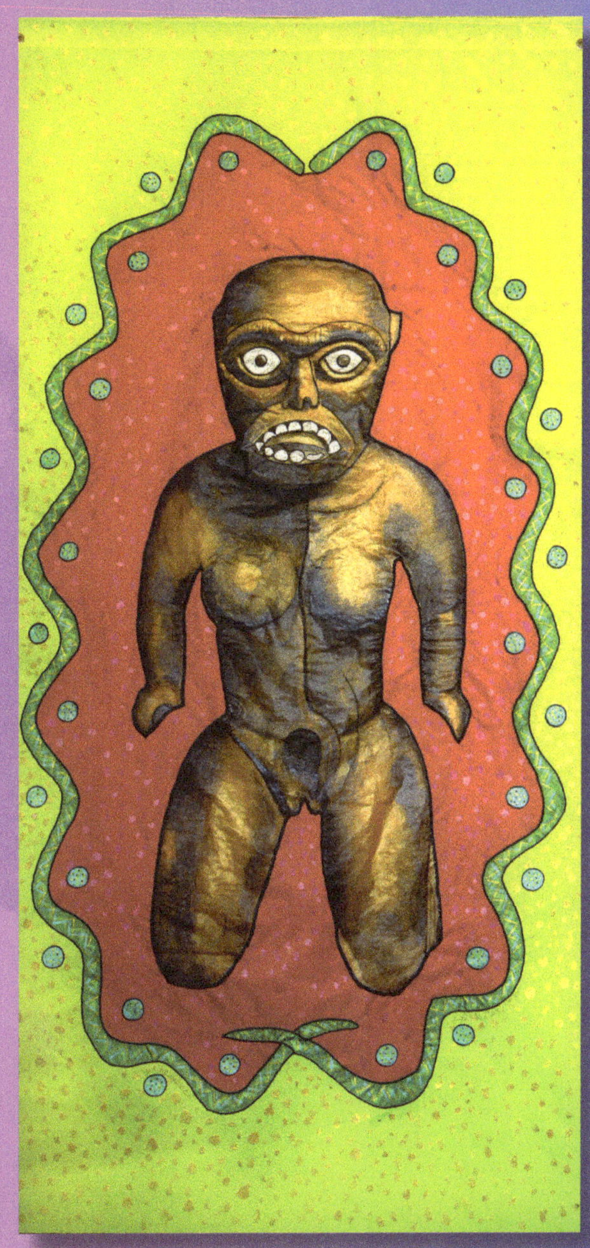

Kihawahine is the oldest *aumakua,* or "spiritual helper," in Polynesia. She is the life energy of fresh water. Her *kinolau,* or "animal form," is the *mo'o,* or "lizard," whose image can be seen in the West Maui mountains. Her home is Moku'ula in Lahaina. A wavy line punctuated with a dot in each dip of the wave symbolizes Kihawahine's perpetual movement. Life both forms and dissolves in her; she is the spirit of conception, birth and rebirth. [viii]

Kihawahine

Source: Kou wood carving with pearl shells and human teeth (back of head is hollow)
Found by natives of Waimanu, 1885
Berlin Museum collection
Information on mythology supplied by Apela Colorado

The Islands of Hawai'i

Laka, the daughter of Kapo, is the goddess of rejuvenation, a celebration of the healing energies of water. In this vibrant banner mandala, Laka and her *ohana,* or "global family," dance the healing energies of the four elements of nature: *honua, ear, ahi* and *wai* which mean "earth, air, fire and water," respectively.

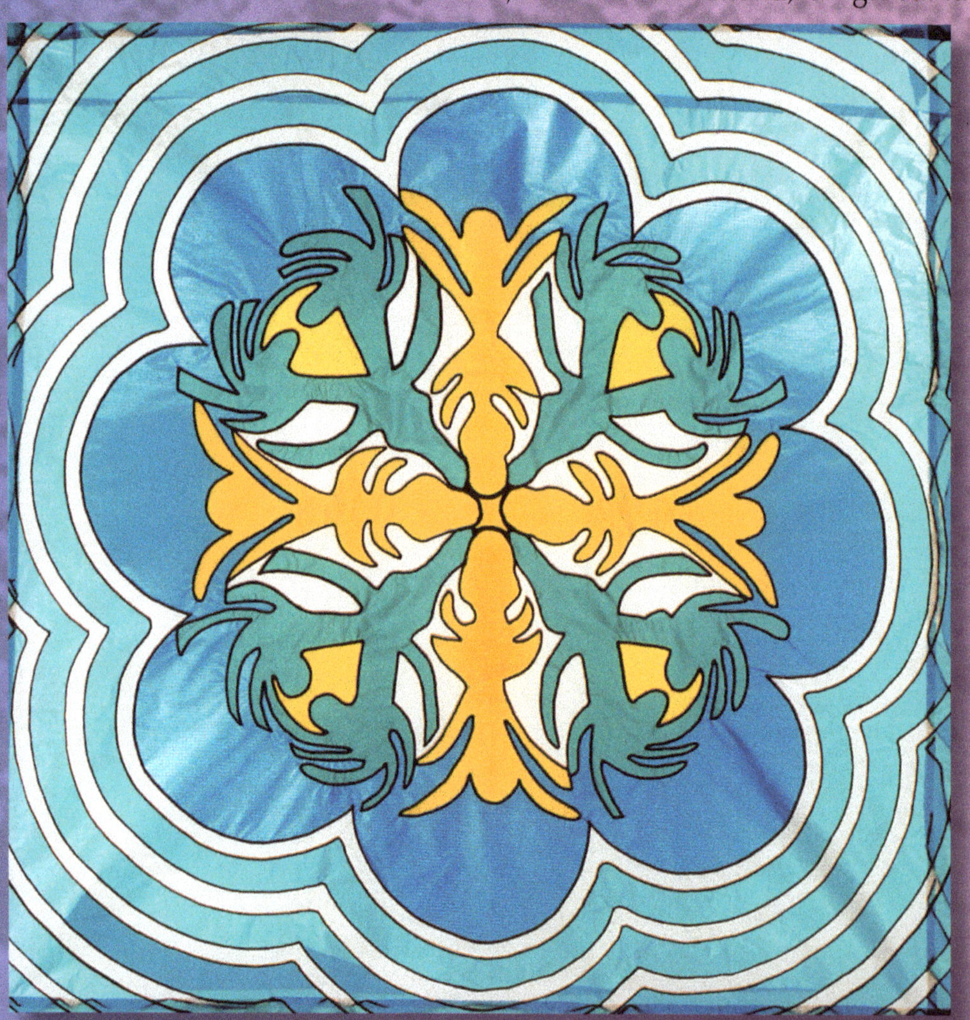

Laka banner

Source: Cut paper quilt pattern, 1996, Lydia Ruyle

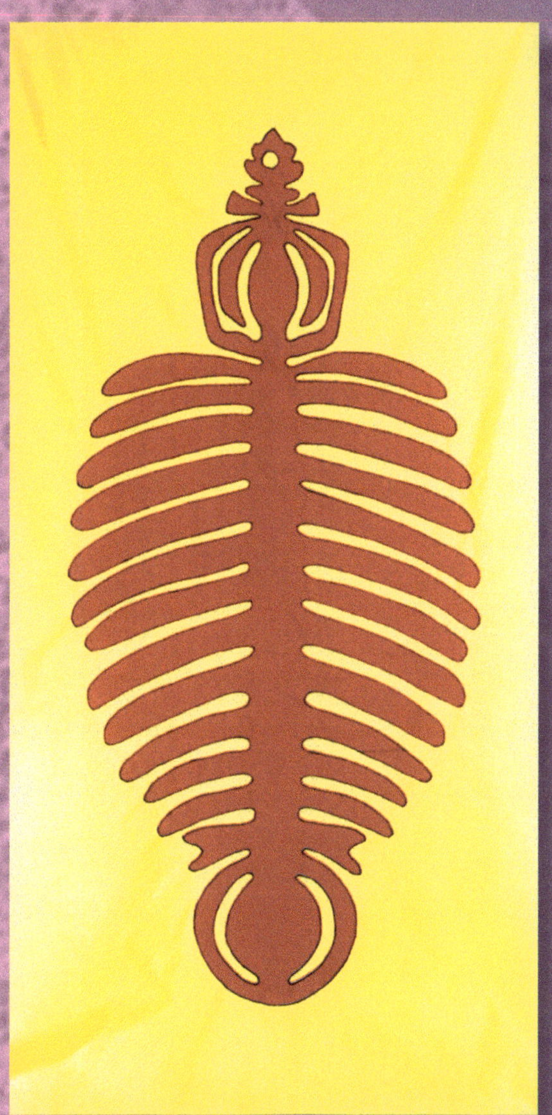

Lilliuokalani, the last Queen of the Islands, reigned until the 20th century. Her scepter fan of authority has thirteen lunar arcs. It becomes a tree of life, which grows from a kekui nut seed. Her scepter is topped by a dancing crowned goddess.

Lilliuokalani banner

Source: Sceptre, The Bishop Museum, Honolulu

The Islands of Hawai'i

Pele Honua Mea is the creatrix of the Hawai'ian Islands, where she is making new volcanic earth each day from lava flowing from her *pu'u o'o,* or "vulva opening." *Honua mea* means "earth mother." Pele dances the hula in a priestess circle mandala framed by her rainbow of transformation at her volcanic home in Halemaumau at Mauna Loa, on the big island of Hawai'i. She is the star of the Kumulipo, the creation story of the Hawai'ian Islands. Pele's dancing *anuenue* or "rainbow trail," connects the islands, ocean, volcanoes, mountains, caves, rain forests, beaches and myths.

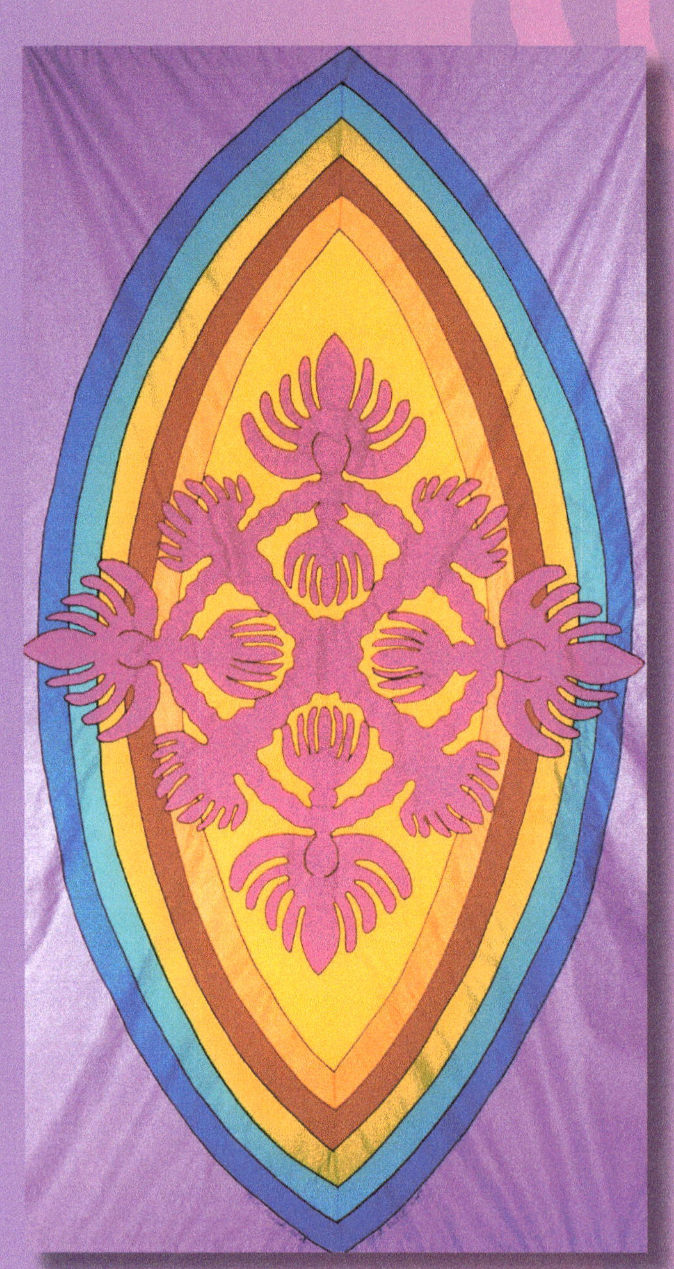

Pele Honua Mea

(vulva with paper cutouts)
Source: Logo,
1997 Goddess Tour of Hawai'i
Photo: Pele's Halemaumau

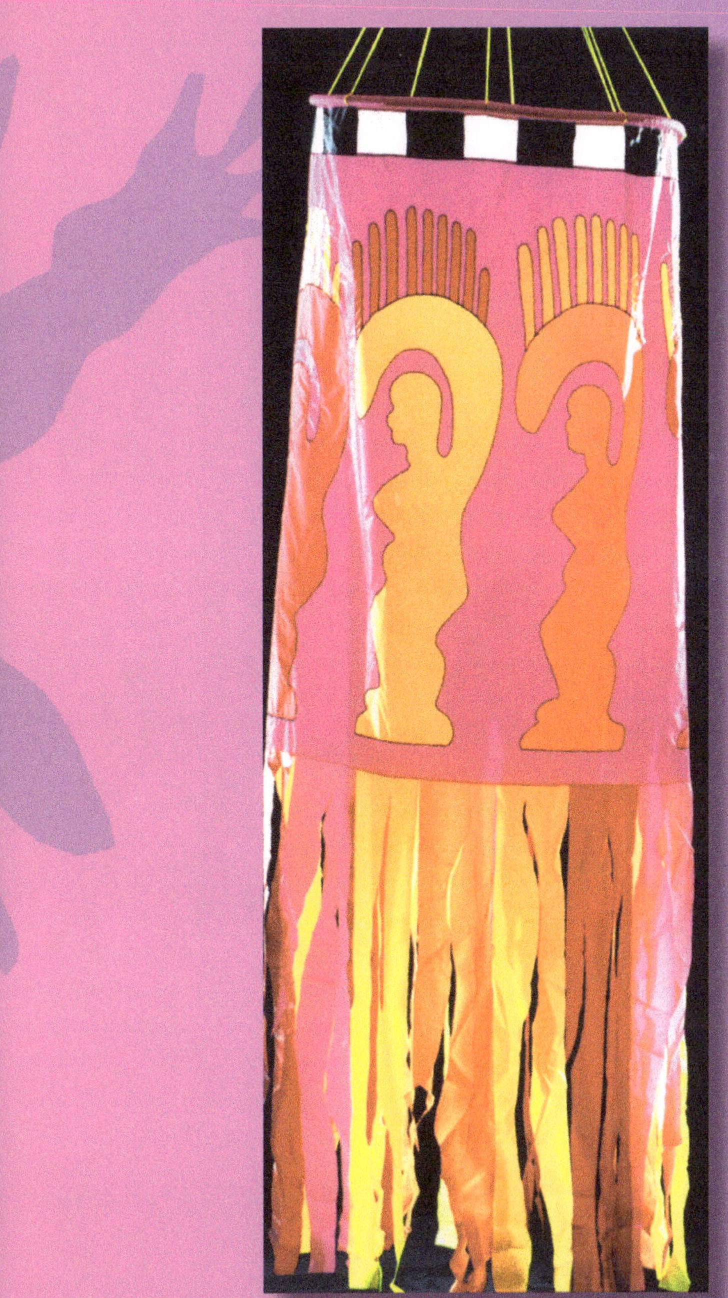

The Pele mandala is a circle of energy of six priestesses dancing and creating fires of creative passion. The feminine energies rising from their crowned heads are triggered by passion. Streams of vitality flow from the twirling figures as the fire grows and burns more radiantly. "Follow your bliss!" is the wise advice of mythologist Joseph Campbell. Pele, the red-haired volcano goddess, is credited with bringing the visual art of image-making to the islands. She is the goddess of sculpture and an artist of the infinite possibilities of lava and earthworks.

Pele Mandala

banner / wind sock
Source: Wood effigy figure
Bishop Museum. Honolulu

Priestesses of Pele use *mana aurae* to call women to create sacred space and do ceremony together. Ritual is a way of saying *mahalo!* ("hello!") to the universe and the Goddess. All spiritual traditions practice ritual and offer thanks to the powers of creation.

Priestesses of Pele

Source: Marks on lava Anaehoomalu petroglyph site South Kohala, Hawai'i

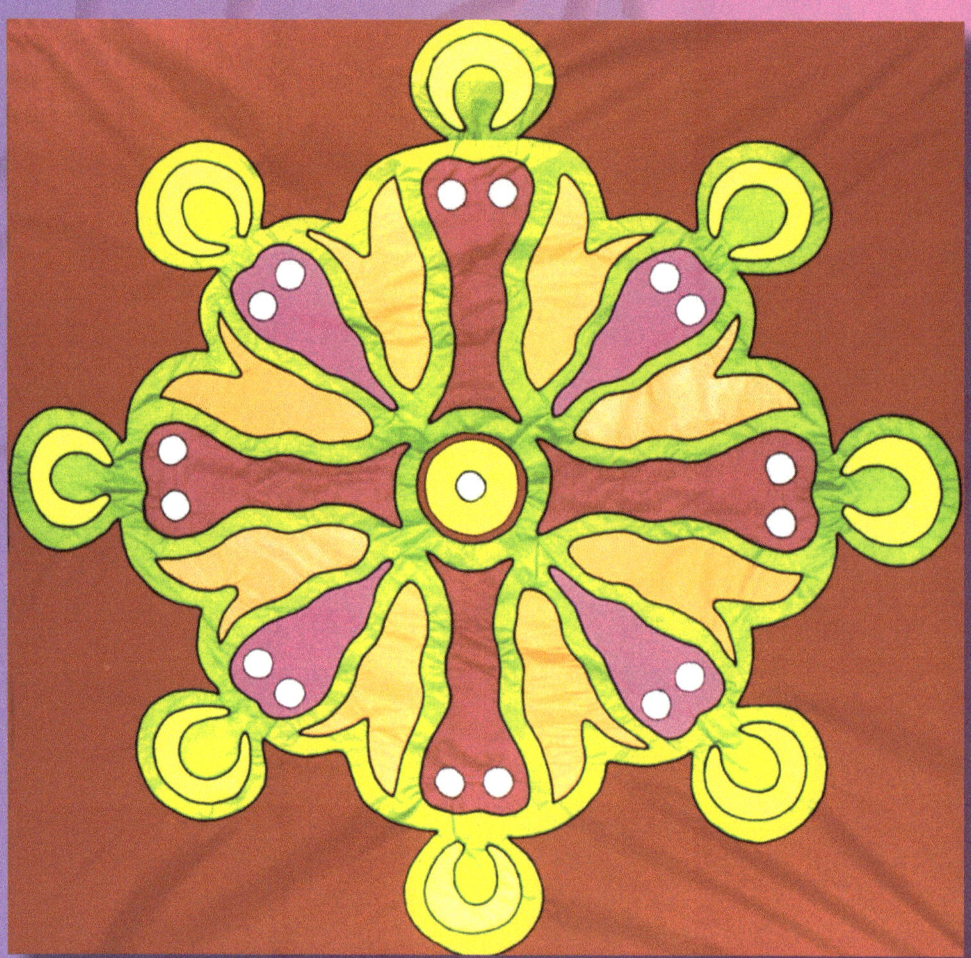

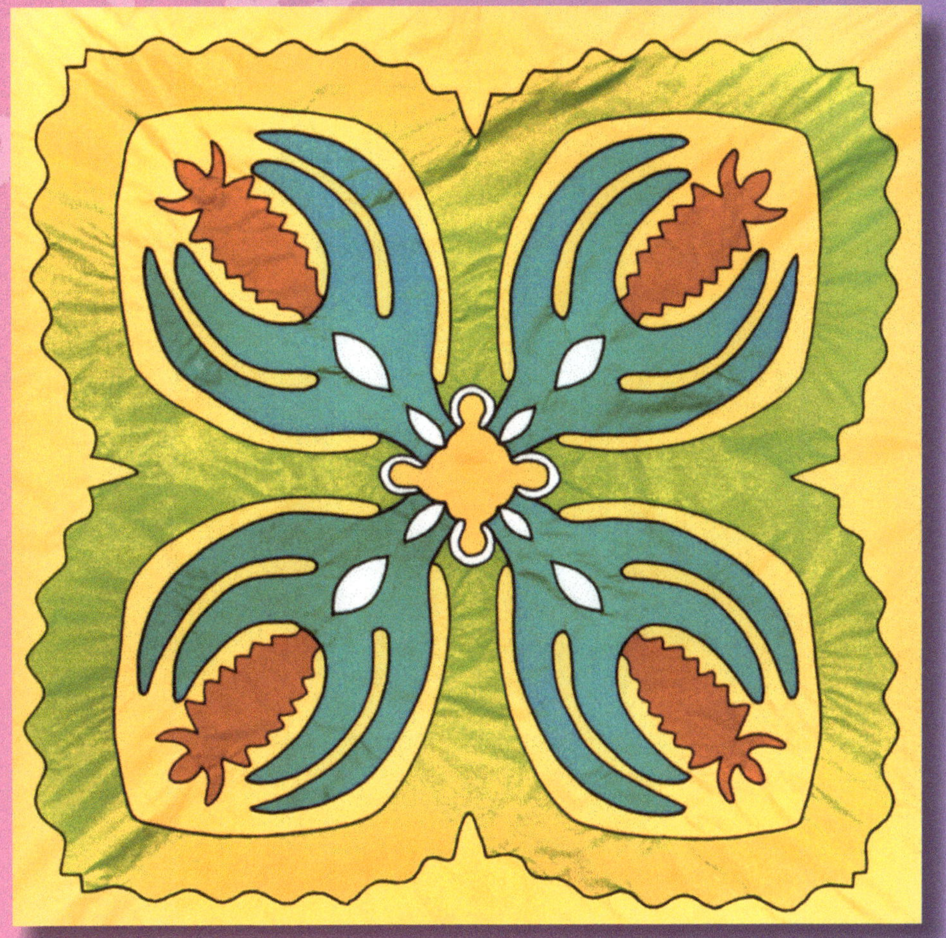

The goddess Uli is continuously changing, birthing, growing, flowering, dying like other vegetation deities. Uli is the grandmother goddess of darkness and the underworld. In the pineapple goddess banner, she represents the great mysteries of creation from a seed to a golden fruit, which nourishes life with its sweet nectar.

Uli

Source: Pineapple quilt pattern, c. 1918
Made for William F. Pogue, Hawai'i;
and Stella M. Jones, 1973
Hawai'ian Quilts, Daughters of Hawai'i
Honolulu

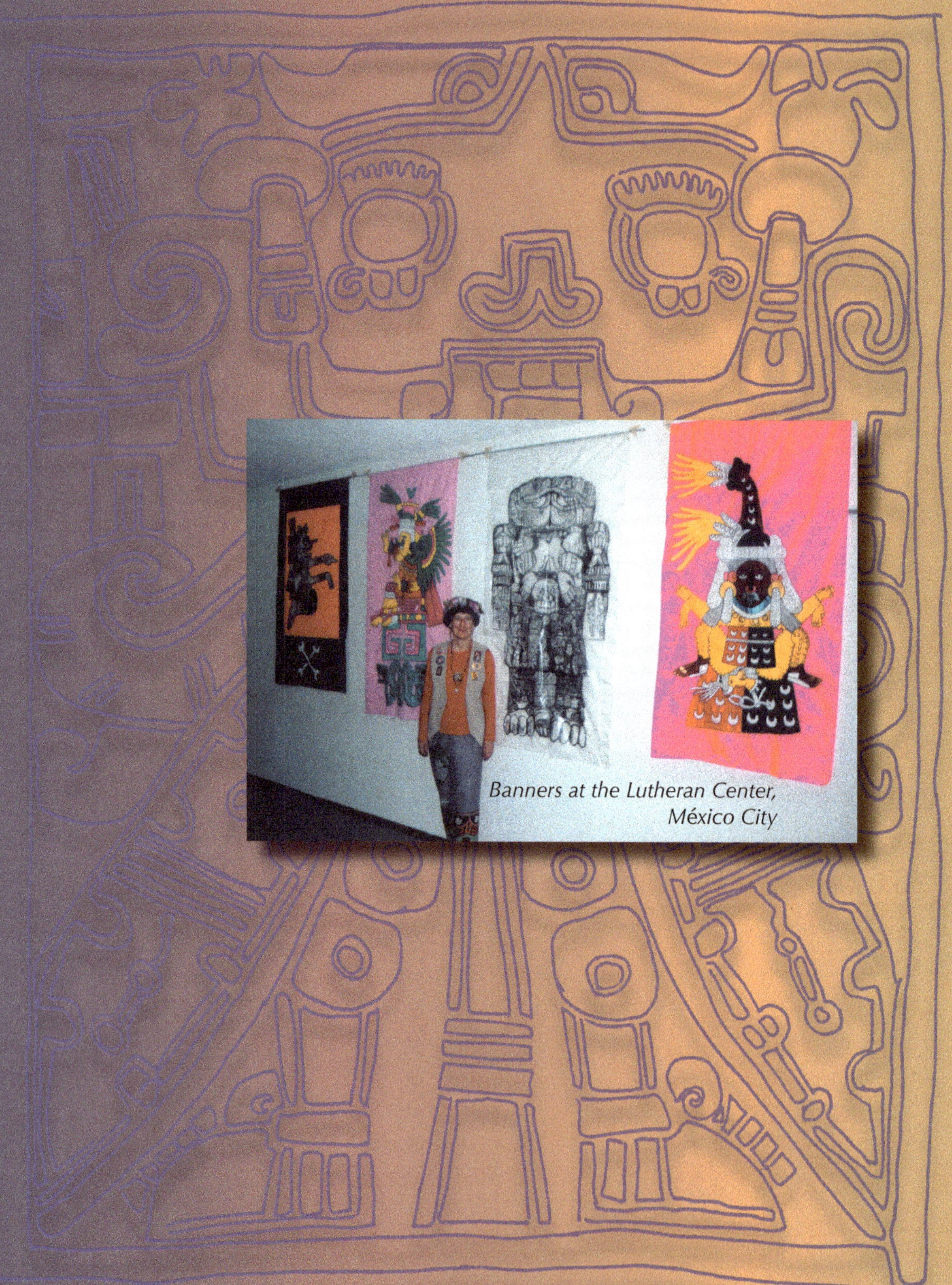

Banners at the Lutheran Center, México City

Mesoamerica

To eyes that are more familiar with the classical western ideal of beauty, Mesoamerican goddesses are unfamiliar, angular and fierce. The pantheon of female deities covered the spectrum of women's lives, from goddesses who embodied a woman's first flowering of maturity and her sexual desires, to those who eased the passage through death. Many goddesses were seen as patrons of weaving because of women's constant engagement with textile production as an economic and artistic activity.

Depending on their needs, women called on young, middle-aged or older goddesses who were knowledgeable midwives with training in the ways of medicinal and edible plants to help with their struggles through pregnancy and childbirth. Because the divinatory (260-day) calendar was related to the human gestation process, the goddesses of midwifery and childbirth also assisted in divining the forces that governed each day of a human's life, from conception to death. These goddesses served as archetypes for the creative energies that danced through the earth and its soil, through the caverns and waters of caves, and in the forms of plants, animals and birds.

Mesoamerican goddesses were primordial creators. Many local societies within the ancient Mesoamerican civilizations—which included the Olmec, Zapotec, Maya, Huastec, Toltec, Mixtec and Aztec—honored a creatrix as half of a divine couple in their mythologies, art and architecture. The powerful flow of cold and hot, female and male energies required humans to engage in rituals aimed at achieving the delicate balance necessary for the regeneration of life, time and the world, life and death joined in a cosmic dance of creation and destruction.

With the conquest of Mesoamerica came the Spaniards, who brought their own images of the divine feminine with them to the Americas in the form of virgin madonnas and saints. Some were black, connecting to pre-Christian goddess traditions of the Mediterranean. The indigenous peoples syncretized their deities with the new hierarchy, revering the earth mother and the queen of heaven as the Virgin Mary; the goddesses live today within Catholic traditions and liturgy. La Virgen de Guadalupe is called the Queen of México (La Reina de México) as well as the Empress of America (La Emperatriz de America). I think of her as the Goddess of México.

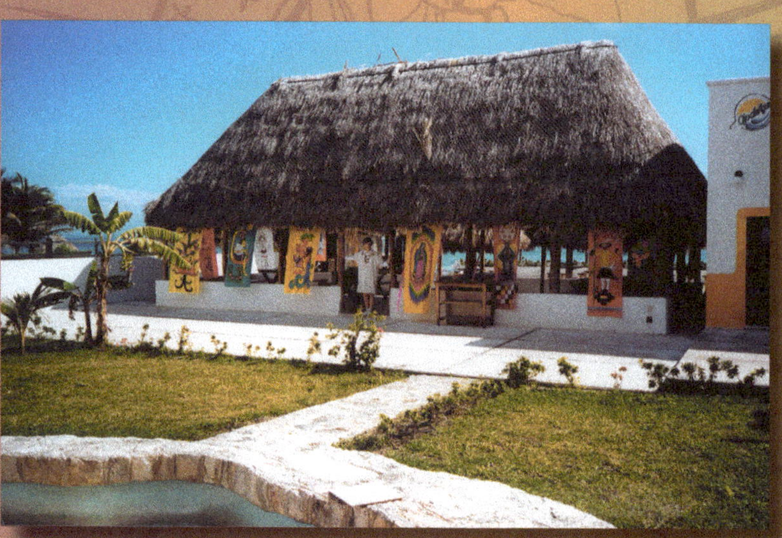

Banners at Ojo de Agua Palapa, Puerto Morelos, México

The easiest way to understand the complexity of the goddesses of Mesoamerica is to study them within both chronological and regional contexts. The chronology includes the formative, classic, post-classic and colonial eras, while the geographic regions primarily include the central Mexican highlands (near present-day México City), the Gulf Coast (the modern state of Veracruz, on the east coast of México) and the Yucatán Peninsula. Mesoamerican civilizational development can be divided into three major time periods: the pre-classic or formative period extending from 1500 BCE–300 CE; the classic period extending from 300–950 CE; and the post-classic period extending from 950–1521 CE.[ix]

Mesoamerica

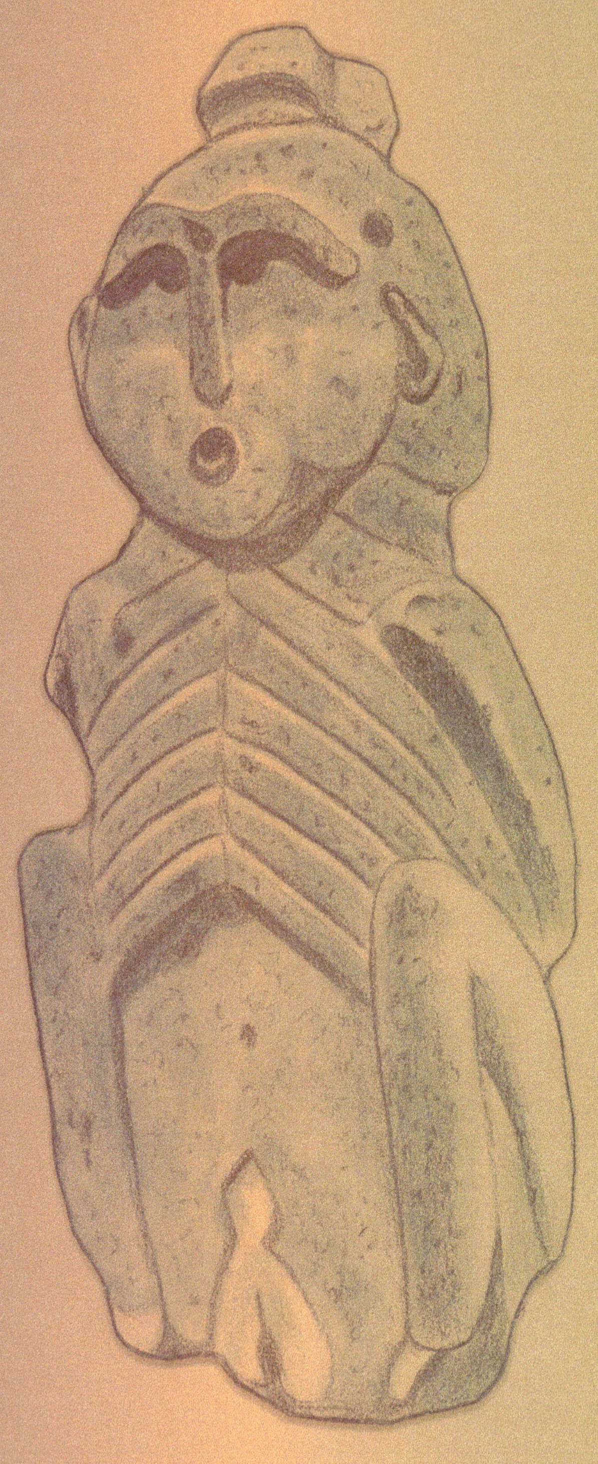

Formative Period

Although there was no single, unified culture in Mesoamerica, in the formative period (1700–400 BCE) all of the area was explored and villages established throughout the southern regions, in the cool highlands, along rivers and in the swamps. Although the peoples of these regions spoke different languages, through trade and travel they gradually developed some shared beliefs and knowledge. These shared traits are evident at several Olmec sites: La Venta (along the Gulf Coast); on the eastern seaboard; and at various sites in the central highlands near modern-day México City, including Chalcatzingo and the lakeside villages of the Valley of México. Women played more prominent roles than in the later classic and post-classic periods.

Gulf Coast Olmecs and La Venta

The great Olmec civilization was nestled in the humid tropical jungle of eastern México, along the southern Gulf Coast. From as early as 1700 BCE, the rise of civilization here was probably assisted by the local ecology of well-watered alluvial soil, which encouraged high maize production. The Olmecs subsisted for many centuries on riverine and wild plants, supplemented by small garden plots, until they began producing large crops of maize as a staple food around 850 BCE. With an ecology comparable to that of other ancient centers of civilization, such as the Nile, Indus and Yellow River valleys of Mesopotamia, the Olmecs could coax two crops a year from the rich soil along some of the rivers.

As a civilization, the Olmec are considered the mother culture of Mesoamerica and are credited with many firsts: permanent city-temple complexes, the Mesoamerican ballgame, sacrificial bloodletting, writing, monumental sculpture, sophisticated jade carving, the invention of the zero and the Mesoamerican calendar. During the formative period, women's knowledge of human gestation and midwifery played a critical role in the development of this complex society. Women learned about plants and their medicinal uses, and probably developed the long-lasting tradition of the sweat bath as a place of healing and regeneration. This knowledge led to the creation of a unique 260-day calendar, which became the fundamental ritual and divinatory calendar for all subsequent Mesoamerican civilizations.

Mesoamerica

It was women's knowledge that led to the development of this calendar, based on the human gestation cycle. Over time, people ascribed deities, animals, birds, color and directional space to each of the 260 days. These energies governed the fates and powers of each day, and diviners used this calendar to guide human decisions and actions and to name each newborn. Although it was born from women's knowledge of childbirth and pregnancy in the formative period, the calendar reached its fullest expression in the post-classic, when the many Aztec goddesses ruled individual days, as well as entire thirteen-day periods known as trecenas.

The Olmecs built the first ritual center in Mesoamerica at El Manatí around 1600 BCE, upriver and inland from the port city of modern day Veracruz. There they emulated the planting of maize in the ground and semen in the womb by depositing hard, phallic-shaped jade axe heads and bouncy rubber balls in a freshwater spring at Veracruz. A few hundred years later, the earliest urban center with monumental sculpture and earthen mounds in Mesoamerica was built at San Lorenzo, near El Manatí. Roughly 600 years later, around 1000 BCE, the Olmecs built enormous and extraordinary offerings of flat, rectangular, green stone blocks at La Venta, on the Gulf Coast. These honored the goddess of lakes and other sources of water, as well as fishing and childbirth. Sadly, the names of the deities are unknown, but their ritual sites communicate a sense of their devotion.

The Olmecs of La Venta commemorated several women, some of whom were probably midwives in a shamanic tradition, on stelae (monuments) and in burial offerings. Nearly every other Mexican and Central American civilization that followed emulated the Olmecs' political system of hierarchical city-states along with their extensive trading network. Researchers believe Olmec deities were the forerunners of many of the later Mesoamerican deities, including Abuela.

Abuela, or "grandmother," is the popular name for a weathered basalt statue from La Venta. The crouched figure holding an offering must have reminded those who named it of their grandmothers holding bowls of food, but recent scholarship suggests it is an image of an infant wearing a raincloud mouth ornament, which refers to the human embryo or mystical principle of life and growth.

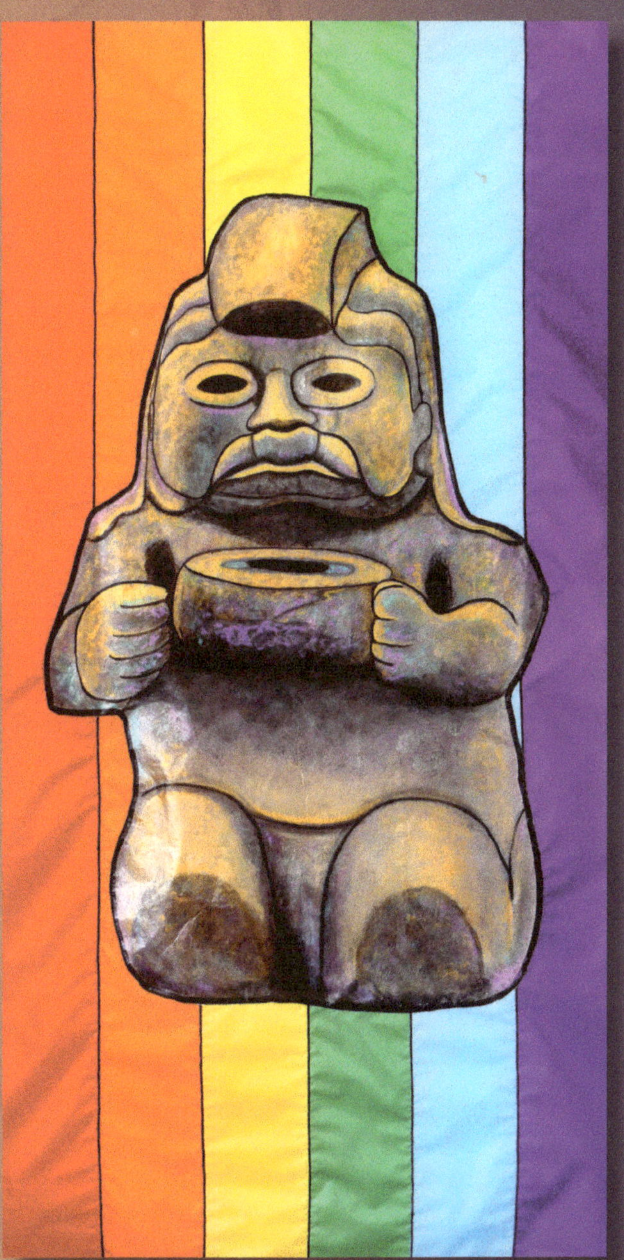

Abuela

Source: Stone sculpture n.d.
Parque Museo de LaVenta
Tabasco, México

Mesoamerica

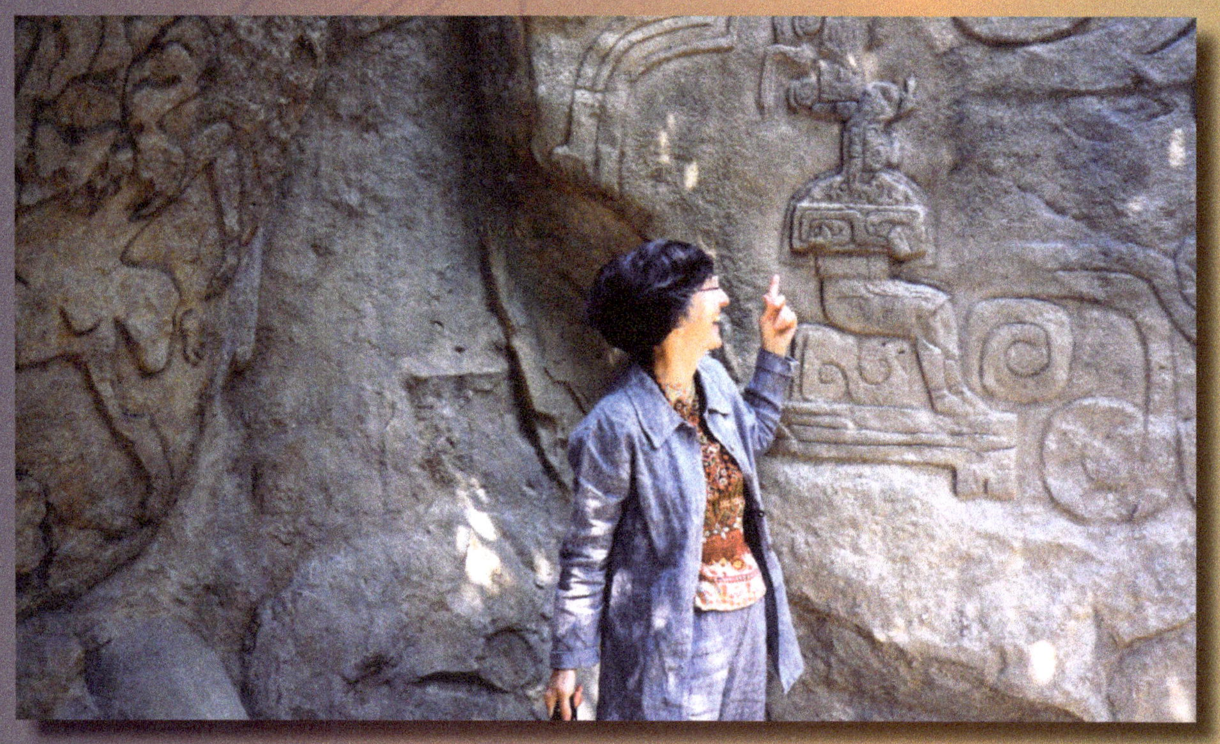

National Museum of Anthropology (Museo Nacional de Anthropología), México City

Central Highlands

In contrast to the jungle climate of the Gulf Coast, the central highlands of México, also known as the Mexican altiplano, is an arid to semiarid desert resting about 3600 feet above sea level. This area begins at the Rio Grande river border with the United States and moves south, through what is now known as México City. Carved into the hillside of Cerro Chalcatzingo, south of México City, a bas-relief figure sits within a stylized cave mouth under three clouds from which raindrops fall. This figure has been referred to as El Rey, or "the king," but can just as easily be interpreted as a female figure; I see her as a goddess. The clouds resemble an ornament worn on the upper lip of the principal Olmec symbol, the human embryo. At six to eight weeks, the human embryo doesn't quite look human, but shares many features with the embryos of other animals. It's a symbol of pluripotentiality; like a seed, it has great transformational possibility.

The cave itself is a mouth with speech scrolls issuing from it in typical Mesoamerican fashion. The divine queen within the cave sits on a throne and holds a bar; throne and bar are both decorated with curving designs that, again, refer to clouds. Her elaborate headdress includes a stylized bird, among other fascinating symbols of her dominion. She controls all the powers of earth, rain, human gestation and seed growth. The carving is located at the head of a main rainwater channel, further emphasizing her connection to growth.

Mesoamerica

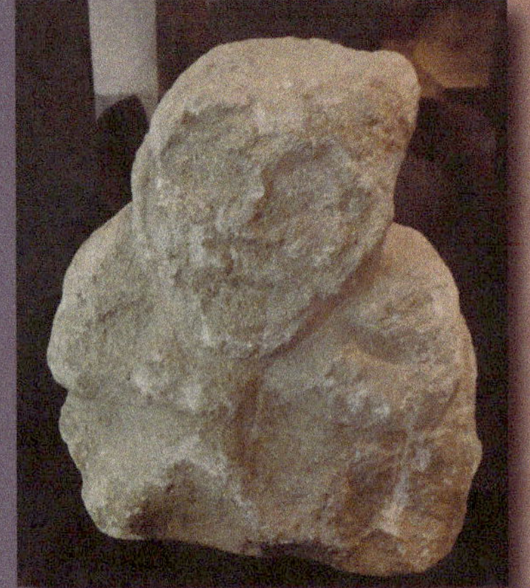

Cuicuilco
Crone

Cuicuilco[x] was an ancient city on the southern shore of Lake Texcoco, what has now become México City. It was occupied from 700 BCE to 150 CE. A circular pyramid on the site, near Universidad Nacional Autónoma de México (the National Autonomous University of México), is believed to be the oldest circular stone pyramid structure in the New World. Cuicuilco may also have been the earliest urban center in the Valley of México, which was roughly contemporary with, and possibly interacting with, the Olmec civilization on the Gulf Coast. In 400 CE, Cuicuilco was covered by a volcanic eruption and resulting lava field.

Cuicuilco's founders were farmers who developed the earliest hydraulic water system of the region, as well as a complex ritual practice that included funerary offerings. Many small ceramic "pretty ladies" were found at the pyramid site, along with a large, fierce stone figure that I call the Cuicuilco Crone.

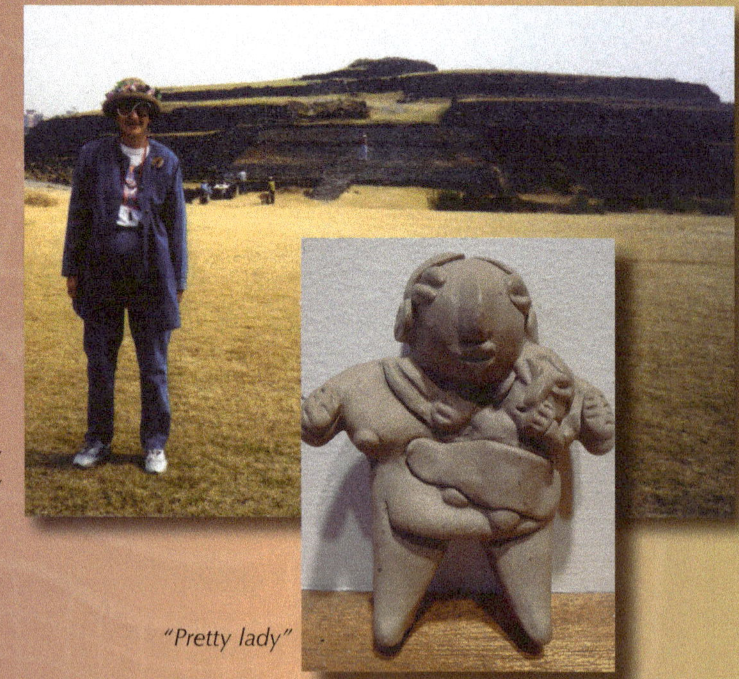

Cuicuilco Archeology site, México City

"Pretty lady"

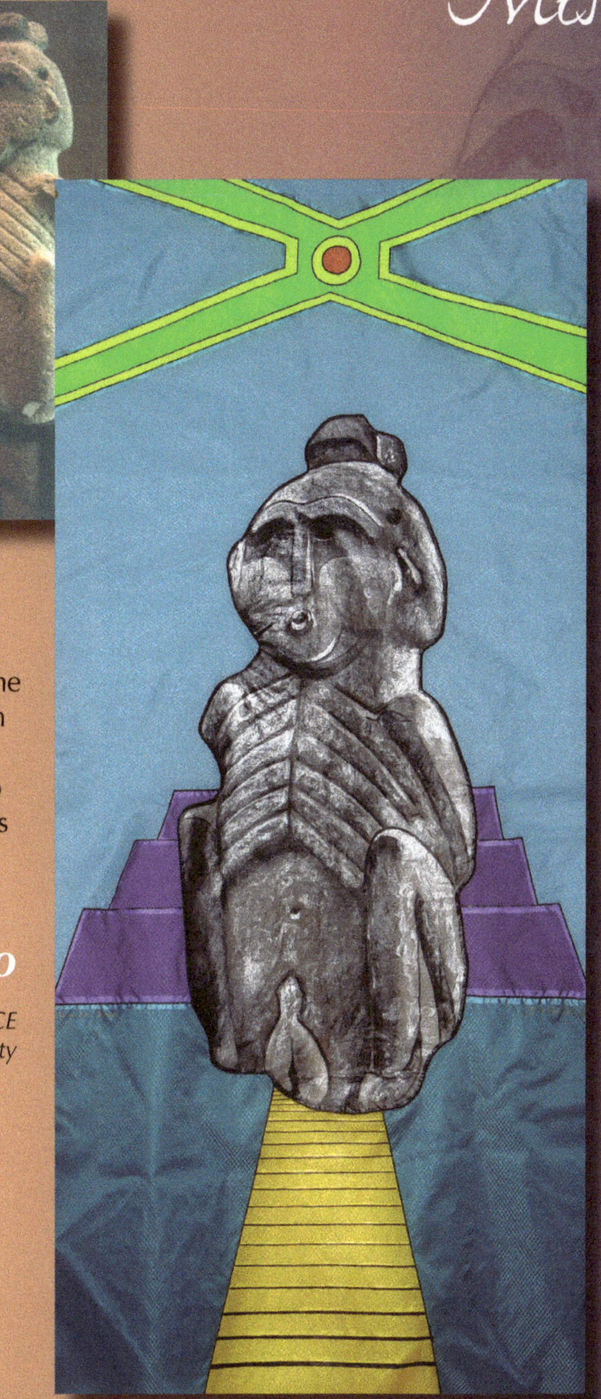

The Cuicuilco Crone is a life-size stone sculpture that now resides in a small museum at the archaeological site of Cuicuilco in México City. Her vulva and skeletal frame crouched in a fetal position symbolize the cycle of life and death. She is similar to other sacred display images found around the globe.

Cuicuilco

Source: Stone sculpture, c. 700–150 CE
Cuicuilco Museum, México City

Mesoamerica

Classic

By 100 CE, Mesoamerican social structure became more hierarchical and new concepts of rulership developed. To document the deeds of rulers, some civilizations, especially the Maya, developed writing and a new calendar, which tallied each day in a linear fashion. This new era is commonly referred to as the classic period and generally defined as the time in which the Maya recorded history in hieroglyphic writing. Where writing was most prominent, as in the Mayan area, the elite rulers, mostly male, downplayed the sacred feminine, but some women were honored with tombs and monuments. Where writing was less prominent, as in Teotihuacan, the sacred feminine remained a powerful force.

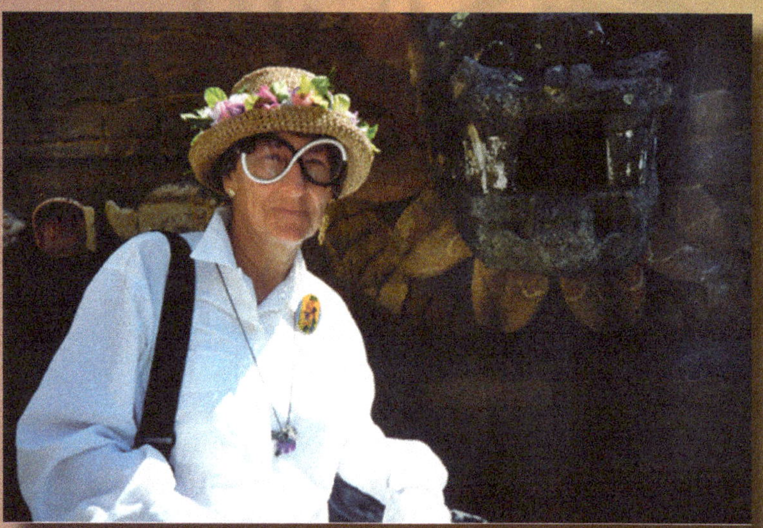

Lydia at Teotihuacan

Teotihuacan

Teotihuacan is the name of both the largest urban center in Mesoamerica and the civilization that centered there. Located in a valley to the northeast of the great lake that once existed in highland central México, where México City is today, the ceremonial center includes three large pyramids and a long avenue situated to echo the surrounding mountains and align with astronomical phenomena. This civilization flourished from about 150 BCE to 650 CE.

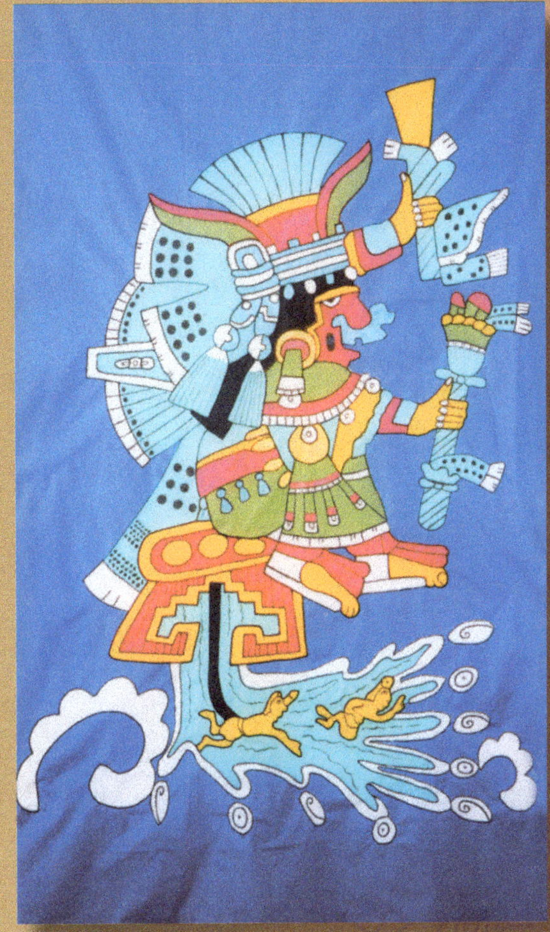

Chalchiuhtlicue

Drawing

The earliest inhabitants were influenced by the Gulf Coast Olmec and the city attracted traders and artisans from other Mesoamerican civilizations.

Like the Olmec of La Venta, the inhabitants of Teotihuacan worshipped a goddess, possibly the embodiment of Cerro Gordo, or "fat hill," a sacred mountain just north of a site associated with the goddess cult and the region's fertility. The Pyramid of the Moon, one of the three pyramids in the ceremonial center, mirrors the shape of the mountain. A monumental sculpture of a goddess placed in front of the pyramid suggests it was dedicated to a goddess who was a precursor to Chalchiuhtlicue, goddess of water, lakes and streams. She is honored on one of my banners.

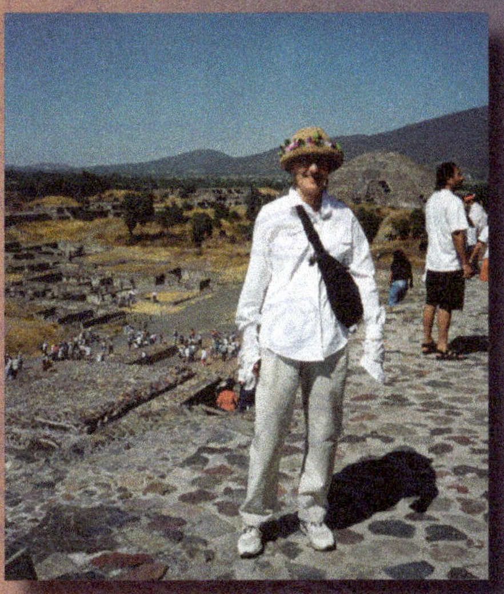

Teotihucan Pyramid of the Moon

On some of the structures within Teotihuacan, brightly painted frescoes represent a goddess of earth and vegetation. These murals feature a gloriously colored goddess adorned with a bird headdress, with the branches of a great tree of life fanning over her head. She sits on a throne of stars, seeds, flowers and roots, with nourishing waters flowing from her hands. The strata of earth, with caves, rocks, soil, plants, trees, spiders and other beings, are considered part of her realm.

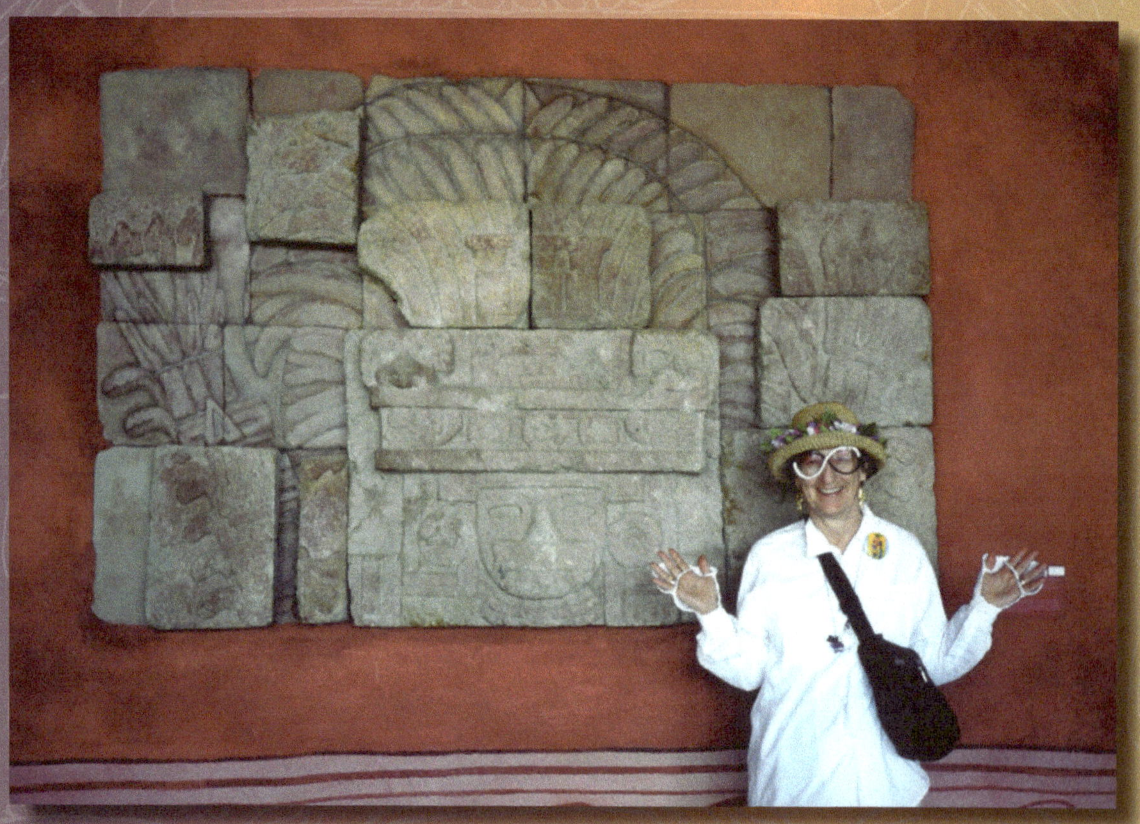

Lydia withTeotihuacan relief

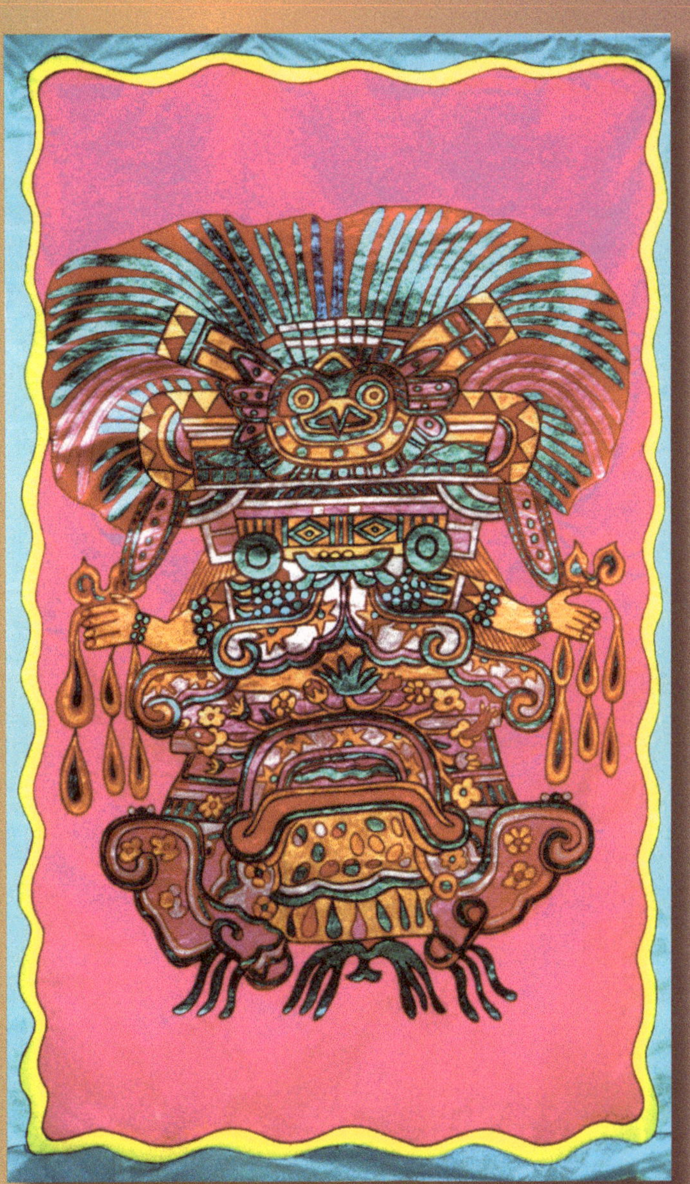

The goddess honored at Teotihuacan is thought to have been a goddess of the underworld, darkness, the earth, water and possibly even creation itself. The Pyramid of the Sun, a main feature of the ceremonial center, was built on top of a cave, which may have been a "place of emergence," the womb from which the first humans came into the world, a key theme in Mesoamerican mythology.

Teotihuacan Great Mother

Source: Fresco mural, c. 600 CE
Teotihuacan
National Museum of Anthropology
México City

Mesoamerica

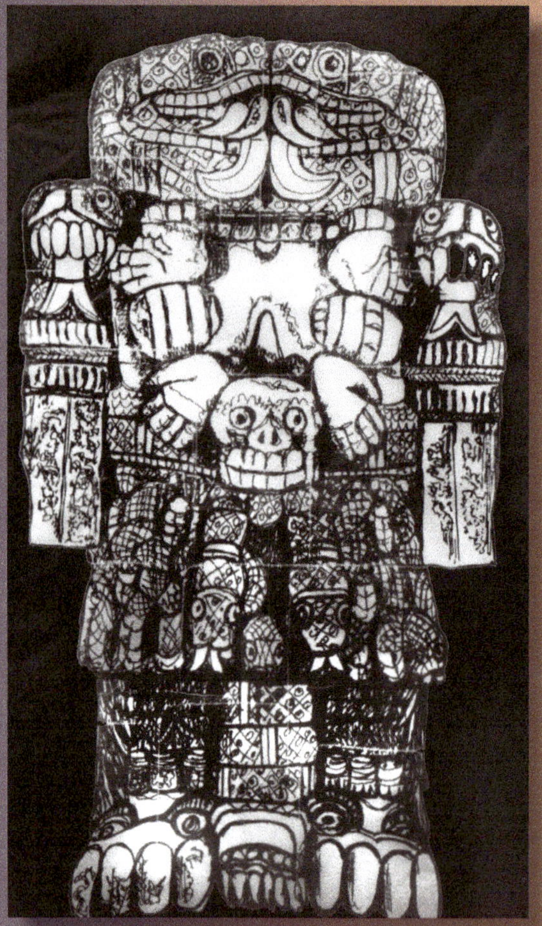

Coatlicue with her rattlesnake skirt, double serpent head and hands is the all-powerful great mother creatrix. In the Aztec myth. She is the mother of Coyoxauhqui, the sacrificed moon daughter. Her pendulous breasts nursed both gods and humans. Coatlicue wears a necklace of hearts, hands and a skull. She is the great duality of life and death.

Coatlicue

Stone sculpture,
National Museum of Anthropology,
México City

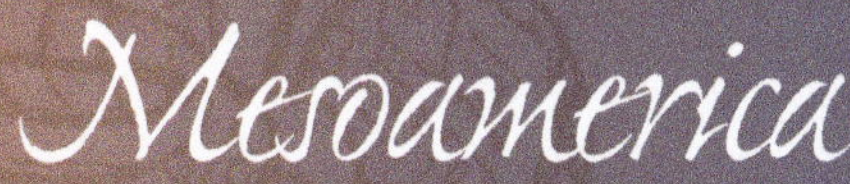

Post-Classic

During the post-classic period (950–1521 CE), regions were governed separately and developed into commercial areas. This was an era that saw a high level of artistic production, unequal to anything produced in the past. Competition for rare and exotic materials was fierce. The Mesoamerican economy traded widely, as evidenced by turquoise imported from the southwestern US.

Mesoamerica

Valley of México

After the fall of Teotihuacan around 800 CE, Mesoamerican cultures remained small and localized for the next several hundred years, until the Aztecs fought their way to prominence. The Aztecs, or Mexica people, adopted many of the religions and traditions they found in Central México, and goddesses played an important role. The goddesses appear in the screen-fold divinatory books, called codex (or codices, plural), produced by the Nahua, a group of people indigenous to Central México, of which the Aztecs are the best known. Although the Spanish destroyed most of these books, about five remain, revealing the important role goddesses played in the lives of the people, particularly the Codex Borbonicus and the Codex Borgia.

Itzpapalotl is a fearsome skeletal goddess with jaguar talons and obsidian-tipped wings. She was a stellar creature, called a *tzitzimitl*, who devoured humans during eclipses (the term *itzpapalotl* can signify either "obsidian butterfly" or "clawed butterfly"). Itzpapalotl was originally a goddess of the Chichimecs, later adopted by the Aztecs. In the post-classic period, Itzpapalotl became the matron of one of the twenty thirteen-day periods in the ancient 260-day divinatory calendar based on human gestation. This time period was related to another group of divine beings, the *cihuateteo*, women who died in childbirth and were honored for their bravery. Itzpapalotl also had a beneficent aspect as the goddess of the paradisical afterworld. called Tamoanchan, a birthplace of gods.

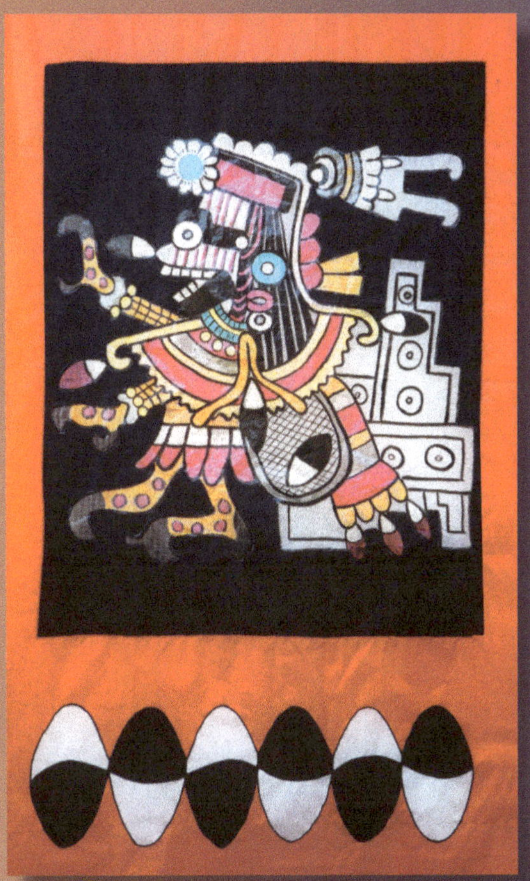

Itzpapalotl

Mayahuel is the goddess of the flowering maguey plant, whose rich sap milk ferments to become *pulque,* a sacred beverage. She is the tree of life growing sisal fibers for rope, thread and clothing, as well as food and drink. She is seated on her turtle throne of creation with her serpents, and she holds sharp thorn knives to cut through ignorance.

Mayahuel

Source: Codex Laud Folio, 9–10 frontal

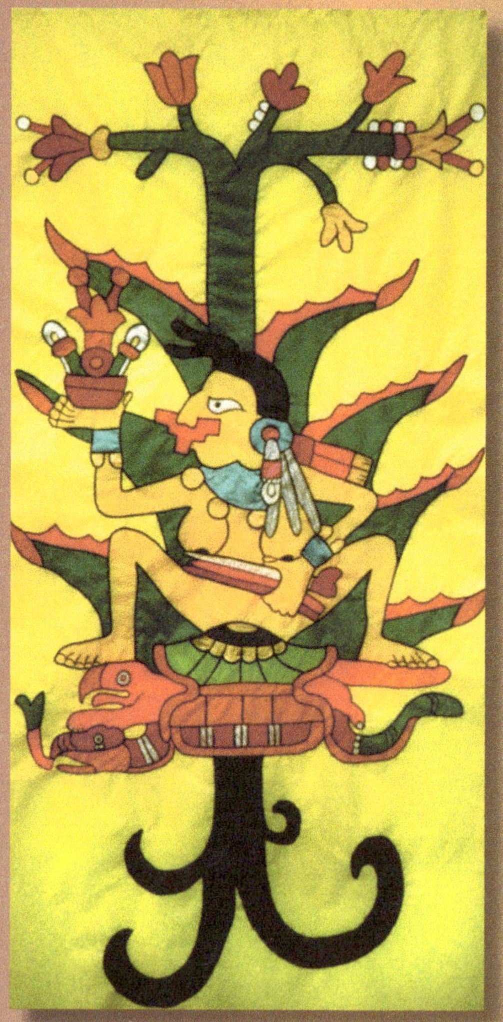

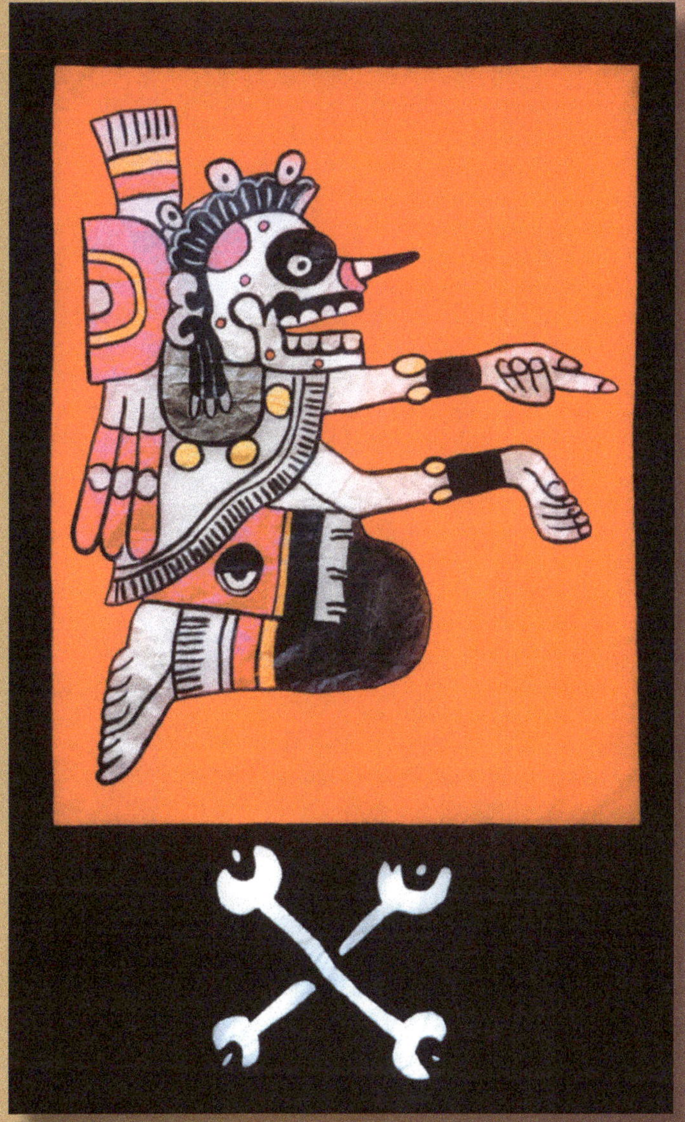

Mictlancihuatl is the lady of the realm of the dead, Mictlan. She is paired with Mictlantecutli, lord of Mictlan. She is the great mother of the cycles of life, creation and destruction, and she kneels on the bones of the ancestors. An eye of wisdom adorns her skirt.

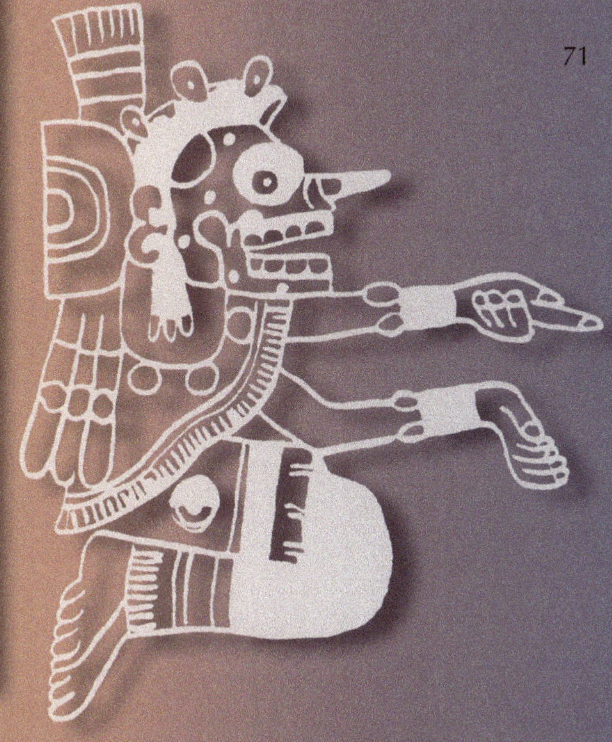

Mictlancihuatl

Source: Codex Fejervary Mayer

Mesoamerica

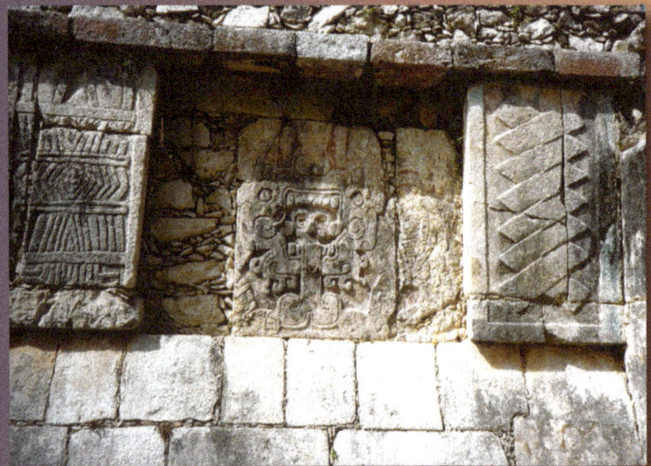

Venus Temple Chichen Itza, México

While visiting the Venus Temple *(Plataforma de Venus)* at Chichen Itza, I saw a stone relief sculpture with deeply inspiring imagery. The sculpture portrays the open mouth of a serpent with a face inside. This image calls to me as one of birth. I have added fierce claws reminiscent of Tlatecuhtli, the earth mother.

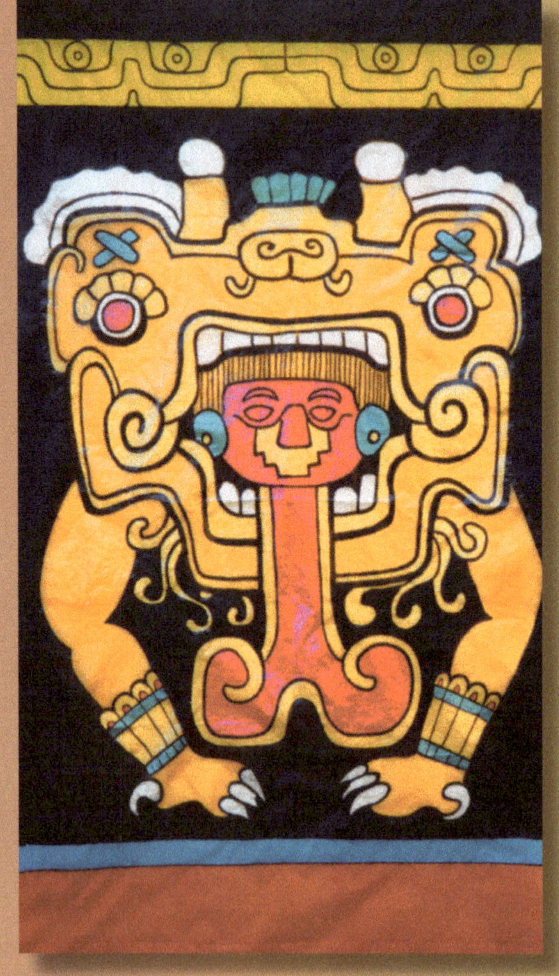

Venus Temple Chichen Itza

Source: Stone relief sculpture, c.1400 CE Temple of Venus, Chichen Itza

Tlazolteotl devours filth and darkness and gives birth to the soul. Crescent moons adorn her and she wears the sacrificed skin of her former innocent self with all its power. Facing the shadow and letting go is the critical part of the healing process. This image, based on her depiction in the Codex Borbonicus, shows her wearing unspun cotton on her headdress and ear ornaments, a symbol of a woman's power as a weaver and creatrix. In this banner, she is squatting to give birth.

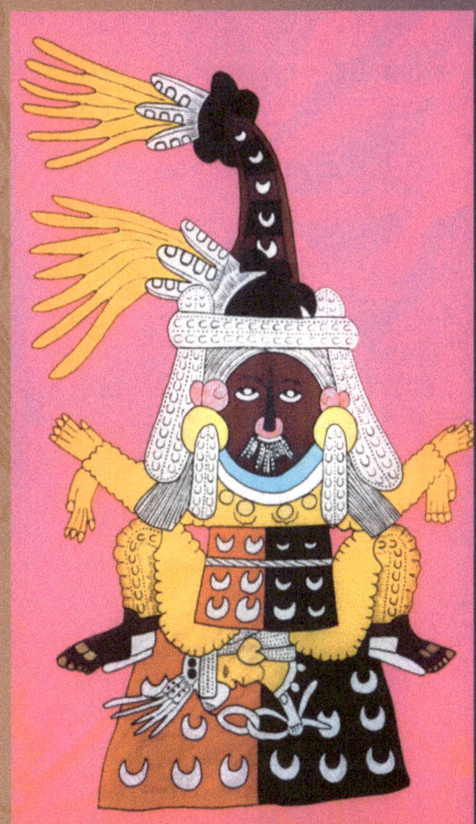

Tlazolteotl

Source: Codex Borbonicus

In this second image of Tlazolteotl, I see her as a magic transformer of energies. The artistic process is one of creation and birth, then death and letting go. This likeness finds her with arms outstretched holding her precious tools; the energies of creation come from understanding this endless cycle of duality. Tlazolteotl represents the positive and negative behaviors of women. She is the patroness of spinning, pregnancy, midwifery and divination, all quite proper behaviors in Aztec thought, but also of excessively carnal behavior and lust. She eats "filth," which could be excrement, but also could be disease or sin, thereby purifying people of the residue of improper carnal behavior. Tlazolteotl encourages the regulation and balance of desires and acts, craving and abstention, leading to the fluid equilibrium that promotes creation and regeneration.

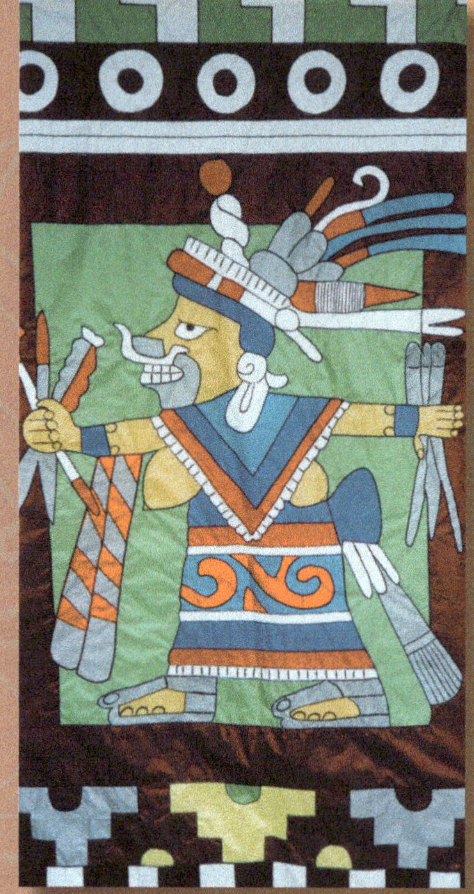

Tlazolteotl Artista

Source: Codex Laud Folio, 1819

Tlazolteotl is shown here squatting in the birthing position; her effort is fierce and unwavering. She is the protector of midwives and guardian of the *temazcal*, a cleansing ceremony like a type of sweat lodge. The waves in the banner are reminiscent of the *temazcal*. The Codex Laud depicts Tlazolteotl in a position of sacred display, suggesting her connection to birth and the gift of life.

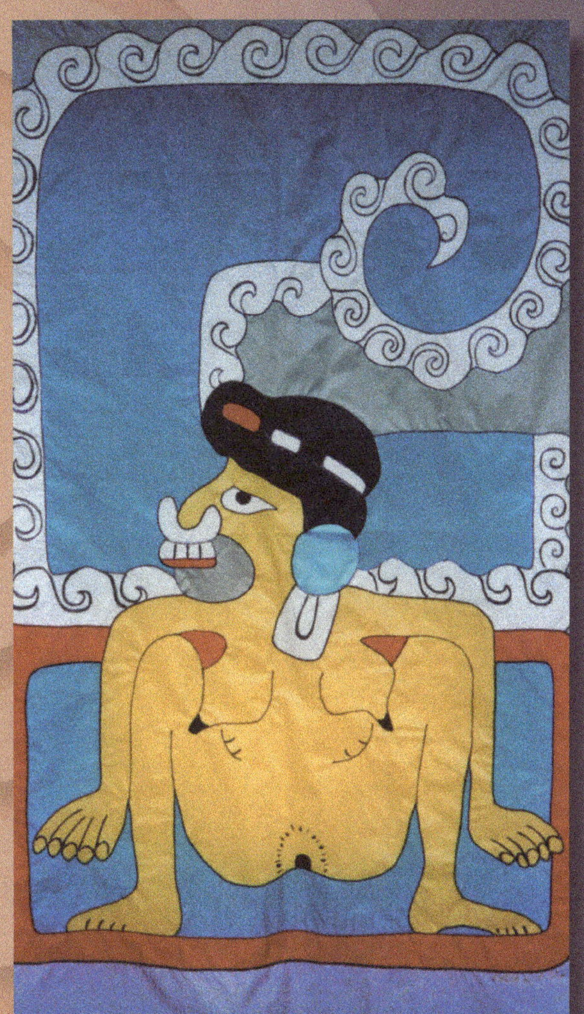

Tlazolteotl Temazcaltoci

Source: Codex Laud Folio 16–17

Tonacacihuatl is the lady of flesh and sustenance. Her roots are in earlier myths of fertility and food. In Nahuatl, the language of the Nahua people, *tonan* means “our mother.” Tonacacihuatl sits on a throne with three circles that symbolize the belt of Orion, associated with the hearth and fire. She wears double tufts of green quetzal feathers in her headdress and a skirt with red diamond designs, both of which are the insignia of Xochiquetzal, goddess of love, beauty and feminine activities. The snake image, such as the one on the bottom of the banner, is a primordial symbol in Mesoamerican culture.

Tonacacihuatl is rarely shown, but she is the female counterpart of Tonacatecuhtli. Together they are primordial gods connected with procreation and sustenance.

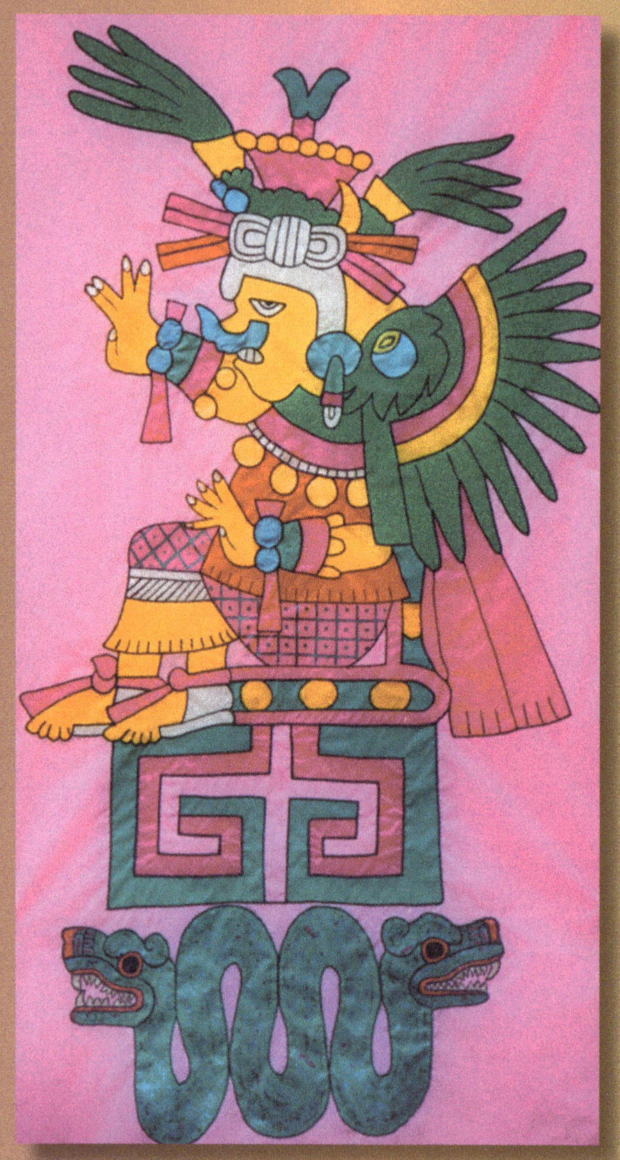

Tonacacihuatl

Source: Codex Telleriano-Remensis

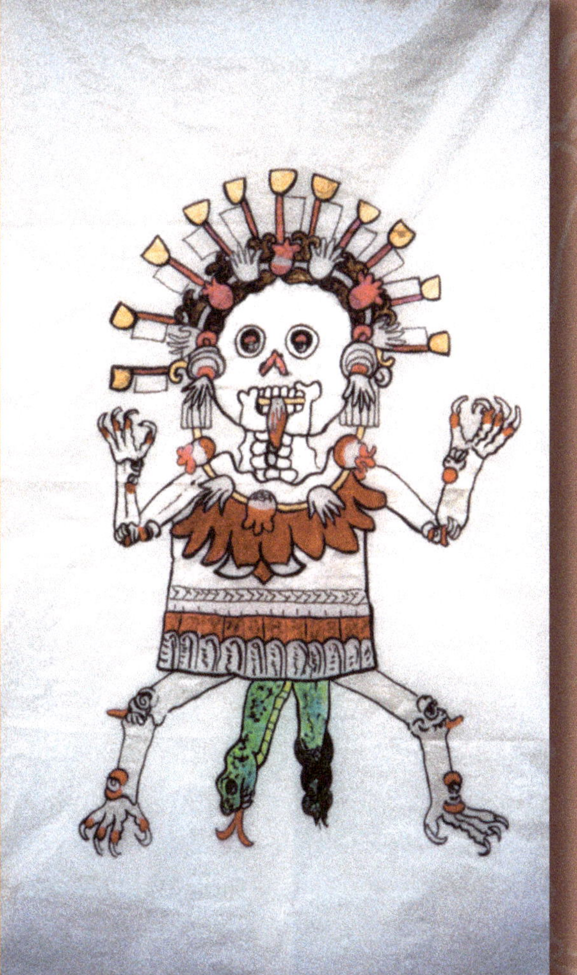

Tzitzimime are fear-inspiring skeletal female star-beings. As night creatures, they descend to earth garbed in skirts fringed with shells. These goddesses were associated with unstable times, such as eclipse. They were powerful and dangerous as well as being protectors.

Tzitzimitl

Source: Codex Magliabechiano

Xilonen, the maiden goddess, is the corn goddess associated with the young, tender ear of corn; her name literally means "young corn." As corn was the main food staple, each step in the growth of the plant and the ear of corn was differentiated with care and veneration. While Chicomecóatl represented the mature ear, Xilonen represented the intermediary stage between the budding corn ear and the mature one, so the goddess was portrayed as an adolescent girl. A temple in Tenochtitlán was dedicated to her, and a priestess danced and sang in her honor at the festival of Xilonen.

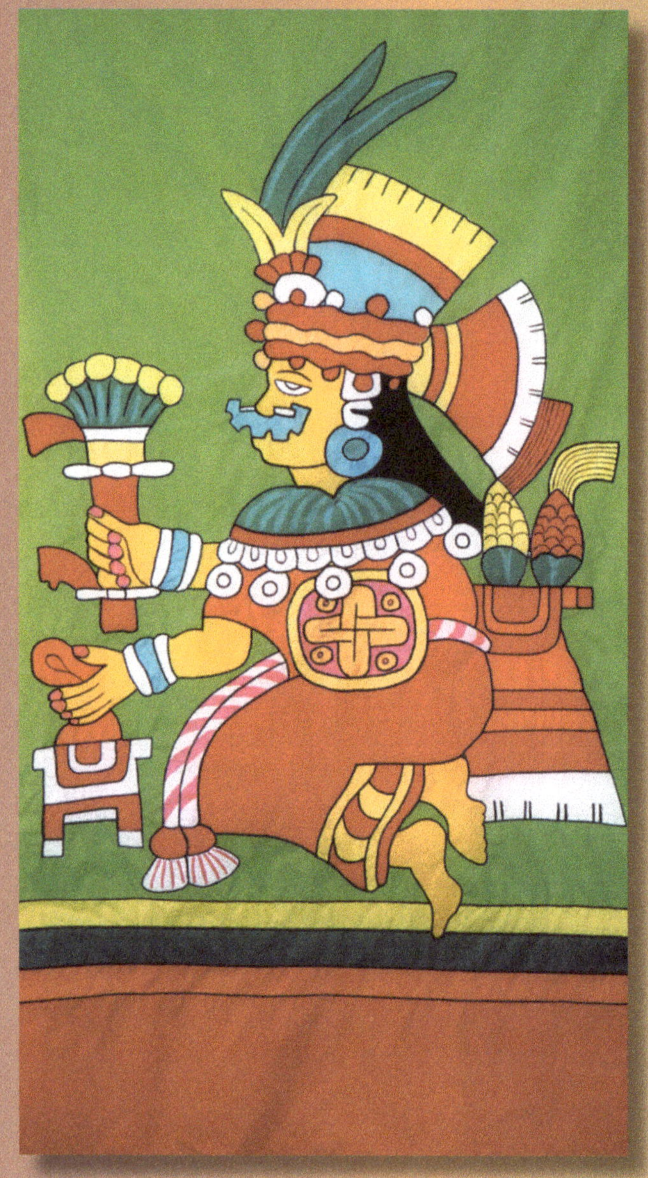

Xilonen

Source: Codex Magliabechiano

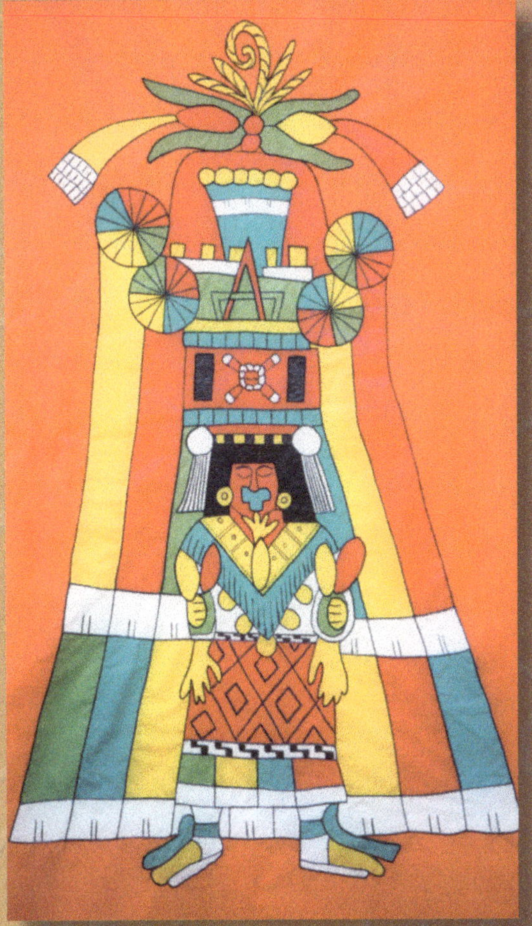

Chicomecóatl

Chicomecóatl is the Aztec goddess of food, especially maize. In this rendition of her, based on her image in the Codex Borbonicus, her face is painted red, and a tall, crown-like structure adorns her head. She wears rosettes and holds double ears of corn. Chicomecóatl's skirt is a vulva-like diamond pattern that represents the germinating power of Mother Earth, but she is also wearing the flayed skin of a human sacrificial offering, embodying the cycle of seed, growth, flowering and death. In the accompanying photo, Chicomecóatl is carved from stone, her head replaced with seven intertwining snakes. She is dressed as a ball player, possibly representing her ties to death and regeneration.

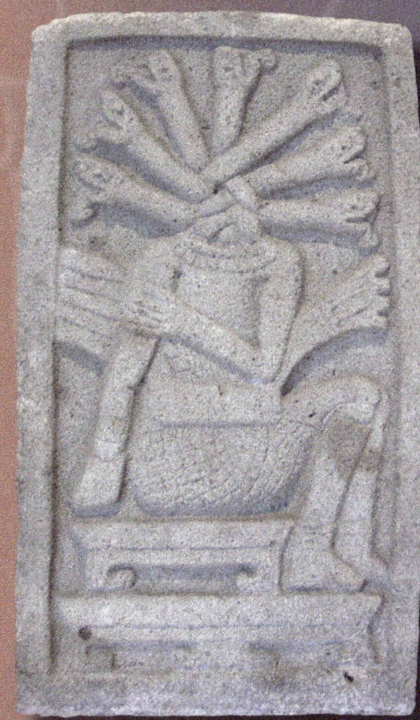

Seven-headed stone Chicomecóatl from the Anthropology Museum (Museo de Anthropología), in Xalapa, Veracruz

Mesoamerica

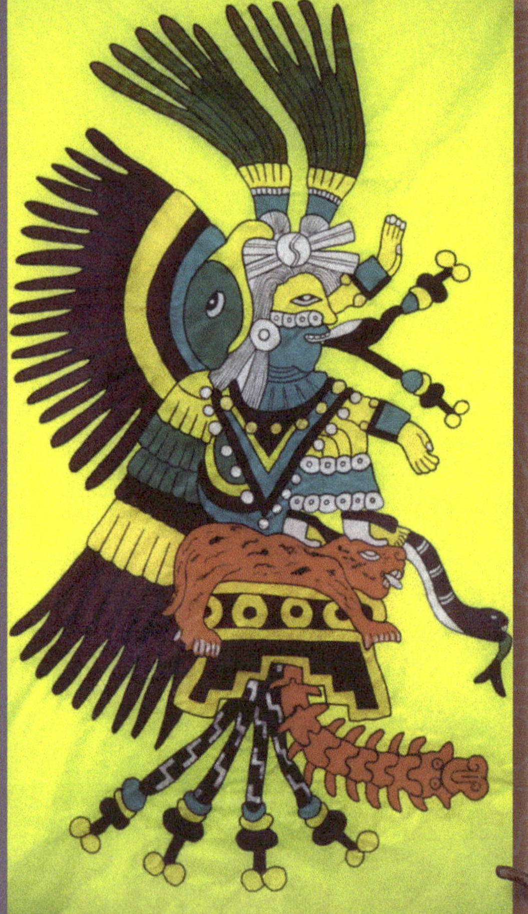

Xochiquetzal

Xochiquetzal represents young female sexual power, pleasure and love. Because weaving is a metaphor for female generative activity, she is patroness of weaving, along with the older goddesses Toci and Tlazolteotl. All fragrant flowers originated from a piece of her fleshy labia that had been bitten off by a bat. She is honored in the divinatory calendar as the patroness of a time when practitioners of luxury arts—including metalsmiths, feather workers, sculptors, painters and weavers—offered a sacrificial woman, who became the Xochiquetzal impersonator. After she was sacrificed and flayed, men donned her skin and sat at a loom while the craftspeople danced in animals costumes.

In this image, based on one from the Codex Borbonicus, Xochiquetzal sits on a throne with a jaguar skin seat, which symbolizes the power and protection of the great mother.

Yucatán Peninsula

The Yucatán Peninsula is located at the southeast tip of what is now México, surrounded by the Gulf of México to the north and the Caribbean Sea to the south. The peninsula is the homeland for the peoples of the Mayan lowlands, where Mayan languages are still commonly spoken. Well-known archaeological sites in the Yucatán include Chichen-Itza, Tulum and Uxmal.

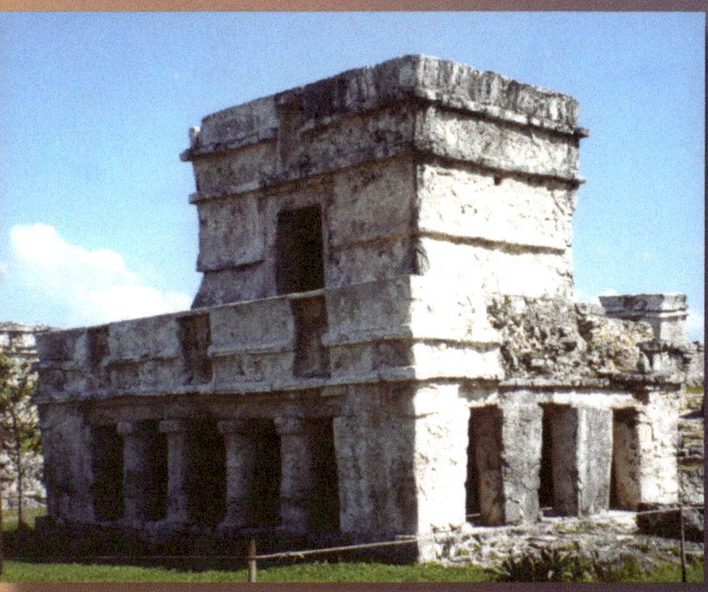

Tulum

This area is also called the Mayan Riviera because of its beautiful white sand beaches. The *cenotes,* which are natural pits or sinkholes filled with water that are common throughout the area, are considered sacred and often associated with goddess worship. Although the *cenotes* are landlocked, they are still connected with the ocean, so the water is saline with sweet rainwater on top. They are truly magical places.

Mesoamerica

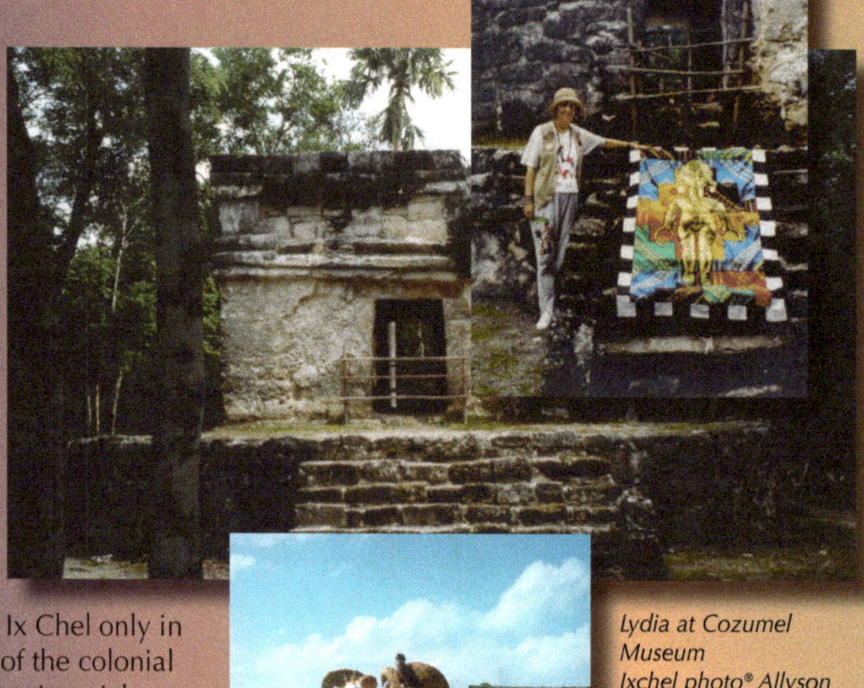

Ix Chel is the divine feminine creatrix specifically of the Maya, whose shrines were islands on the Caribbean coast, Cozumel and Isla Mujeres (Island of Women). In 1998 and 1999, I was with a group that performed ceremony here.

We find the name Ix Chel only in writings by Spaniards of the colonial era. According to the testimonials of the Maya, Ix Chel only appeared during a ritual that honors Bacabes, one of the oldest of four pre-Hispanic deities. Ix Chel was the wife of Itzamná, the supreme deity of the Maya; together they formed a divine couple and created the world.

Lydia at Cozumel Museum
Ixchel photo® Allyson Rickard 1999

Lydia at Isla Mujeres

Mesoamerica

She was known as "Our Mother" and "Our Mother of Sustenance." In the Yucatán, she was known as Ix Chel, Acna, Uo, The White Lady and Ixchebelyax. Her name means Lady (Ix) of the Rainbow (Chel or Cheel). She is sometimes depicted with blonde hair (Ch'el), suggesting a relationship with the moon.[xi]

Ix Chel is the archetype for women's activities. She is creative inspiration for artists and craftspeople, weaving the web of life; she is also patroness of weavers and clothing makers. She is associated with gestation, birth, midwifery and healing, learned in the use of medicinal plants and the healing gifts of nature.

Mesoamerica

Ix Chel sits on the moon as it moves through cycles of waxing, fullness, waning and darkness, mirroring women's blood mysteries and the cycles of human life. She is associated with divination in the pregnancy-related 260-day calendar, and related to lunar influences on tides and the germination of seeds. Ix Chel holds her rabbit of fertility and abundance.

Inspired by the stone relief sculpture at Tulum, a depiction often identified as the Diving God, I have reimagined this image as a Diving Moon Goddess, with aspects of Ix Chel. In this banner, serpents crown her and she carries sacred plants, a mirror and ritual objects. I envision Ix Chel diving into the universe, bringing sacred accoutrements with her.

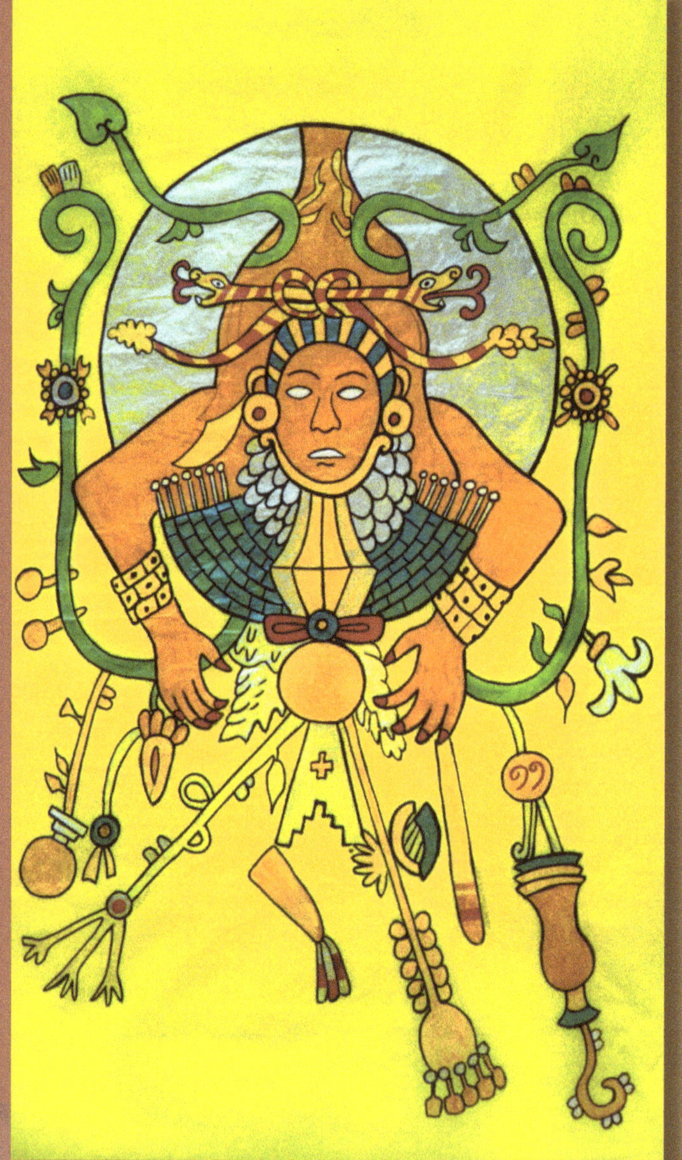

Ix Chel Moon Goddess

Source: Stone relief at Tulum

Another depiction of Ix Chel is that of a young woman, as in this representation of her holding a rabbit and sitting on a moon sign. In Copan, a Mayan archaeological site, there is a bench with a similar image of the young woman with the rabbit and the moon glyph.[xii] Ix Chel is a moon goddess; sometimes she looks like the crone, and sometimes the maiden, as she moves through her phases.

In this banner, I have taken a well-known image of Ix Chel with her iconic rabbit symbol and added a design inspired by the symbols in the temple at Uxmal in the upper corner.

Ix Chel
Queen of the Moon

Source: Clay vessel
Late classic Mayan
From Dumbarton Oaks Museum in Washington, DC

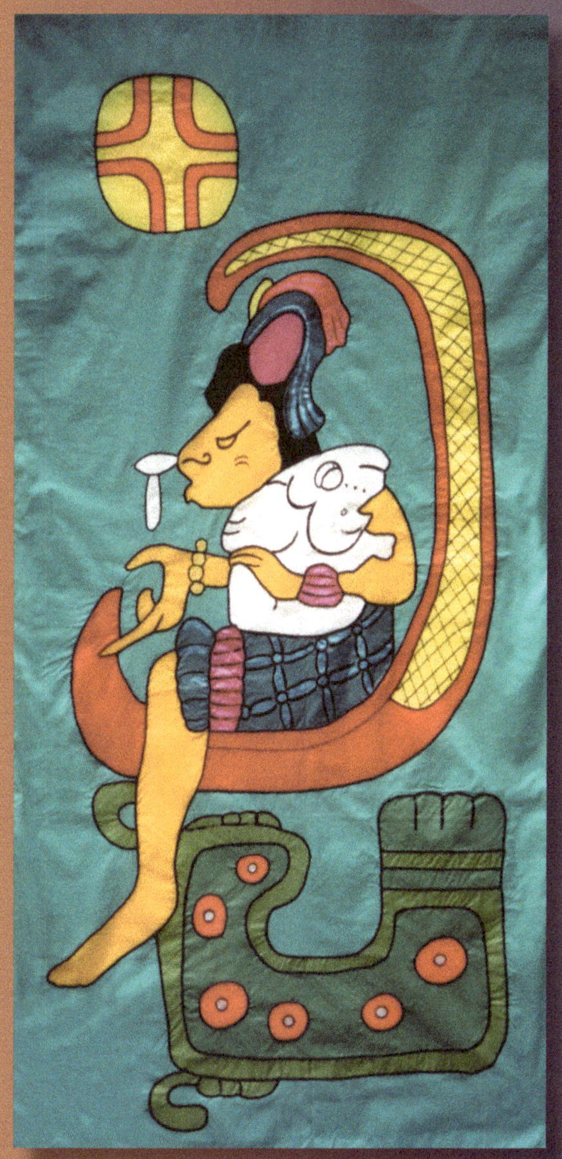

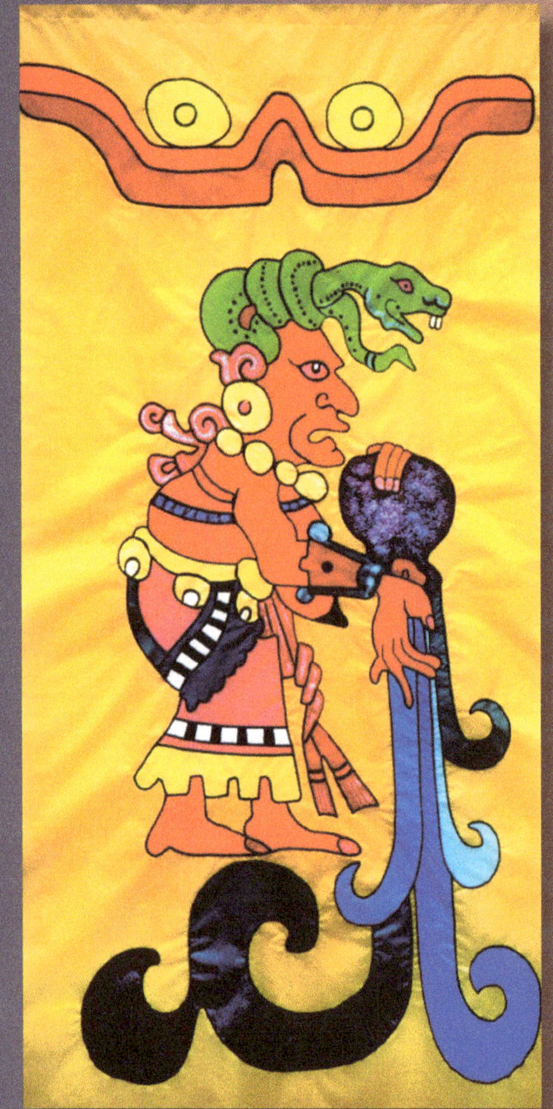

I also see Ix Chel as the old crone of wisdom pouring the waters of life from her vessel cauldron. The design at the top of this banner was inspired by the stone relief at Uxmal; I see it as reminiscent of the eyes of wisdom. One of the possible meanings of her name is Lady Rainbow, and her totem animal spirit is the snake, which sheds its skin and is continually reborn, like the moon. A serpent crowns her.

Ix Chel Crone

Source: Dresden Codex page 74
background drawing of Dresden Codex page 74

Ix Chel, fierce and strong, protects women and children. Rays of power extend from her breasts and between her legs; I interpret this exquisite force as representing the nourishing milk that flows from her breasts and the sacred blood of life that flows from her womb. Ix Chel's temple at San Gervasio on Cozumel was a pilgrimage destination for women seeking healing, pregnancy and a safe childbirth.

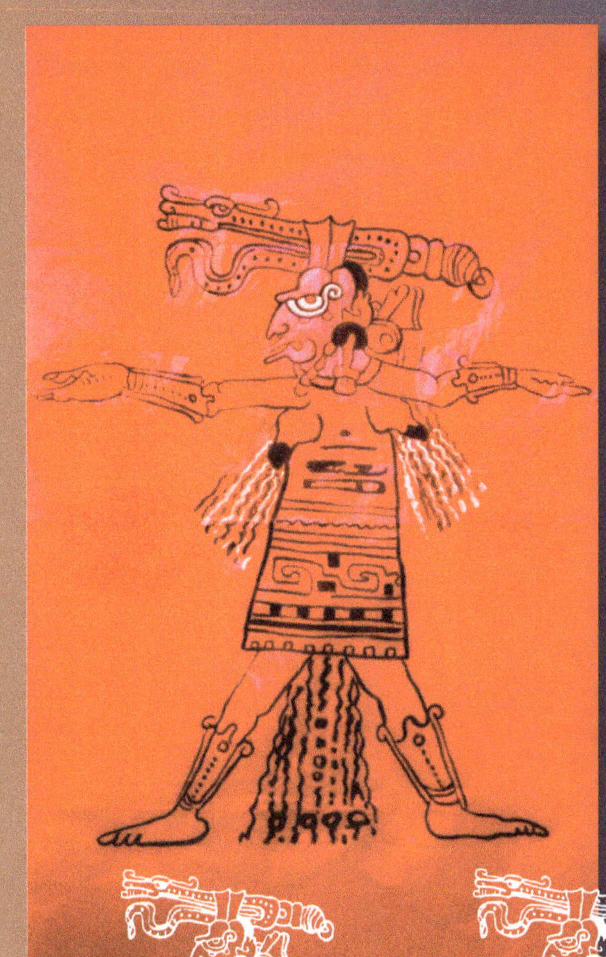

Ix Chel Tree of Life

Source: Codex Madrid lamina 27

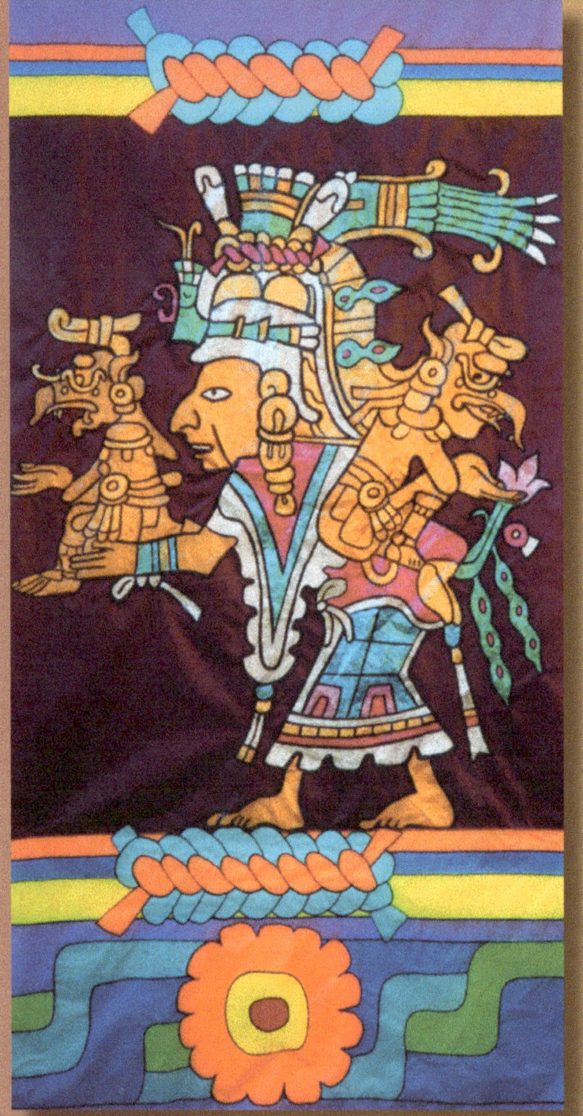

Ix Chel is the Mayan Great Mother Goddess, the cosmic feminine duality. In this image from Tulum, she carries two images of Chaac, the deity of rain. I have drawn both young and old versions of Chaac. All humans have both male and female energies within their psyches, and when they come together, all life flowers and grows. This rendition of Ix Chel is unique because it is in the Mixtec-Puebla style rather than Mayan, showing the cross-pollination of these cultures. On the banner, the knotted threads symbolize Ix Chel weaving the threads of life.

Ix Chel
Mayan Great Mother

Ixcacauix is the name of the Goddess of Cacao, who is referred to in the Popol Vuh, the Mayan creation story. She is mentioned in the invocation of the Blood Moon, the mother of the divine twins. Blood Moon asks Ixcacauix for help, specifically to bring food to her mother-in-law:

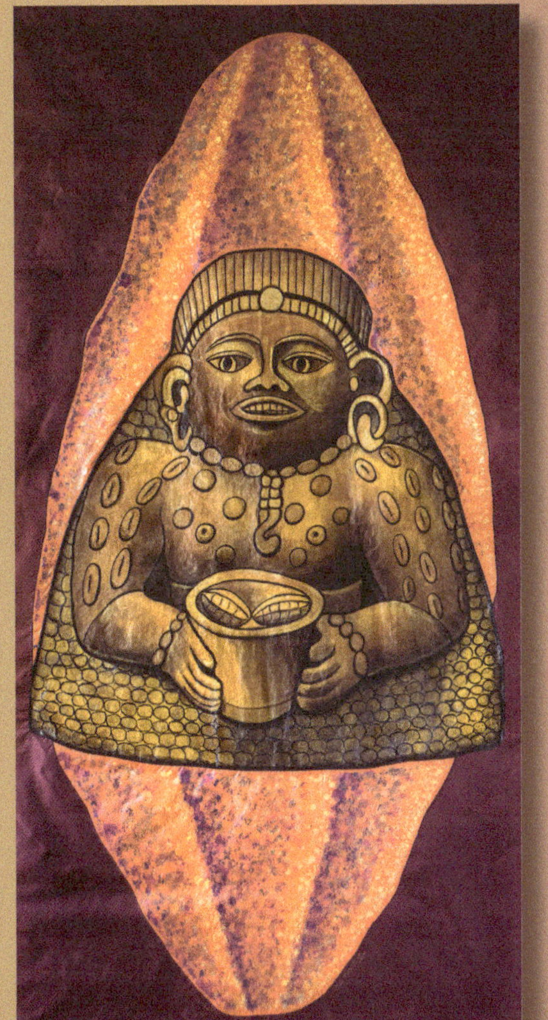

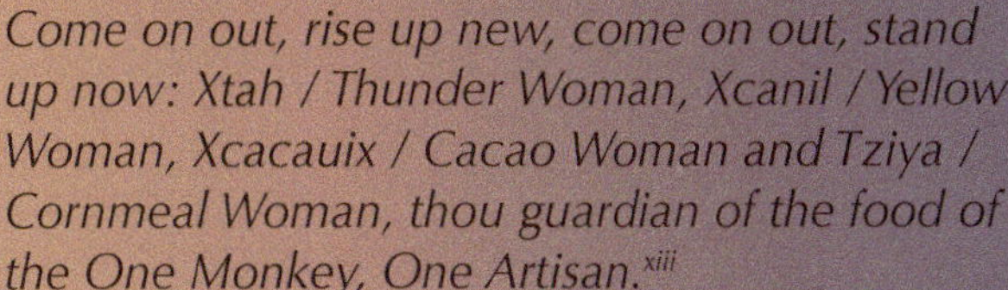

Come on out, rise up new, come on out, stand up now: Xtah / Thunder Woman, Xcanil / Yellow Woman, Xcacauix / Cacao Woman and Tziya / Cornmeal Woman, thou guardian of the food of the One Monkey, One Artisan.[xiii]

I see Ixcacauix as connected to matriarchal societies where women gathered the crops and saw to it that everyone was fed. Her wisdom is a counterpoint to the economic hustle of our modern world with its frantic buying and selling for profit and greed. She reminds us that a luxurious world unfolds when you take a moment to quiet your "busy-ness" and rejoice in what gives you pleasure. The shape of the cacao pods reminds me of the vulva.

Ixcacauix

Source: Clay sculpture. Mayan. n.d.

Mesoamerica

Colonial

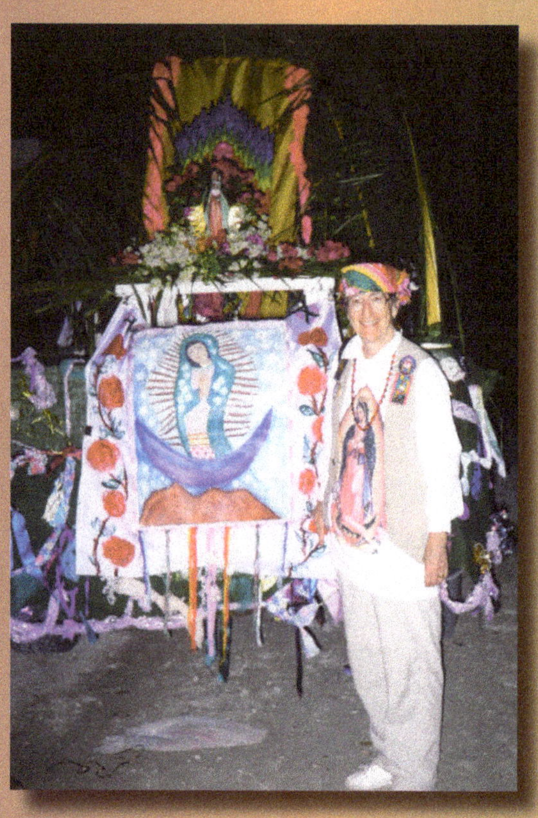

Lydia at Guadalupe celebration 1999

Female images have deep roots in time. Blackness is associated with the earth and fertility as the sources of life and death. These sources come to us with dark images of a sacred female from Africa, the Middle East, Old Europe, Asia and the western hemisphere. Some of her names are Isis of Egypt, Diana of Ephesus, Crow Mother of the Hopi, Aumakua of Hawai'i and Kali of India.

During the first millennium, as Christianity gained power, it took over the sacred images of previous cultures and religions. During the 12th and 13th centuries, crusaders carried images of Notre Dame, Unsere Schwarze Frau, Santa Maria, Nuestra Señora and La Madonna on their journeys to and from the Holy Land. Over 200 churches, shrines and cathedrals were built on the pilgrimage routes in Europe. In the 15th century, Europe discovered the New World. People brought their images with them to the Western Hemisphere, where they joined with indigenous images and were exchanged and absorbed into new images and herstories.

Nuestra Señora (Our Lady) is a sacred image—an icon. All people and cultures create icons to honor the sacred dimension. Images are powerful. The essence of spirituality and religion is kindness, unconditional love and acceptance of human imperfection. The Black Madonna, as the mother of us all, embodies this ideal.

Nuestra Señora La Virgen de Guadalupe is the present name of the goddess in the southwestern United States. The Spaniards brought black madonnas with them to the western hemisphere and carried them north from México with traders and priests. Presently, immigrants from México bring Guadalupe with them. She reigns in churches, santos, murals, shrines, jewelry, cars, tattoos and prisons. La Virgen is the most beloved goddess of all the Americas today. At Zuni Pueblo in New Mexico, a mosaic of Guadalupe stands over the main altar, and the Zuni goddesses and gods bring their offerings to her in a fresco on both sides of the mission church.

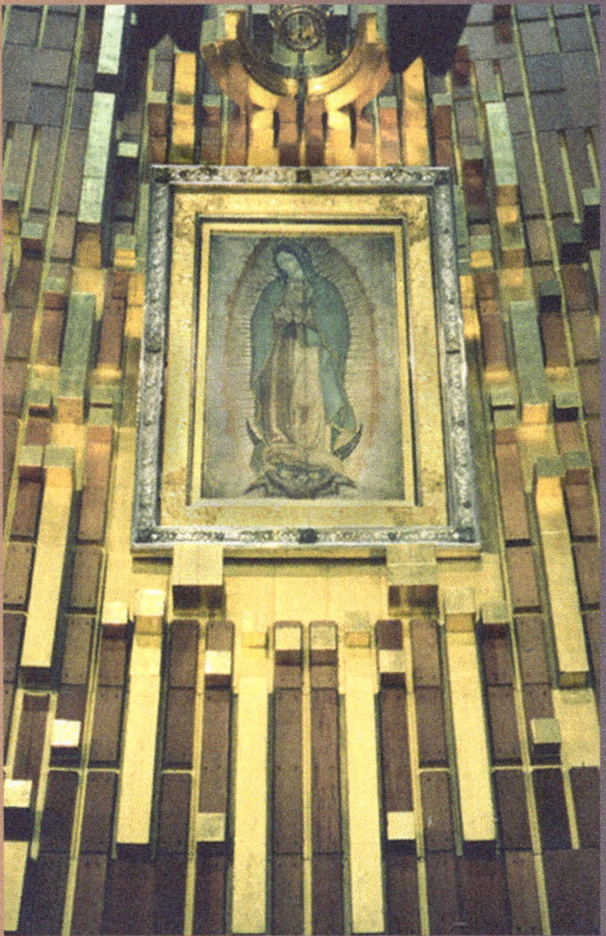

Basilica of Our Lady of Guadalupe

Mesoamerica

Nuestra Señora La Virgen de Guadalupe is also the present name of the Great Mother Goddess of México, an emanation of Tonantzin, the Aztec Mother Goddess. La Virgen spoke to Juan Diego, who was an indigenous man rather than one of the Spanish colonialists, and asked him to build her a church at Tepeyac, a hill (located in present-day México City) where the Aztecs had traditionally revered Tonantzin. Miraculously, La Virgen's image appeared on his *tilma*, or "cloak," wrapped around many red roses as proof of his vision. The *tilma* hangs in the basilica dedicated to La Virgen de Guadalupe. Today she is considered the queen of heaven and earth in México and the American southwest.

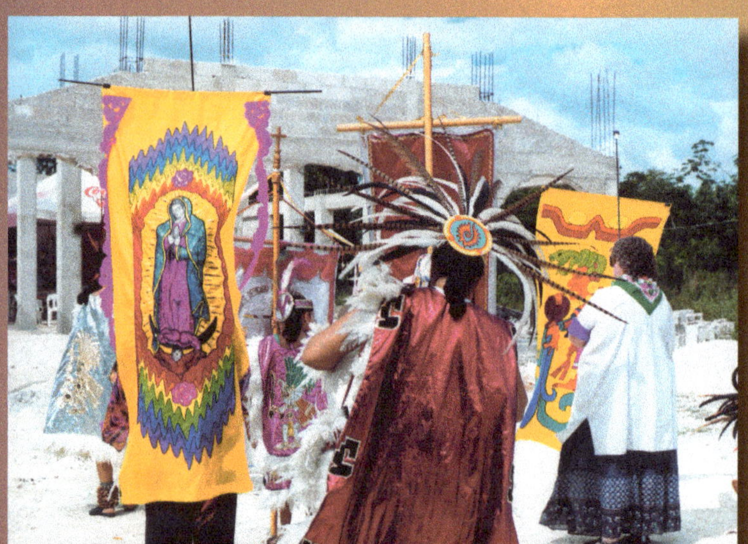

Maya Colona, Yucatan

My banner of Guadalupe has been exhibited in México and around the globe since 1998. Copies of her hang at the Mayan Women's Center in Puerto Morelos, México, and with the Franciscan Sisters of Perpetual Adoration in La Crosse, Wisconsin.

Guadalupe

Source: Painting on cloth, c. 1534
Basilica of Our Lady of Guadalupe
Tepeyac, México City

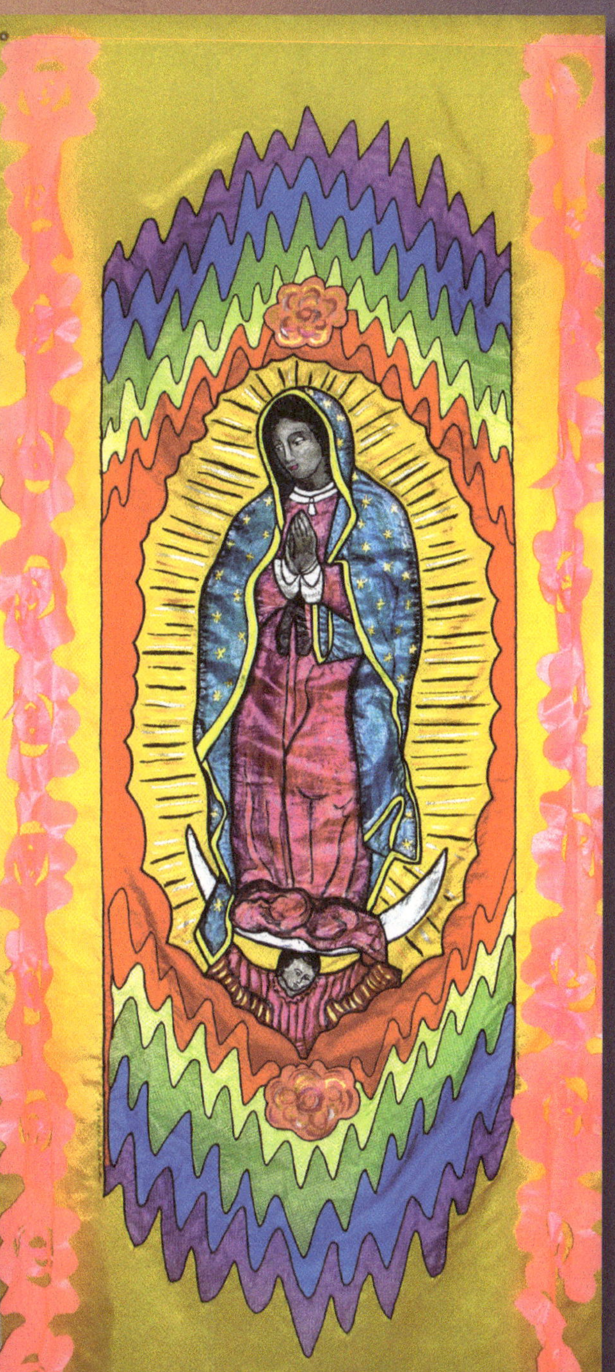

Land of High Mountains

Ayiti, "land of high mountains," is the indigenous Taíno name for the present-day Republic of Haiti, one of many Caribbean islands inhabited at the time of European arrival by the Taíno, a matrilineal culture who spoke an Arawakan language. Queen Anacaona is revered as one of the country's founders because of her role in fighting the Spanish conquistadors.

Haitian Vodou is a rich spiritual tradition that originated in the French slave colony of Saint-Domingue. Taíno beliefs were syncretized with practices descended from West African religions, European spirituality (including Roman Catholic Christianity) and mysticism, Freemasonry and other influences. To navigate daily life, vodouisants (followers of vodou) cultivate personal relationships with the spirits by presenting offerings; creating personal altars, devotional objects and colorful banners; and participating in elaborate ceremonies of music, dance and spiritual possession.

I first saw the Black Madonna Ezili Danto at a fantastic exhibition on Vodou art at the Fowler Museum at UCLA. She became a banner in 2009 and has joined my other black madonnas and dark mothers flying in exhibitions around the globe. She reminds me of the Black Madonna of Czestochowa in Poland.

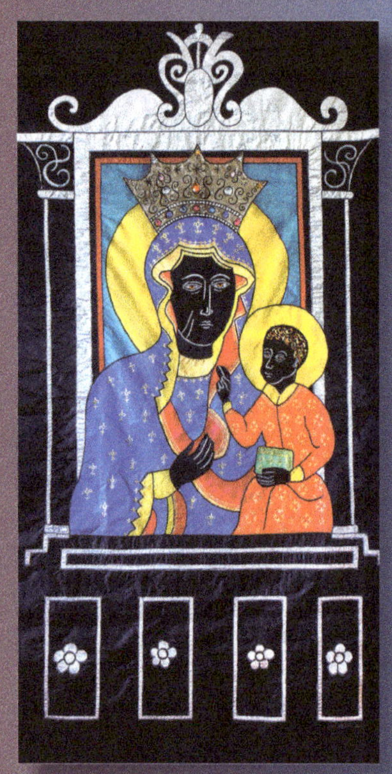

Madonna of Czestochowa banner

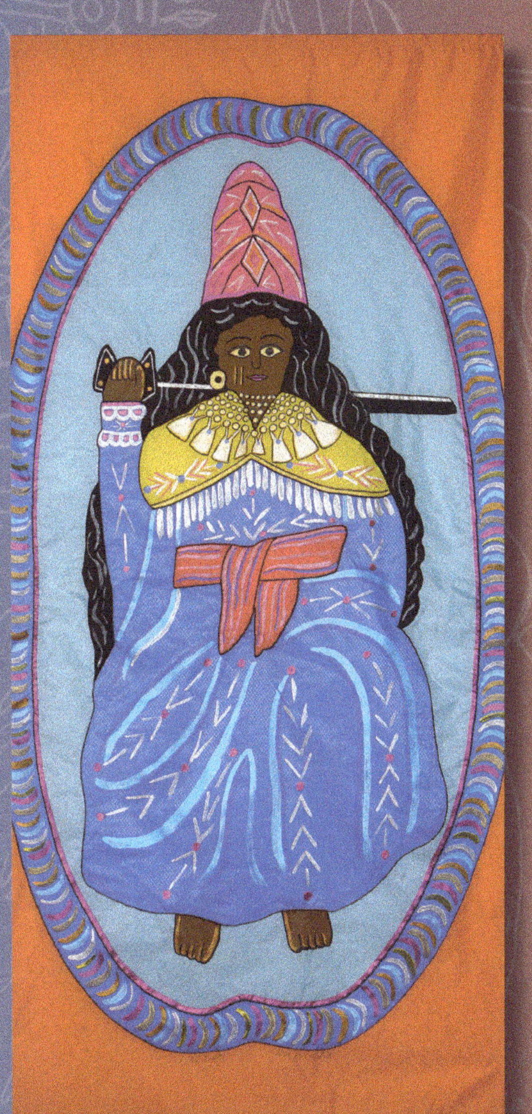

Ezili Danto, often depicted as a scarred and buxom black woman, was a hardworking and fiercely protective mother of Haitian Vodou. She was a particularly ferocious protector of women and children and is often identified with lesbian women. The scratches on her cheek remind us of her bitter rivalry with Freda and her connection to the Black Madonna of Blood. Knives persist in her iconography. Ezili dresses in blue, red and gold. She likes to be sprayed with Florida Water, drinks Barbancourt rum and prefers to eat fried pork.

Goddess Banner of Haiti

Source: Calabash painting by Andre Pierre, 1950s [xiv]

The Taíno, the indigenous inhabitants of the Caribbean islands and the first to encounter the Spanish, were Arawak people who migrated from the coastal regions of northern South America around 600 CE. In the matrilineal Taíno culture, the family name, material property, social status and power were passed down on the mother's side of the family, and mothers, sisters and grandmothers enjoyed a privileged social status. Yet less than fifty years after contact with the Spanish, the Taíno culture was virtually extinct—the population reduced to fewer than 500, primarily due to smallpox.

One of the few extant sites of the Taíno culture is preserved in the Indigenous Ceremonial Center of Caguana (Centro Ceremonial Indígena de Caguana) of Puerto Rico, located in the midst of a tropical forest. The site contains ball courts as well as a large plaza of stones etched with petroglyphs on boulders thought to have been carried from the nearby Tanama River. The three peaks of Cemi Mountain (Montaña Cemí), symbolic of Taíno ancestral spirits, rise above the site.

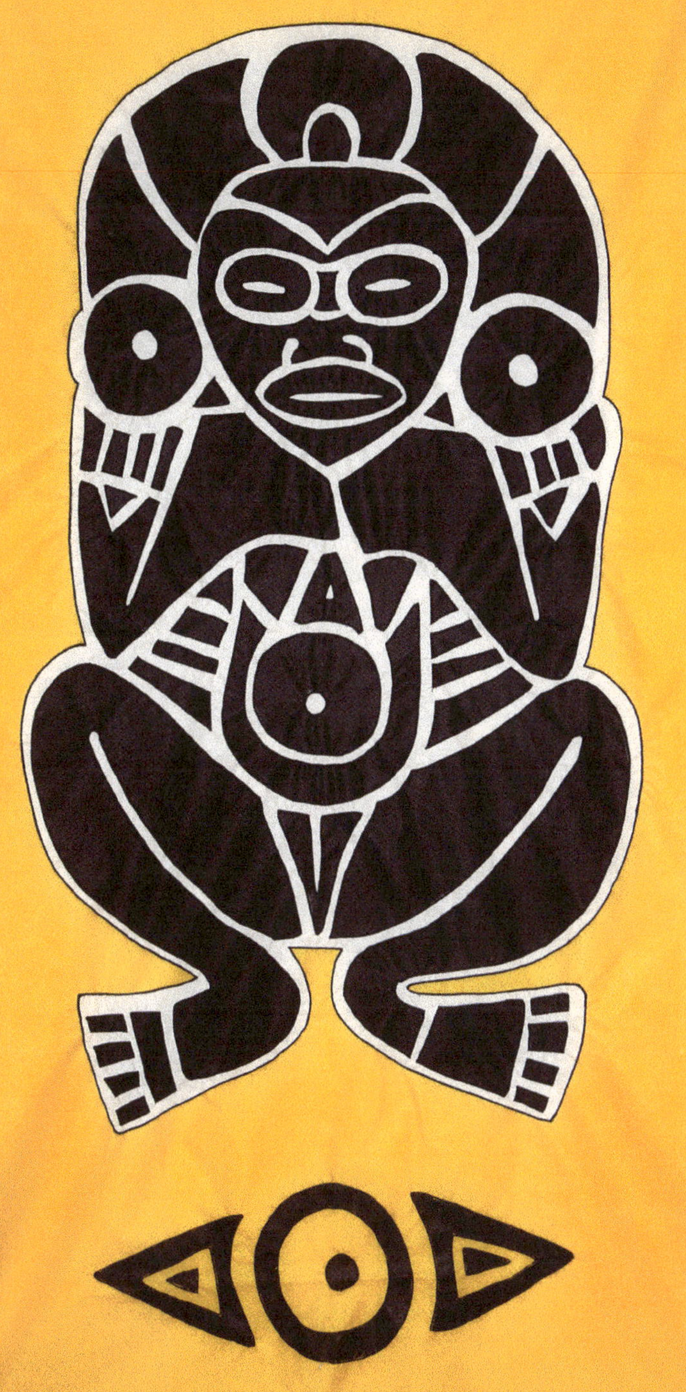

Puerto Rico

One of the most famous petroglyphs of the Taíno culture is Atabey, meaning "mother earth," also known as *mujer de caguana*, or "mother of creation," a form of the earth goddess. Atabey's image, with her splayed legs, echoes female figures of sacred display found throughout the world.

Goddess Banner of Puerto Rico

Source: Petroglyph. n.d.
Ceremonial Park
Cangianas, Puerto Rico

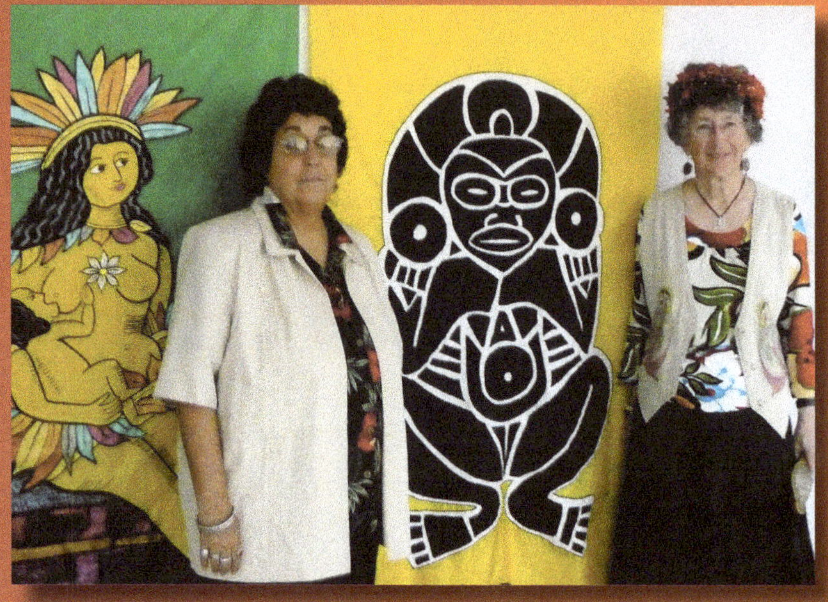

Maria Suarez and Lydia in Costa Rica

I met Maria Suarez at The Second World Congress on Matriarchal Studies in San Marcos, Texas in 2005. She invited me to display the goddess banners at the premiere of her musical, *Wings of the Butterfly,* in San José, Costa Rica, in 2008. For this event, I created the banner of Atabey, as Maria is from Puerto Rico.

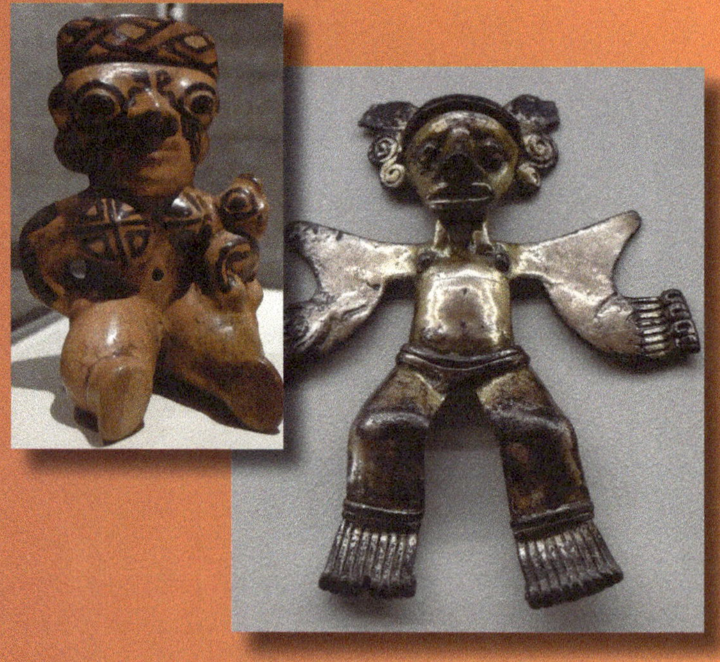

Central America | Costa Rica

While in Costa Rica, I delivered a presentation and hung the banners at the University of San José; I also visited the Museo Banco Central de Costa Rica, taught a workshop at one of the Planned Parenthood clinics and visited Irazu Volcano National Park. I then traveled onward to the town of Cartago, which served as the capital of Costa Rica until 1823, but more importantly is the home of a tiny Black Madonna called La Negrita or La Morenita. Historians have classified the indigenous people of Costa Rica as belonging to the intermediate area, where the peripheries of Mesoamerican and Andean native cultures overlapped. The region includes Nicaragua, Costa Rica, Panamá, Colombia, Venezuela and Ecuador. This area may have played a critical role in the transmission of culture to the north and south.

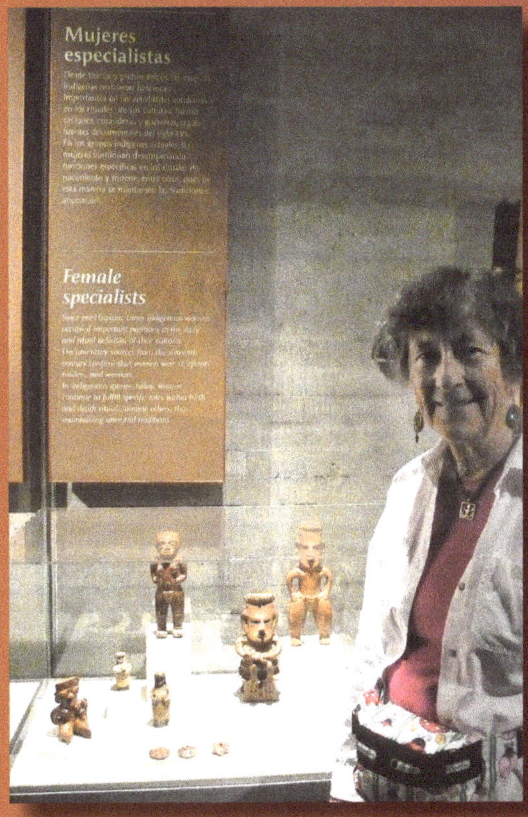

Mujeres de Arcilla and Lydia in the Gold Museum (Museo Oro)

Arcilla Mujer is one of the clay figurines recovered at burial and domestic sites in pre-Columbian Costa Rica. *Arcilla* means "clay," and these statuettes are the oldest pieces from the Guanacaste region, along the Pacific Coast. The nude figures are adorned with black lines, possibly representing garments, necklaces, bracelets, tattoos and other body art.

Arcilla Mujer

Source: Clay sculpture
500–800 CE Guanacaste-Nicoya
Museos Banco Central de Costa Rica
San Jose, Costa Rica

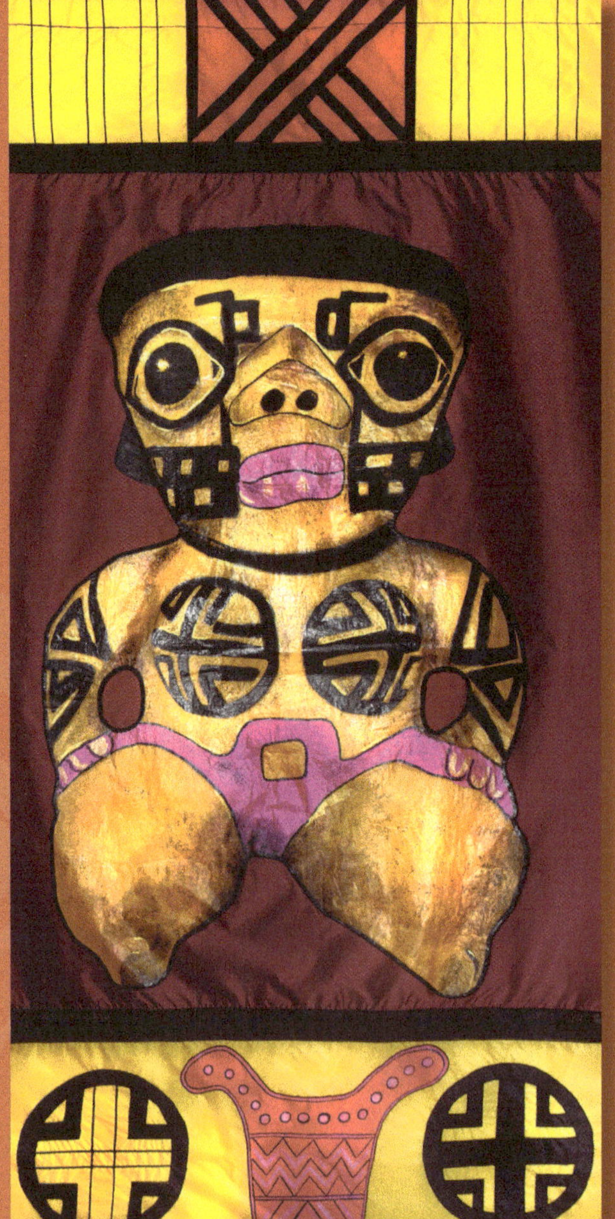

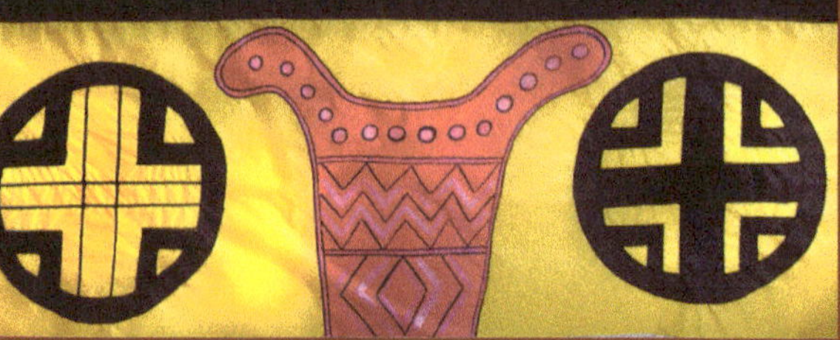

La Morenita / La Negrita is the *reina de los angeles*, or "queen of the angels," and patroness of Costa Rica. Her feast day, a national holiday, occurs on Virgin of the Angels Day, August 2. Pilgrims come from all over Costa Rica to pay homage to her in the Basilica de Nuestra Señora de los Angeles. On her feast day, her statue is carried through the town.

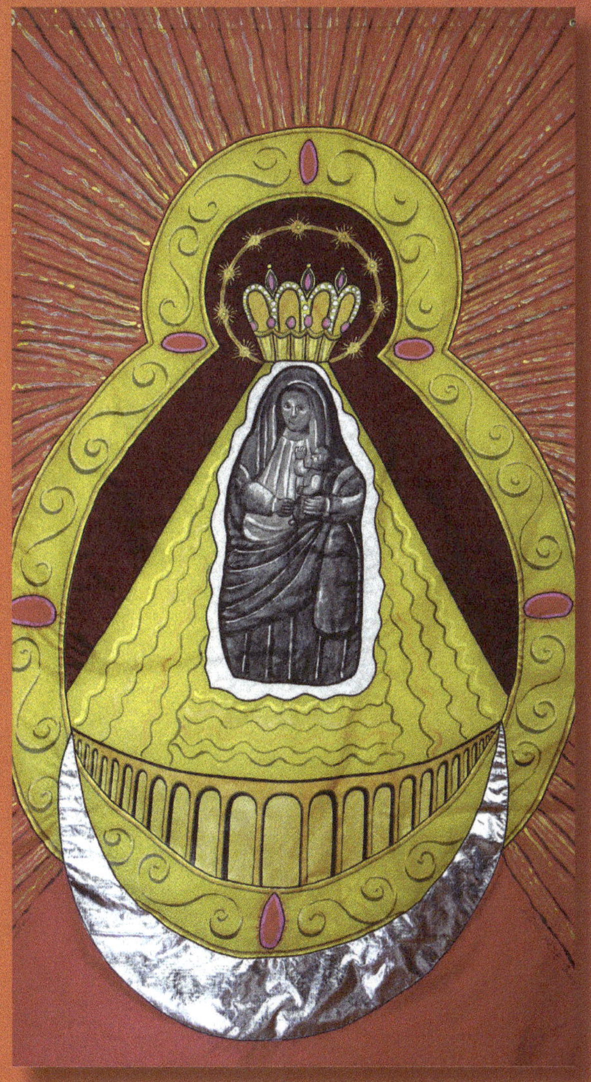

La negrita, literally "small, black woman," is just that. She is a small, dark sculpture, less than three feet tall; she is surrounded by white lace and resides in an elaborate gold setting on the altar. According to legend, the statue of La Negrita was found by an indigenous girl in 1635. She carried it home, but it miraculously reappeared where she found it. The rock where the statue originally appeared is also in the basilica. After performing many miracles, La Negrita was enshrined by the bishop. Nearby is a sacred well for healing and a *milagro*, "miracle," shrine.

La Negrita

Source: Dark stone sculpture, c. 1600 CE
Santuario Nacional de Nuestra Señora de los Angeles
Cartago, Costa Rica

102

The Valdivia culture in Ecuador,

which emerged between 3500 and 1800 BCE, is one of the oldest settled cultures in the Americas. The Valdivia were sedentary people who lived in a community that built houses in a circle or oval around a central plaza, and subsisted through farming and fishing. Valdivian pottery evolved from simple to more complex works, particularly Venus female figurines, which may represent actual women, as each is individual.

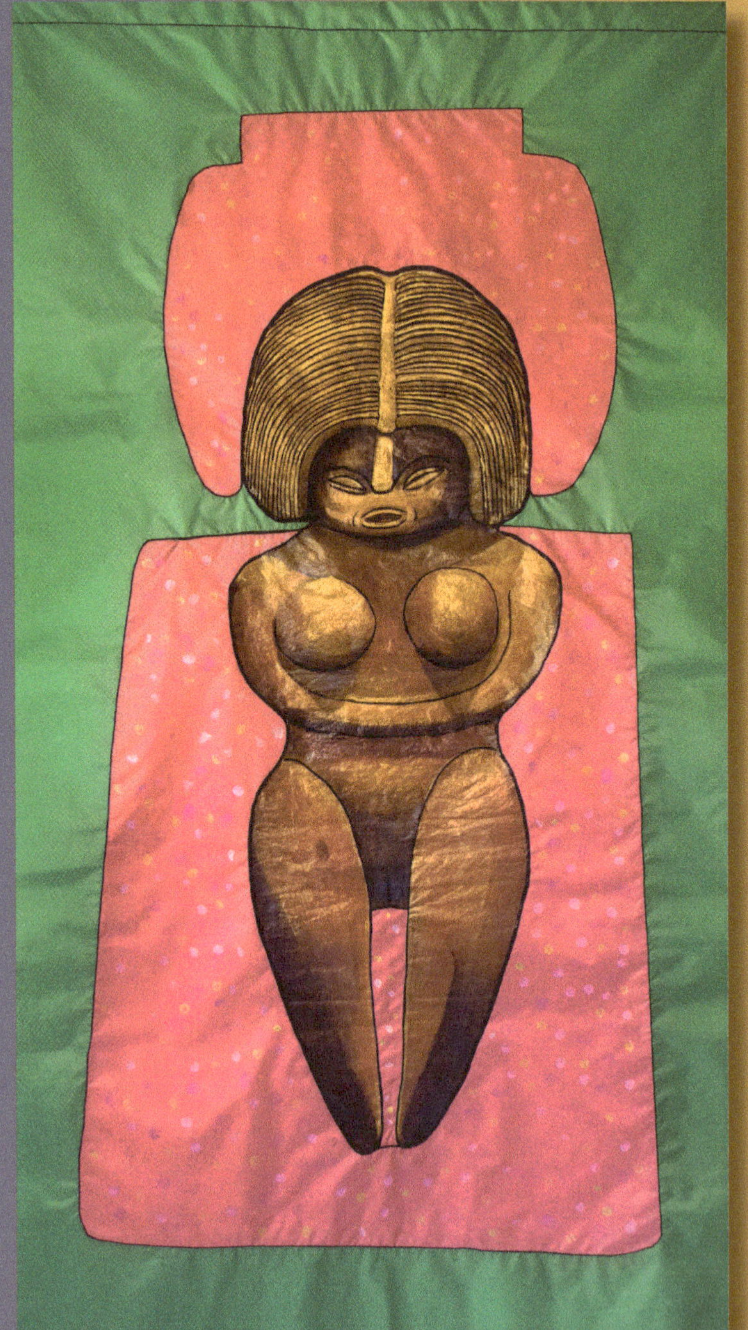

Most Valdivia clay figurines are standing females with pronounced breasts, pubic area, a small face and a distinctive hairstyle; many are covered with a red slip. The context in which most were found suggests they were associated with agricultural rituals and calling for rain. The background figure on the banner is a Valdivian *celt* (a polished stone ax head or adz that was attached to a wooden handle).

Valdivia Venus

Source: Clay, c. 3500 BCE
Valdivia, Guayas Province, Ecuador
Background: Stone celt, c. 3000 BCE
Valdivia, Ecuador

Vieja Arrugada of Ecuador was an elderly Bahia woman. The cheeks of her likeness show scarification, her eyes are shaped like coffee beans and she wears ear spools; these attributes mark her as a respected woman in the community. The Bahia culture occupied a landscape covering the foothills of the Andes and the Pacific Ocean. Wooded hills and expansive beaches supplied ample resources. Archaeological investigations have established that Ecuador was inhabited at least 4500 years before the Incas.

Vieja Arrugada de Ecuador

Source: Clay Bahia Figure Vessel, 100–300 CE
Coastal Manabi Province, Ecuador

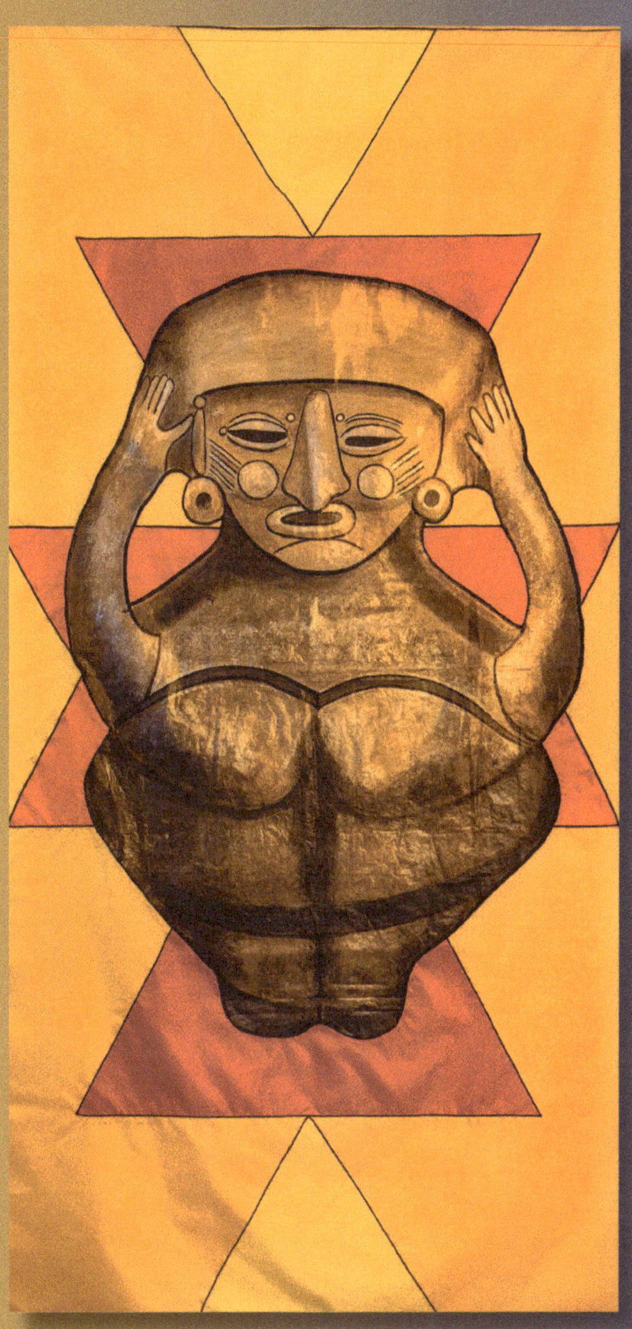

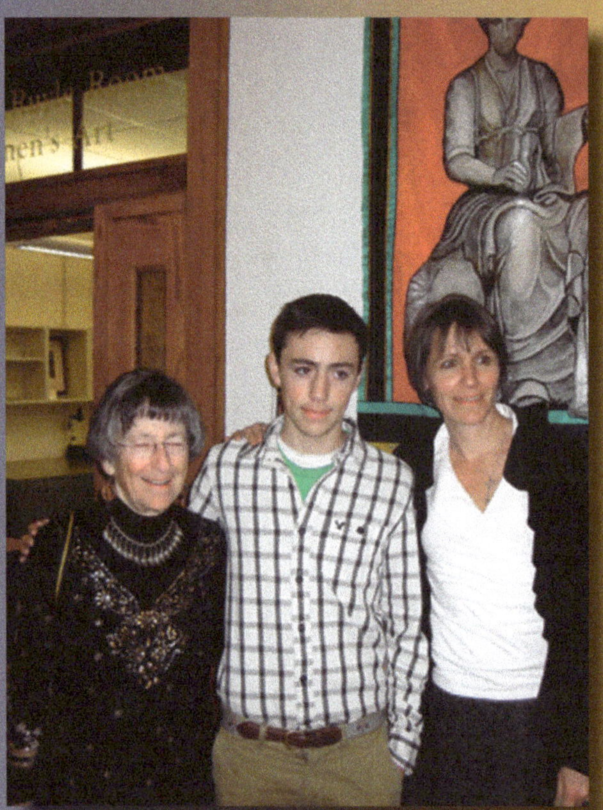

Opening of the Lydia Ruyle Room of Women's Art at the University of Northern Colorado in 2010. Lydia, grandson, Bridger and daughter-in-law, Stephanie Zacharer Ruyle

My family has lived with and supported my art for over half a century. Our only grandson, Bridger Ruyle, spent six weeks in the summer of 2014 in El Alto, near La Paz, Bolivia working with an NGO. I sent a dozen goddess icon prayer flags with him to leave at sacred sites. Bridger showed them to the NGO and they wanted to have an exhibition of the prayer flags featuring the Andean goddess banners. I got busy and created six new goddess banners, including Pachamama from Bolivia, Venezuela, Chile and Ecuador. Some were based on rock art images, others ceramic figurines. I had prayer flags made of the Andean goddesses and sent them to Bolivia with our son Stephen, daughter-in-law Stephanie and granddaughter Remington, who went to visit Bridger. They hung the prayer flags for an exhibition and the NGO has exhibited them several times since. I created and sent a booklet about the Andean goddess banners, which Bridger translated into Spanish. It is a precious gift to me to have three generations of my family teaching about the Goddess!

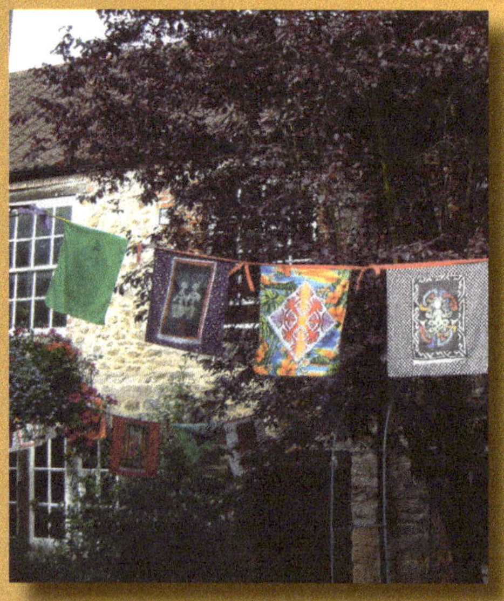

Prayer Flags

Land-locked Bolivia is a country of dramatic landscapes and fascinating native cultures and traditions. Bolivian rock art consists of a wealth of petroglyphs and rock art paintings in small caves, rock shelters, vertical cliffs and on large boulders, concentrated mainly in the Andean region and in the eastern lowlands. The earliest seem to date to the Paleo-Indian period, which some researchers suggest may be 7000 BCE. When I discovered the image of a splayed figure with another figure inside, I knew I had found Pachamama. She became a goddess banner.[xv] The name Pachamama translates into English as "mother earth." *Pacha* is a word in both Quechua and Aymara that means "earth, cosmos, universe, time, space." Pachamama is concerned with the feminine, fertility, abundance, generosity, ripening crops and protection. Pachamama also causes earthquakes and can take the form of a dragon. She is an ever-present and independent deity who has her own self-sufficient and creative power to sustain life on this earth.

Pachamama is known to the Andean people as a good mother. They usually toast her honor before every meeting or festivity by spilling a small amount of *chichi*, "beer," on the floor before drinking the rest. The toast is called *challa* and is made almost every day.

Rituals to honor Pachamama take place all year, but are especially abundant in August, right before the sowing season. Because August is the coldest month of the winter season in the southern Andes and regarded as a tricky month, people feel more vulnerable. Families perform cleansing rituals by burning plants, wood and other items to scare evil spirits and stay on good terms with mother nature, thus keeping themselves, their crops and their livestock healthy and protected. People also drink a kind of tea called *mate*, which is thought to bring good luck.

On the night before August 1, families prepare to honor Pachamama by cooking all night. The host of the gathering then makes a hole in the ground. If the soil comes out nicely, it will be a good year; if it does not, the year will not be bountiful. Before any of the guests are allowed to eat, the host must first give a plate of food to Pachamama. Food is poured into the ground and a prayer to Pachamama is recited.

The main attraction and climax of the Pachamama festival is the Sunday parade. The oldest woman in the community is elected Pachamama Queen of the Year. Indigenous women, in particular senior women, are seen as incarnations of tradition and as living symbols of wisdom, life, fertility and reproduction.

South America | Bolivia

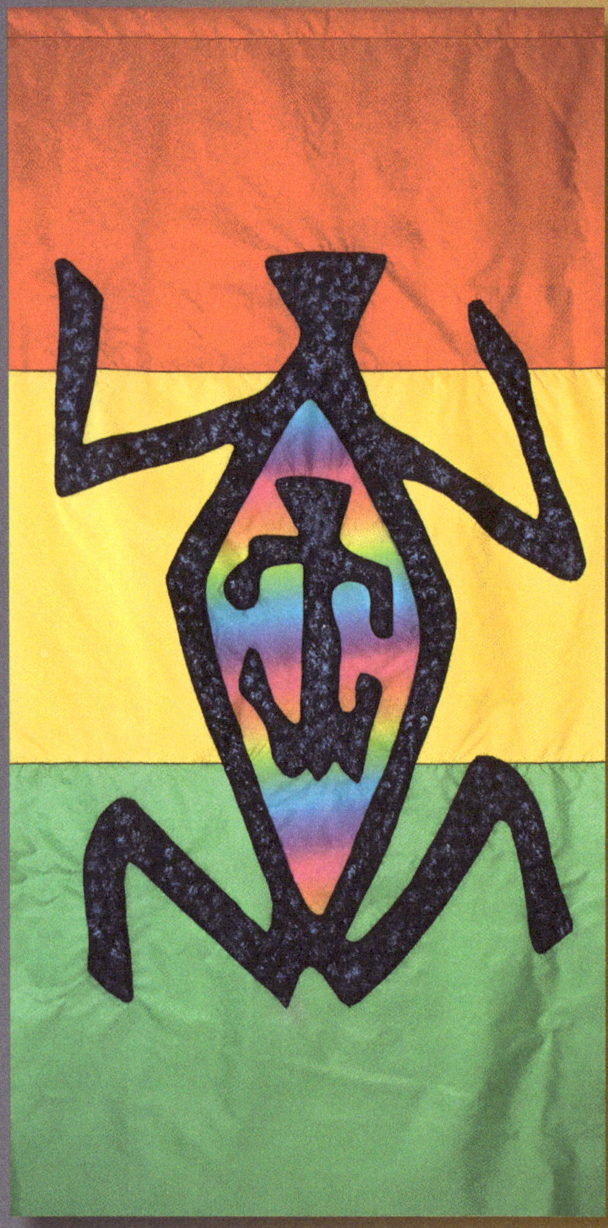

This Pachamama is a rock art image from a site in southern Bolivia. Pachamama contains all life within her vulva-shaped body, upraised arms and splayed legs. In Bolivia, mother earth is protected in the constitution. The banner background combines the two flags of Bolivia. The rainbow colors in the center of the figure represent Wiphala, the flag of the Aymara Quillasuyu (*quilla* means "people" and *suyu* means "region"). Wiphala represents all the native peoples of the Andes and is established in the new Bolivian constitution. Red, yellow and green stripes represent the flag of Bolivia.

Pachamama of Bolivia

Source: Rock art n.d. Orozas site
Bradshaw Foundation
South American Rock Art Archive
Tarija, Bolivia
Background: Internet image of Wiphala of Aymara Quillasuyu
Bolivian altiplano and southern Andes

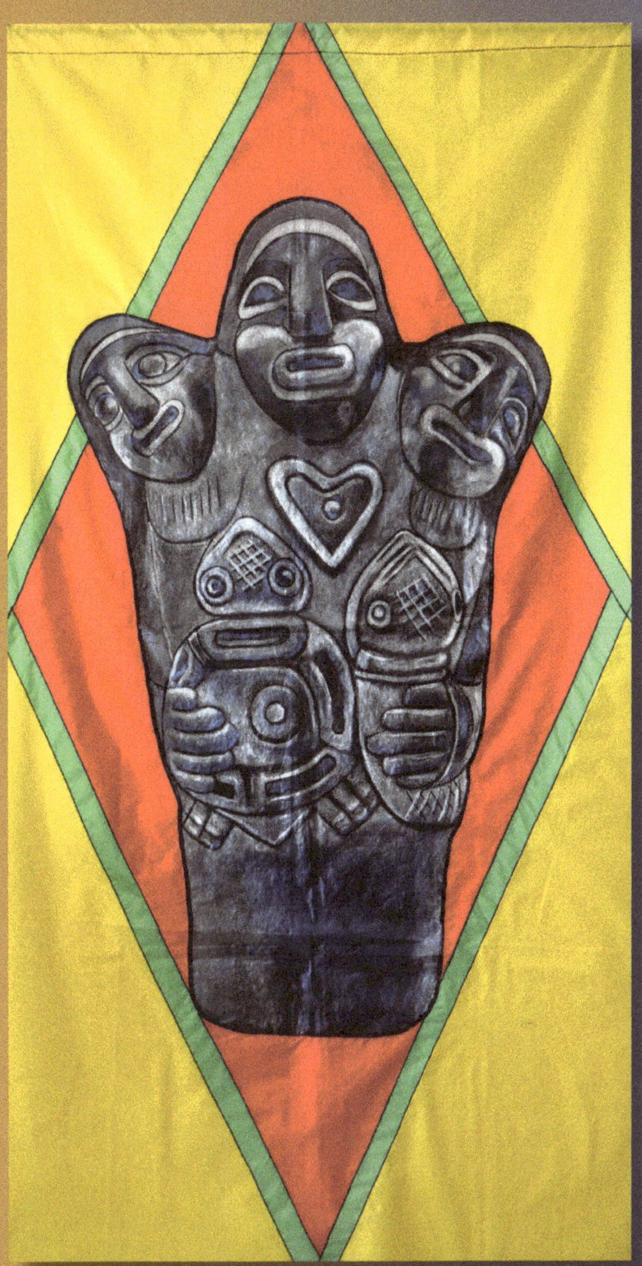

La Pachamama, Mother of All in Bolivia, has a large heart. She is holding two children, a turtle and a snake in her arms. Her cloak encloses all within her protective embrace. On her back is a frog in the birthing position. La Pachamama signifies the interwoven connection between the Goddess and nature.

La Pachamama

Source: Clay figurine from a mold
n.d. Witches Market
La Paz, Bolivia

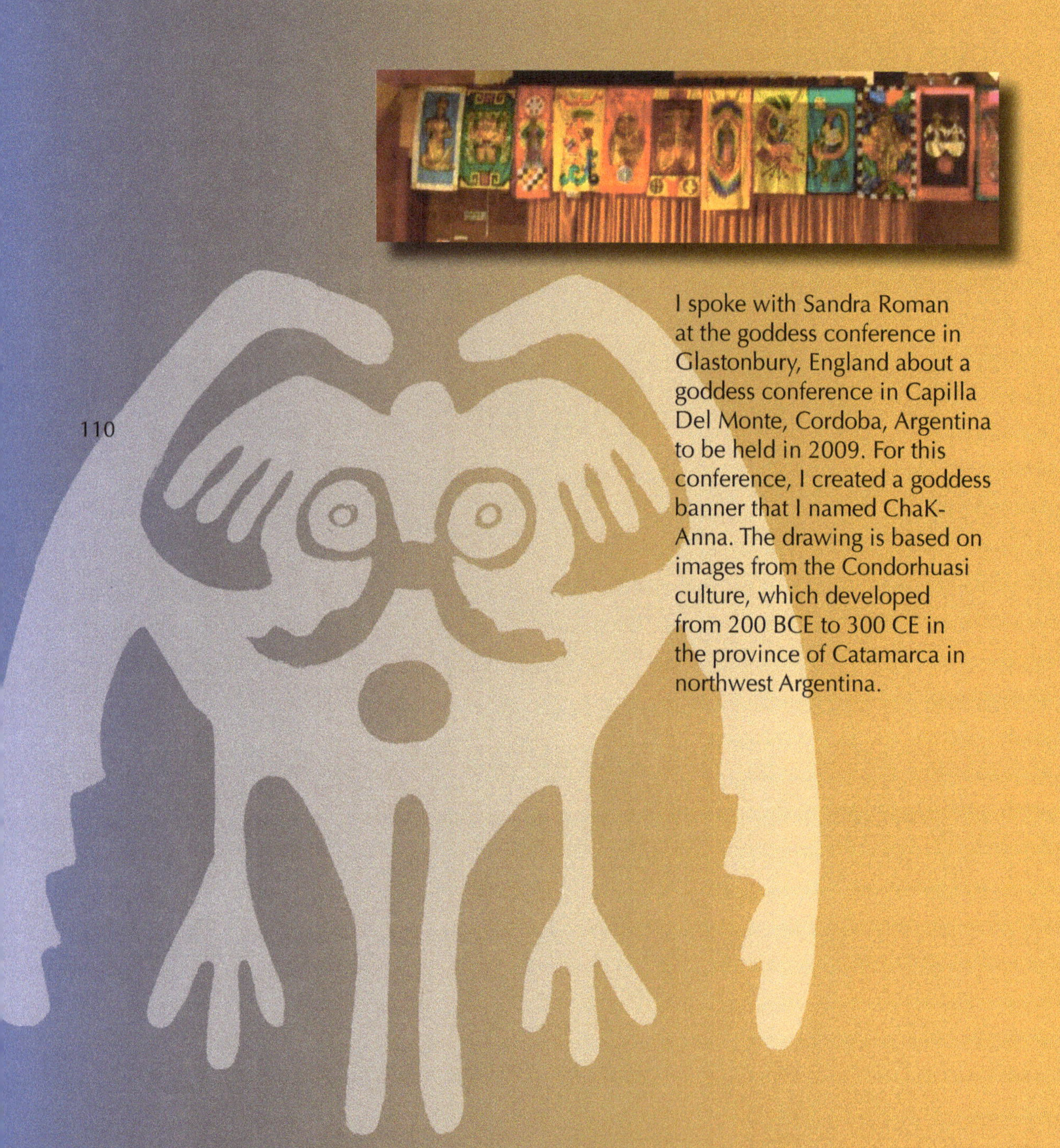

I spoke with Sandra Roman at the goddess conference in Glastonbury, England about a goddess conference in Capilla Del Monte, Cordoba, Argentina to be held in 2009. For this conference, I created a goddess banner that I named ChaK-Anna. The drawing is based on images from the Condorhuasi culture, which developed from 200 BCE to 300 CE in the province of Catamarca in northwest Argentina.

Using clay, stone and fiber, the Condorhuasi people created many images of women and decorated them with richly painted patterns reflecting the ancient South American tradition of ritual body painting, which also influenced surrounding Andean cultures. These hollow red clay figurines appear to be for ritual use, as they are found in graves. Some images are referred to as "crying ladies" because of the lines around the eyes. For the goddess banner, ChaK-Anna sits in a stepped pyramid of the Southern Cross enclosed in a yoni *mandorla*, a design in the shape of an almond.

ChaK-Anna

Source: Clay figurine, 200 BCE–300 BCE
Condorhuasi culture
Catamarca, Argentina

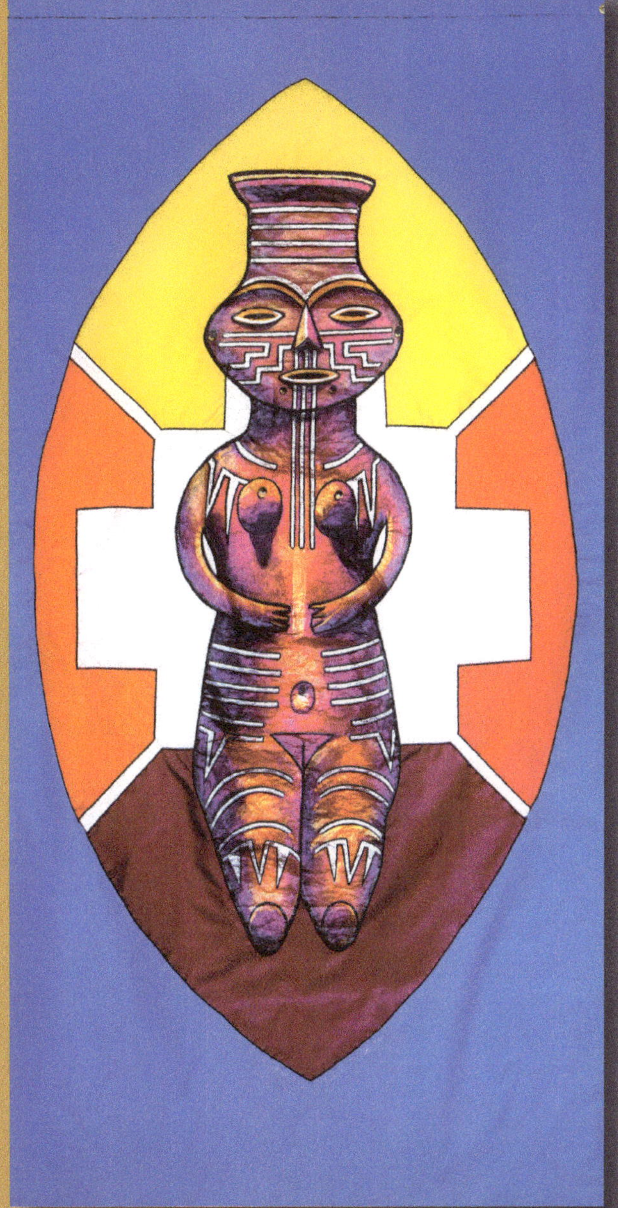

Markawasi

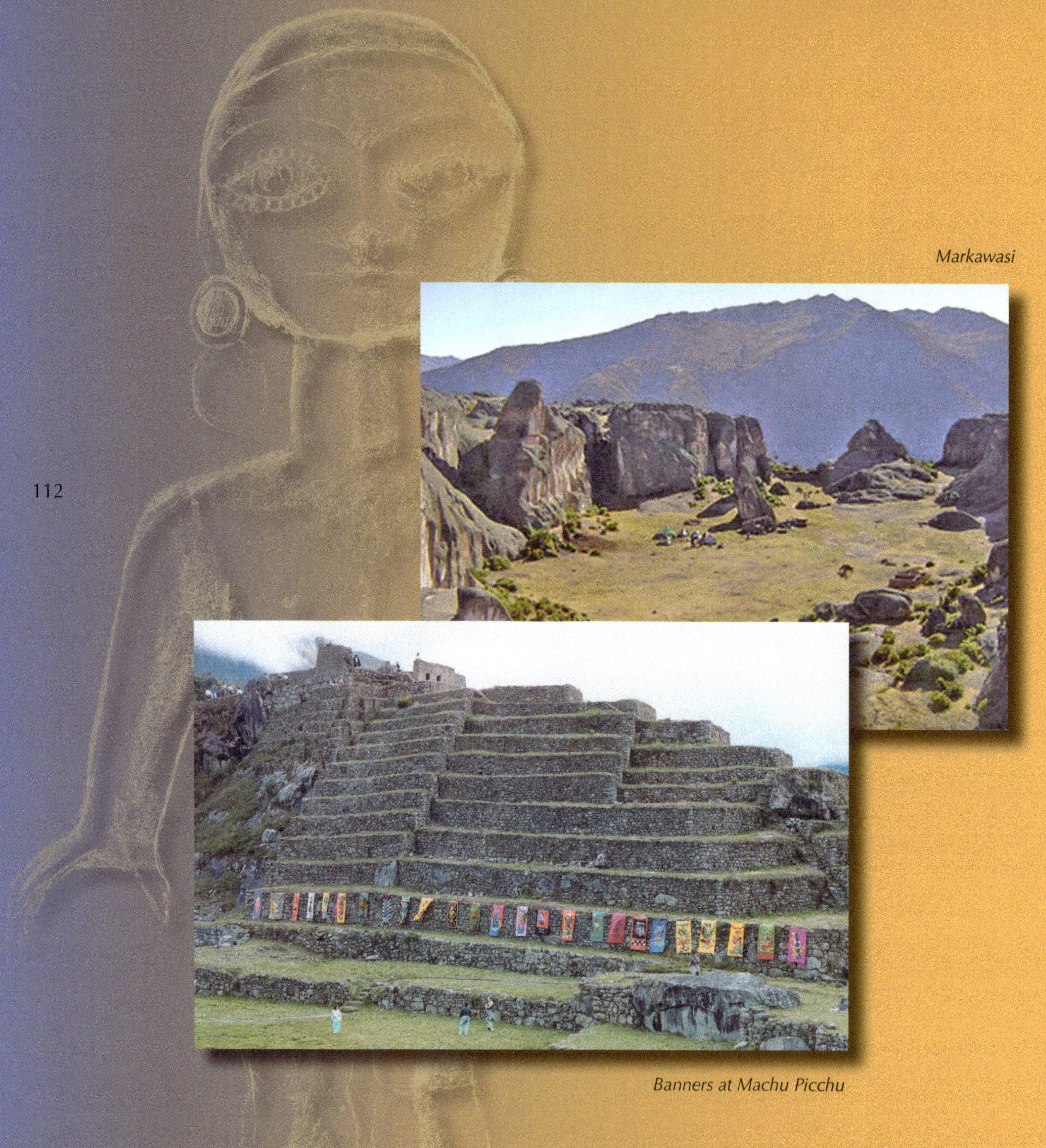

Banners at Machu Picchu

In 1999, Kathy Doore[xvi] invited me to participate in a goddess gathering she was sponsoring at Machu Picchu. She asked if I would provide an exhibition of banners of Pachamama, the earth mother of the Andes, and the goddesses of the world. I collected images, drew plates and designed and painted seven Peruvian goddess banners based on 3000 years of textiles and art. Peru's rich textile tradition continues today.

My niece, Katie Hoffner, and I flew to Lima a few days in advance of the gathering to explore sites and museums including: Huallamarca, a mud-brick stepped temple in Miraflores; the Museo Oro of Peru with its collection of gold, stone and ceramics; the National Museum of Archaeology, Anthropology and History in Lima; and the Larco Museum, which has a fantastic collection of Moche ceramics and other treasures. They are all great resources about the cultures of Peru.

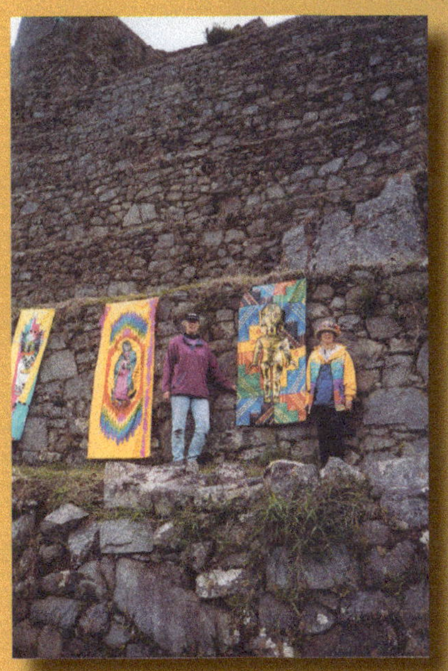

Katie Hoffner and her Aunt Lydia with banners at Machu Picchu

The goddess gathering began in Cuzco, tucked between the peaks of the Andes. José R. Altamirana Vallenas, who made arrangements with the Peruvian Government to sponsor my banner exhibition at Machu Picchu, was our guide at Ollantaytambo, Sacsayhuaman and Tambo Machay. These are all large ceremonial places made of stone as large as any of the megalithic sites I have visited in Europe. The stones are sculpted and placed in the landscape. Our group visited several sacred sites around Cuzco and the Urabamba valley on the way to Machu Picchu.

South America | Peru

Machu Picchu is a three-dimensional, mountainous, sacred space constructed to create a mythic landscape of the three worlds: upper, middle and lower. The condor represents the upper world, the puma the middle world and the caiman serpent the lower world. Machu Picchu is a feminine peak, Huyna Picchu a masculine peak and Putacusi is in between—the coming-together mountain.

Banners at Machu Picchu

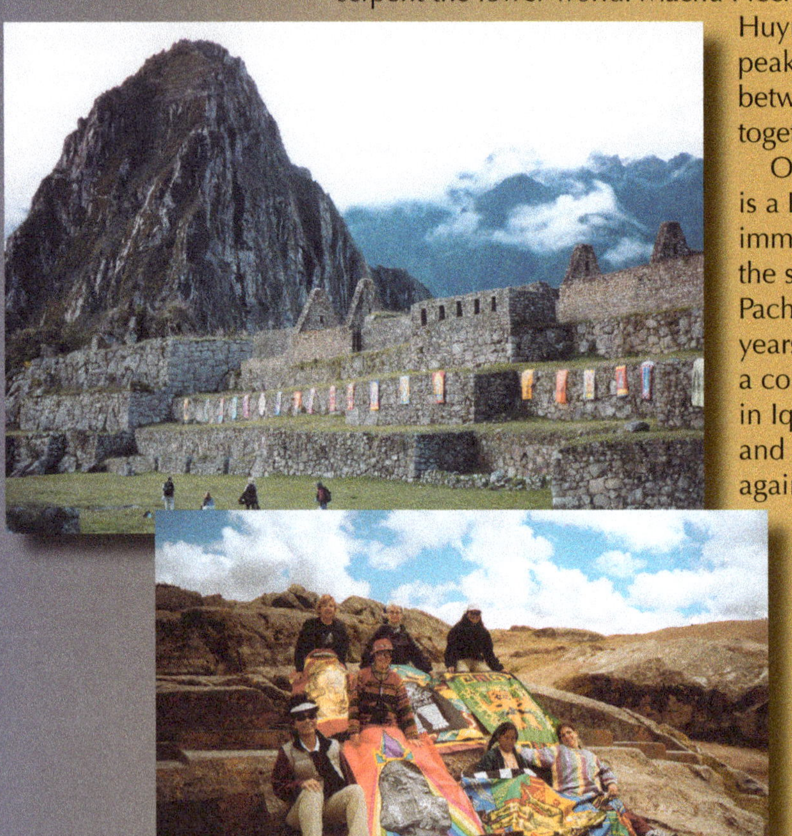

Banners at Sacsayhuaman Altar

Our guide, Kucho, who is a Peruvian shaman, immediately recognized the sacred energies of my Pachamama banner. Twelve years later, Kucho was part of a conference on shamanism in Iquitos, where Pachamama and her sister banners flew again. The banners were hung on the Inca stones and a group of fifty women celebrated the Wesack moon with a sacred ceremony at night. The feminine divine goddess energies were sent around the world for the new millennium.

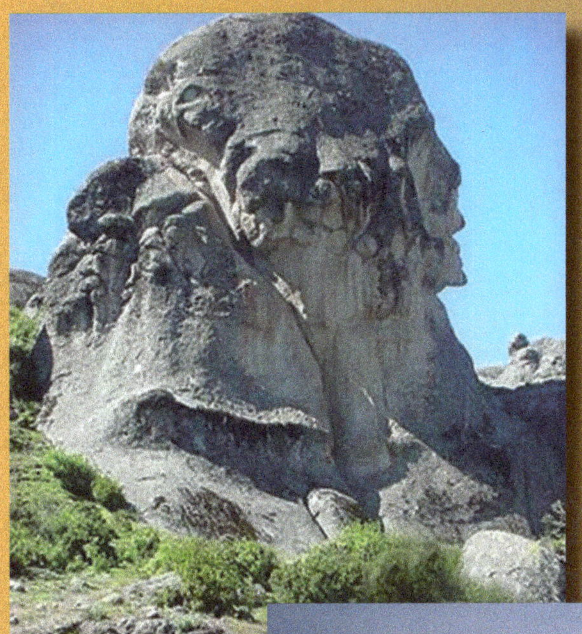

Markawasi

On another journey in 2001, I visited Markawasi, one of the places in Peru that has reported UFO sightings. Immense rock sculptures of heads and figures, fifty to a hundred feet tall, appear in the high mountain landscape. Some look a bit like the statues on Easter Island. There are many theories about their creation, including wind and erosion. The sculptures seem too sophisticated for that to me. I also flew over the Nazca lines, which are desert geo-glyphs, and saw an amazing collection of carved Inca stones. Peru is a rich treasure of sacred sites in both the Andes and on the plains.

Lydia visiting Nazca Lines

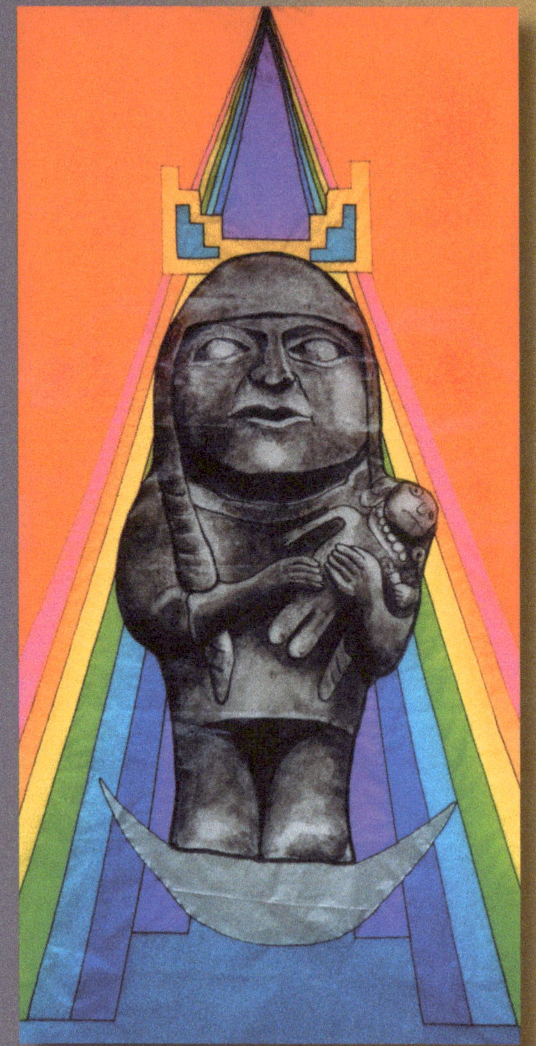

I based the banner Black Madonna of the Andes on a clay Moche figurine. Here she stands on the moon and a stepped pyramid. The Inca and earlier cultures were master builders, shaping stone into sacred ceremonial places such as Machu Picchu and Saksaywaman. The Peruvian Black Madonna has the features of an indigenous native mother and child, not the European version brought by the Spaniards. She is surrounded by a *k'uychi*, which means "rainbow, aura of light." Her crown is a golden-stepped gateway of wisdom and compassion.

Black Madonna of the Andes

Source: Clay figure, 500–800 CE
Moche, Peru

My Cuchimilco Mama raises her arms in a gesture of power, energy emanating from her eyes and crowned head. Her clay body is a Chancay vessel containing seeds and ashes from which new life is born. Her vulva-pubic triangle focuses on the origin of life. The patterns surrounding Cuchimilco are serpents, stones and crescent moons, which frame a gateway opening.

Cuchimilco Mama

Source: Clay figure, 1200 CE
Chan Chan, Archaeology Museum, Lima
Background: Patterns from litter, 750–1250 CE

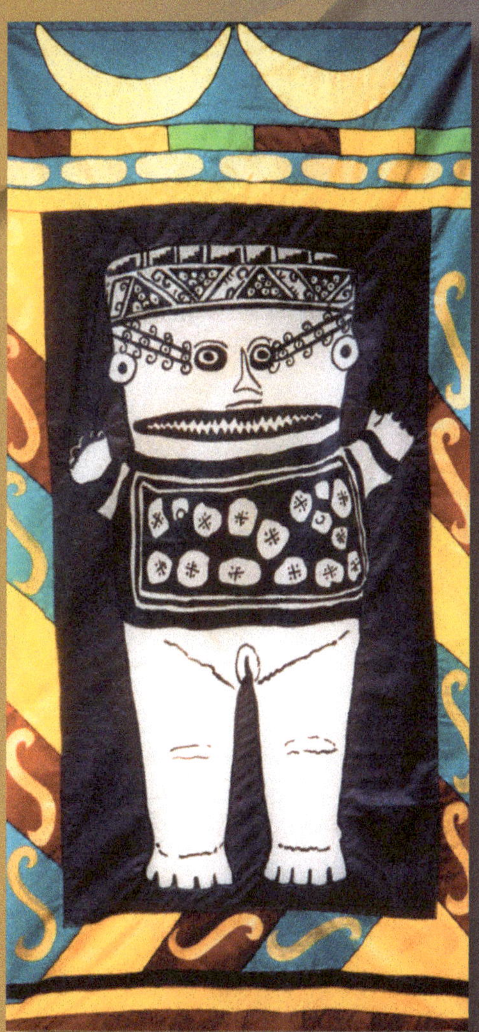

South America | Peru

The Curayacu Venus is a clay figurine that was found in a fishing village south of Lima. Her body is in the shape of a fish and she stands in a frontal hieratic attitude. Curayacu Venus holds her hands over her ample belly, which appears pregnant, and her visionary eyes see into another dimension.

Curayacu Venus

Source: Clay figurine, c. 900 BCE (lower formative period) San Bartolo, National Museum of Archaeology, Anthropology and History (MNAAH) Lima, Peru

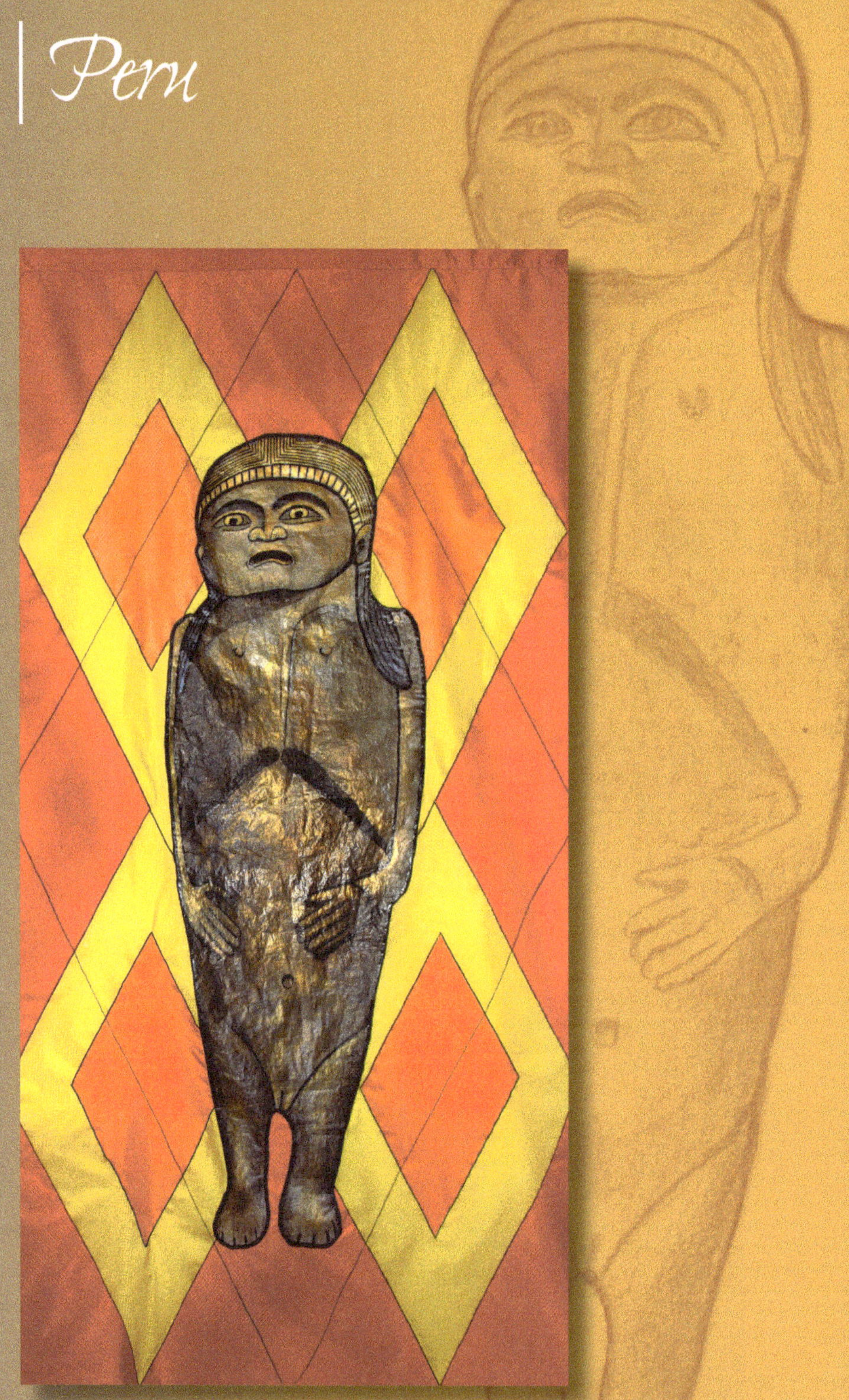

In the Museo Oro, I was drawn to a beautiful golden statue labelled Erotica Mama. This banner is my interpretation based on a Peruvian gold relief image with a woman in a typical sacred display position, with her legs apart and her hands on either side of her vulva. The water of life drips from her vagina. Humans come into the world through the mother and return to her at death. Humans are nurtured in the waters of the womb, but only survive after birth if there is a source of water for them.

Erotica Mama

Source: Gold relief
Museo Oro
Lima, Peru

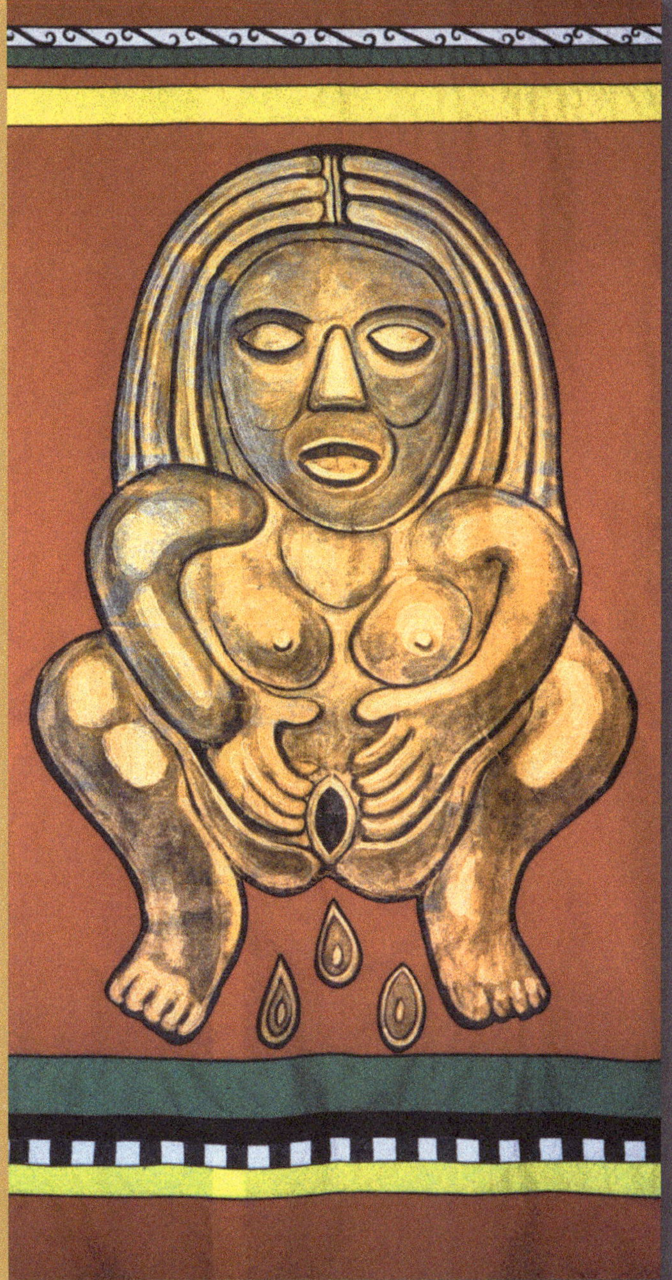

Inca Venus is based on a gold figure from 1500 CE. She is a precious, golden goddess holding spirals of energy as flowering trees of life and the world of the spirit. She is using her inner vision and her ears hear spirit messages. The Inca *cumbi* textile in the background was woven by young priestesses in the *acclahuasi,* the "house of the chosen women." *Mamacunas,* or "great mothers," were abbesses and teachers of ritual to the young girls, who were sent to the *acclahuasi* at Cuzco and Pachamac.

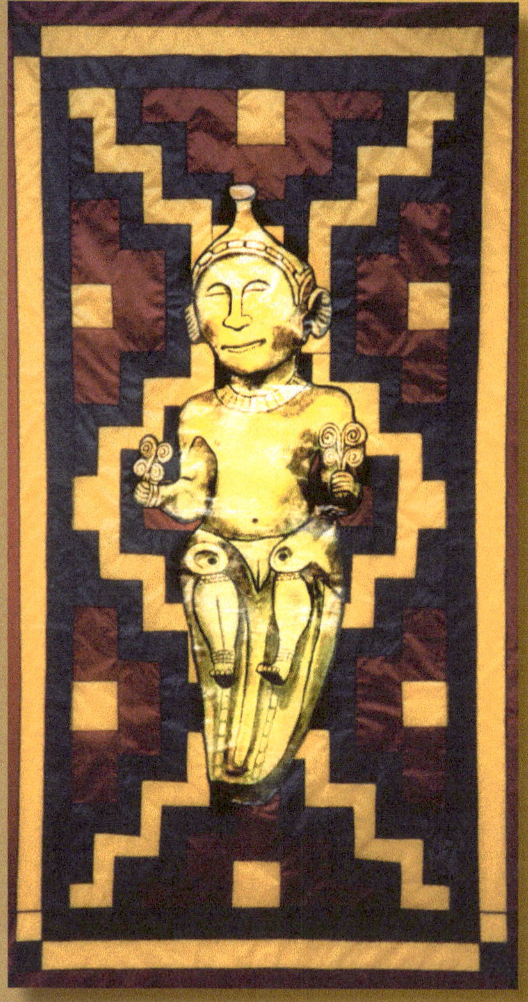

Inca Venus

Source: Gold figure, 1500 CE
Background: Cumbi textile
1500 CE. Inca

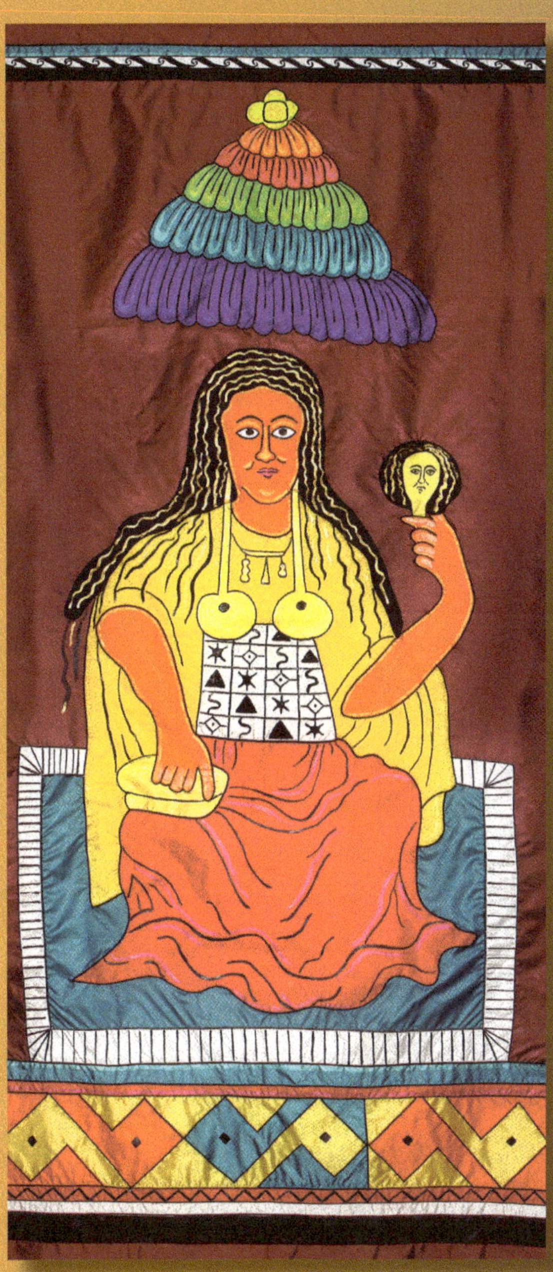

Mama huaca means "sacred stone mother." The Inca creation myth centers on four couples who emerge from a cave near Cuzco. Mama Huaca is the partner of a male trickster who was rowdy and cruel. When the people decided he must return to the cave, they sought Mama Huaca's help, as she was forceful, clever and wise. She tricked her partner back to the cave, where he remains today.

Mama Huaca planted the first field in the Cuzco valley. After she died, people made *chicha,* fermented corn beer, every year in her honor. In my banner, Mama Huaca sits on a throne under a sacred parasol with one hand in a bowl of water. She holds a mirror in her left hand, acknowledging her power.

Mama Huaca

Source: Ink drawing,
Guaman Poma de Ayala
16th century

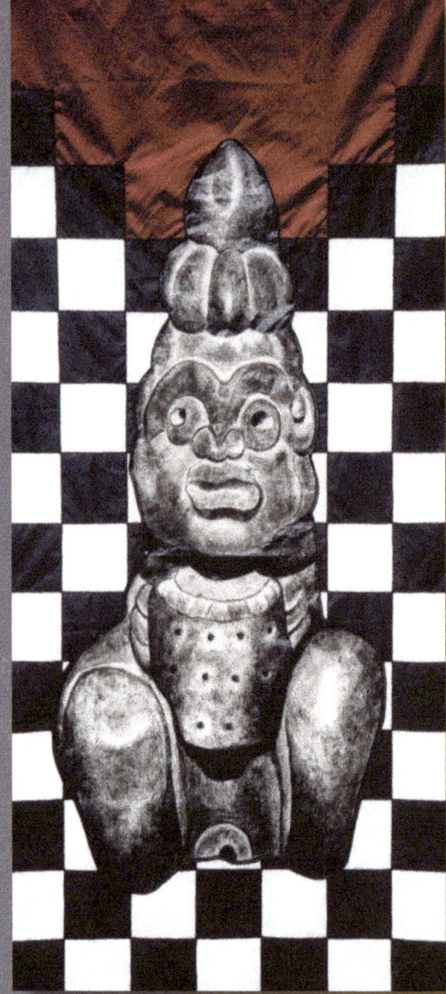

Pachamama is the earth mother creatrix of Peru. Her partner is Pachamac, the masculine divine energy and the name of a stepped pyramid sacred site. Together they create all. Pachamama is a *machukuna,* an "ancient being." She holds an ear of corn with enormous kernels. She squats on her legs displaying her sacred vulva. Corn, the food of life, crowns her head.

Peruvian Pachamama

Source: Stone figure
Pre-Columbian
Background: Inca textile worn for outstanding bravery

Saramama is the great mother of the Chavin culture, a corn mother. Both arms hold sprouting staffs of food and amaru, which are serpentine energies. Food grows from her head and snakes from her hips. She is fierce and powerful. Stepped pyramids and patterns of energy are mirrored on the top and bottom of the banner.

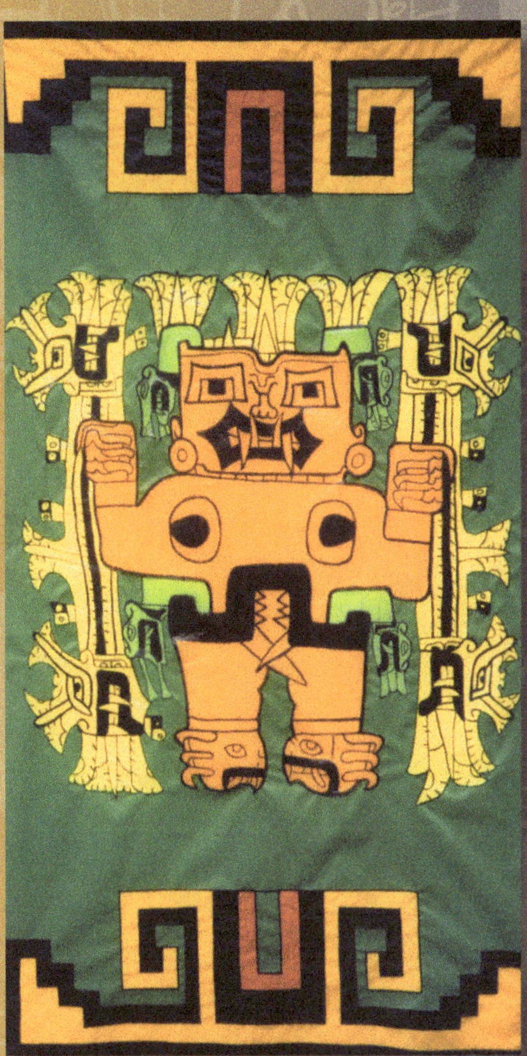

Saramama

Source: South Coastal Figure Textile, 500 BCE South Coastal Karwa
Background: Textile, c. 500 BCE Inca Valley

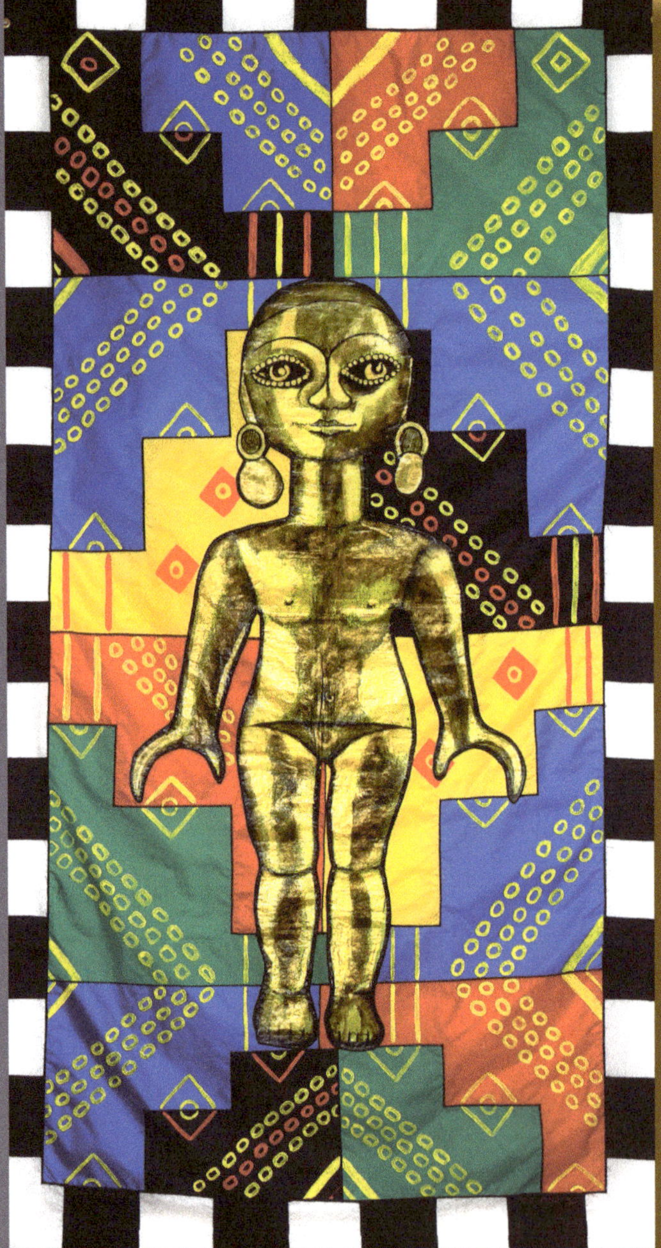

124

The Venus de Fria is a young, golden beauty. She is surrounded by stepped patterns of color, diamonds and circles of light that create a field of energy. The black-and-white frame encloses the energy and celebrates the duality of life. Venus looks into the spirit world with her powerful eyes, hands and pubic triangle.

Venus de Fria

Source: Gold figure, 400–800 CE Mochica
Background: Tie-dyed textile, 500–800 CE Nasca / Wari, Rafael de Larco Musuem Lima, Peru

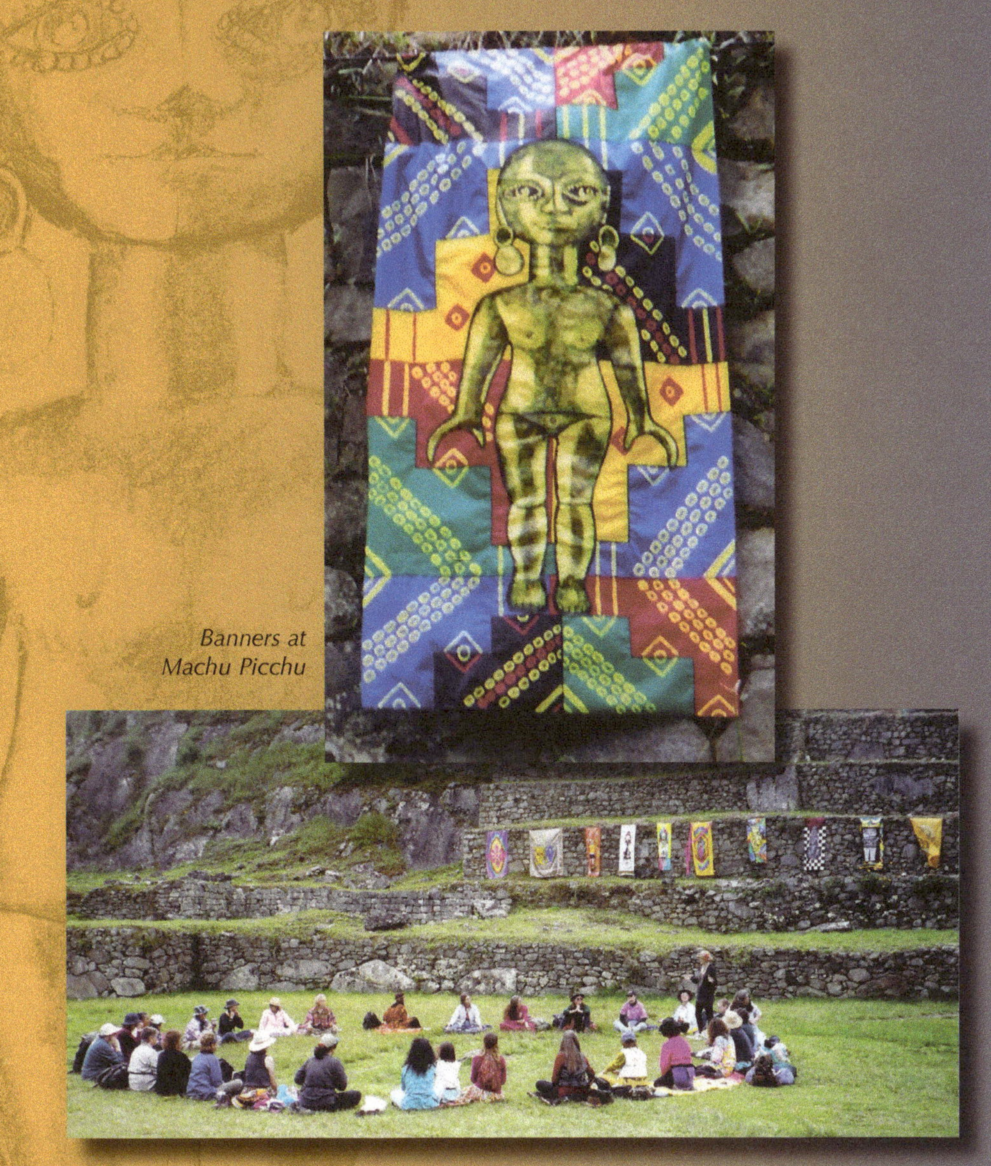

Banners at Machu Picchu

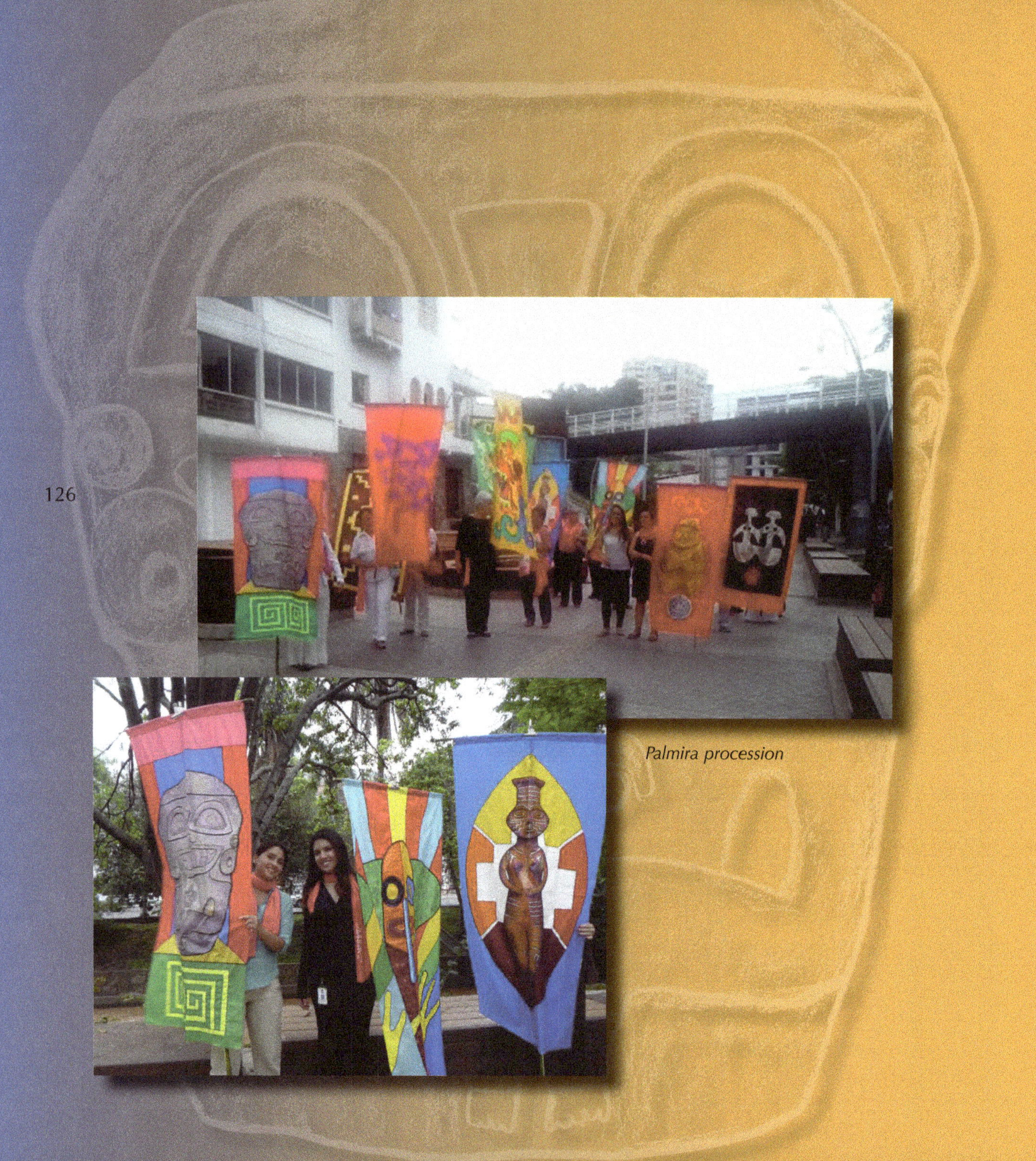

Palmira procession

Due to its geographical location,

the present territory of Colombia was a corridor of population migration from Mesoamerica and the Andes to the Caribbean and the Amazon. The first settlements were in an area where three Andes mountain cordilleras and three rivers come together. Archaeological finds from the Magdalena Valley date to 14,400 BCE. The oldest pottery discovered in the Americas dates to 5000 BCE. The San Agustin culture, 100–800 CE, which is now a UNESCO world heritage site, created structures and the largest library of stone statues in the Americas. Colombia has the highest biodiversity of any place on mother earth.

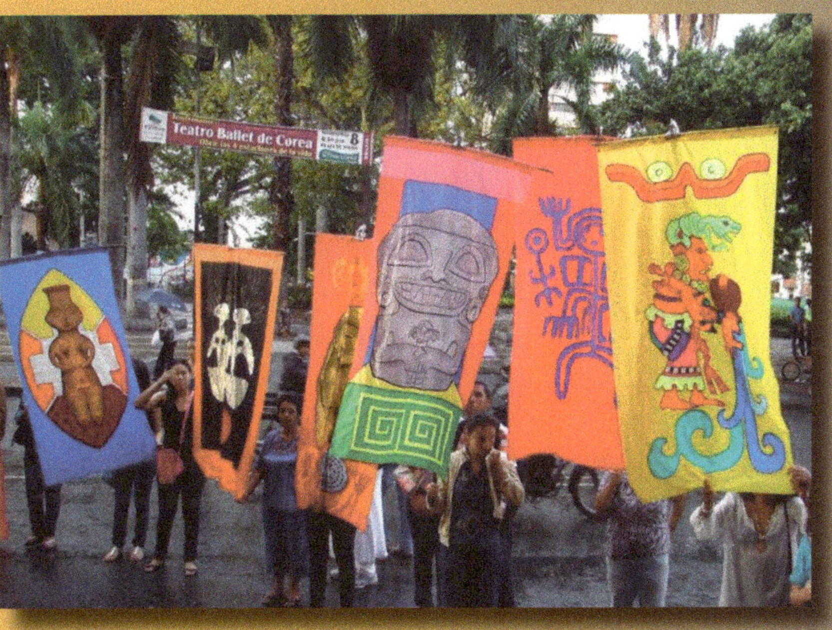

Palmira procession

South America | Colombia

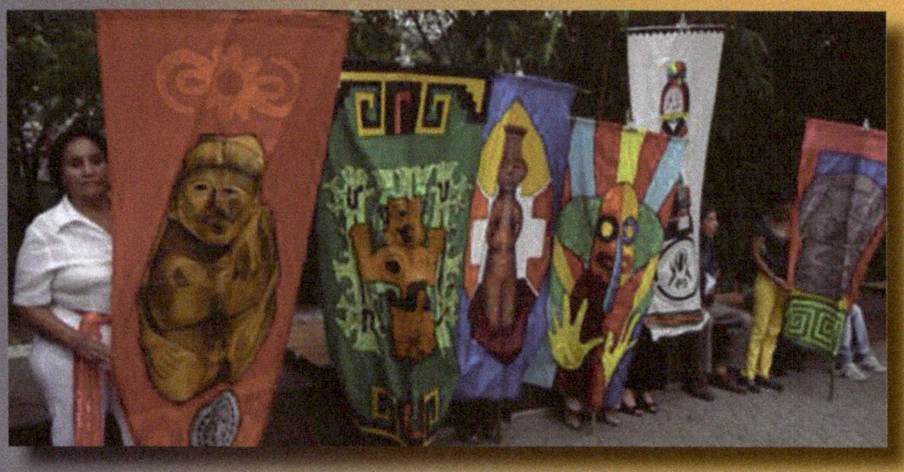

Goddess Conference 2013, Colombia

In 2013, Angela Dolmetsch invited me to create goddess banners for the International Matriarchal Circles Conference at Nashira Eco-Village, a community of low-income women striving to live on matriarchal principles in Palmira, Colombia. The conference grew out of the vision of Dr. Heide Goettner-Abendroth's work[xvii] on matriarchal societies. The mayor of Palmira opened the event. My banners hung over the participants in a large *palapa*, a type of hut. The image of El Abra was painted on the concrete entrance. Prior to the conference, the banners were paraded in the streets of Cali and Palmira and appeared on television and on the front page of the newspaper.

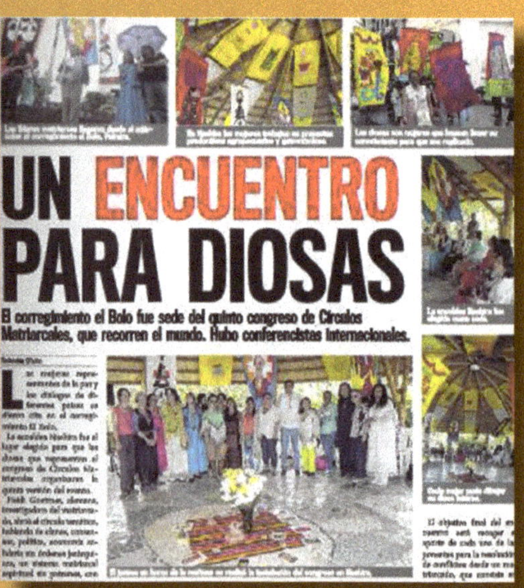

UN ENCUENTRO PARA DIOSAS

El corregimiento el Bolo fue sede del quinto congreso de Círculos Matriarcales, que recorren el mundo. Hubo conferencistas internacionales.

The rock art image I have named El Abra Matriglyph is from one of the first human settlements in the Americas, a cave system in the *altiplano*, Spanish for "high plain," of Colombia. With her arms upraised and rooted on Mother Earth, the matriglyph is calling in spiritual energy for the human at her side. The universal mother creatrix is the central figure of the indigenous Kogi people of Colombia today.

El Abra Matriglyph

Source: Rock art, c. 12,000–10,000 BCE
El Abra, Cundinamarca, Colombia

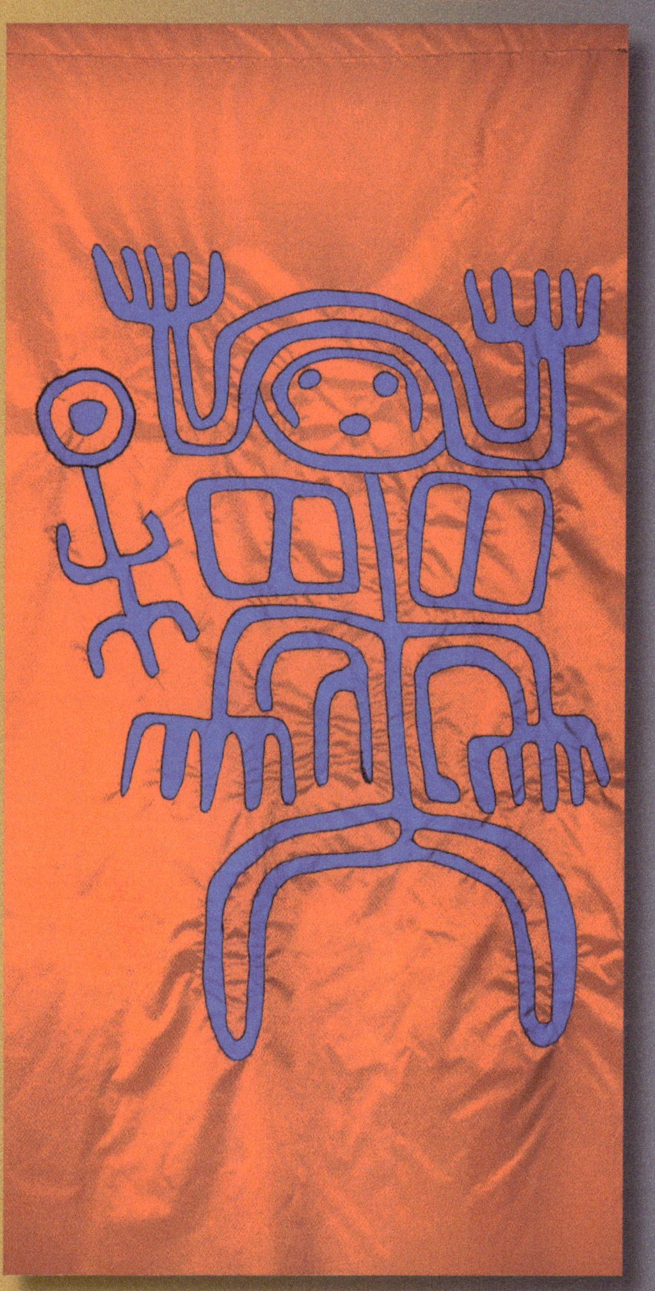

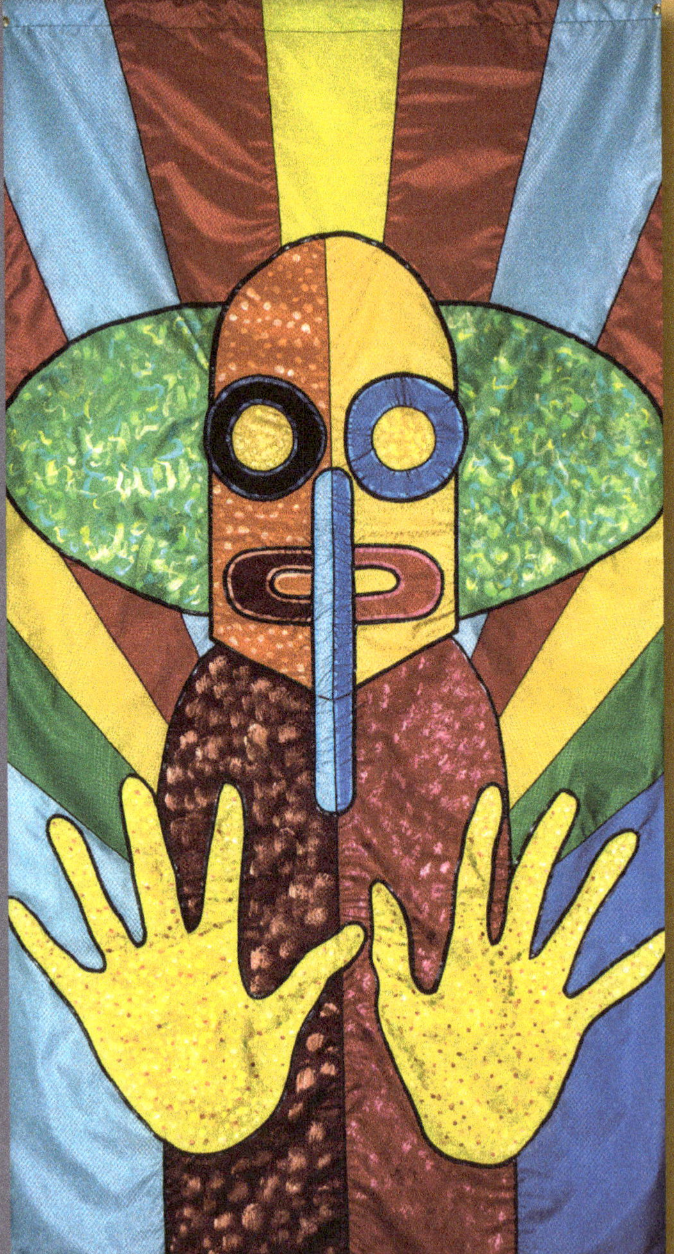

Madremonte or Marimonda lives in the mountains and jungles of Colombia. She is covered in leaves and moss, and has large hands, a long nose and glowing eyes. Madremonte rules the winds and the rains, and groans on stormy nights. Those who invade her territory lose their way. Her role is to protect her forest animals and Mother Nature.

Madremonte

Source: The costumes of Carnival of Barranquilla, Colombia, a UNESCO cultural treasure
A hooded figure with a long nose, Madremonte is the most popular and the only costume that originated in Barranquilla
Hands are those of the artist

There is a stone sculpture found in the San Agustin Archaeological Park that I have named Pachamama of Columbia. She is holding a soul or shaman for protection and rebirth. Her thumbs and hands form a diamond, a symbol for the vagina. Her huge eyes are in an altered state and her fierce grin protects the soul / shaman. This is the culture that created the largest library of stone statues in the Americas, which can be seen as based on a mythological world view of death and rebirth from Mother Earth.

Pachamama of Colombia

Source: Sculpture
San Agustin Archaeological Park, Colombia

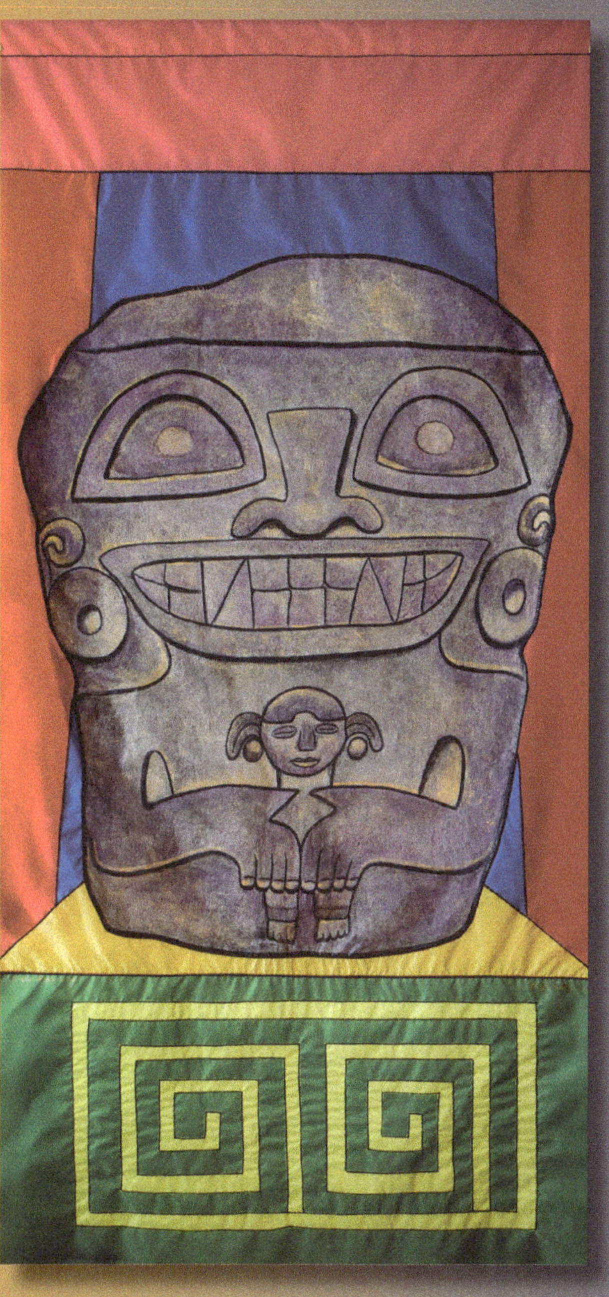

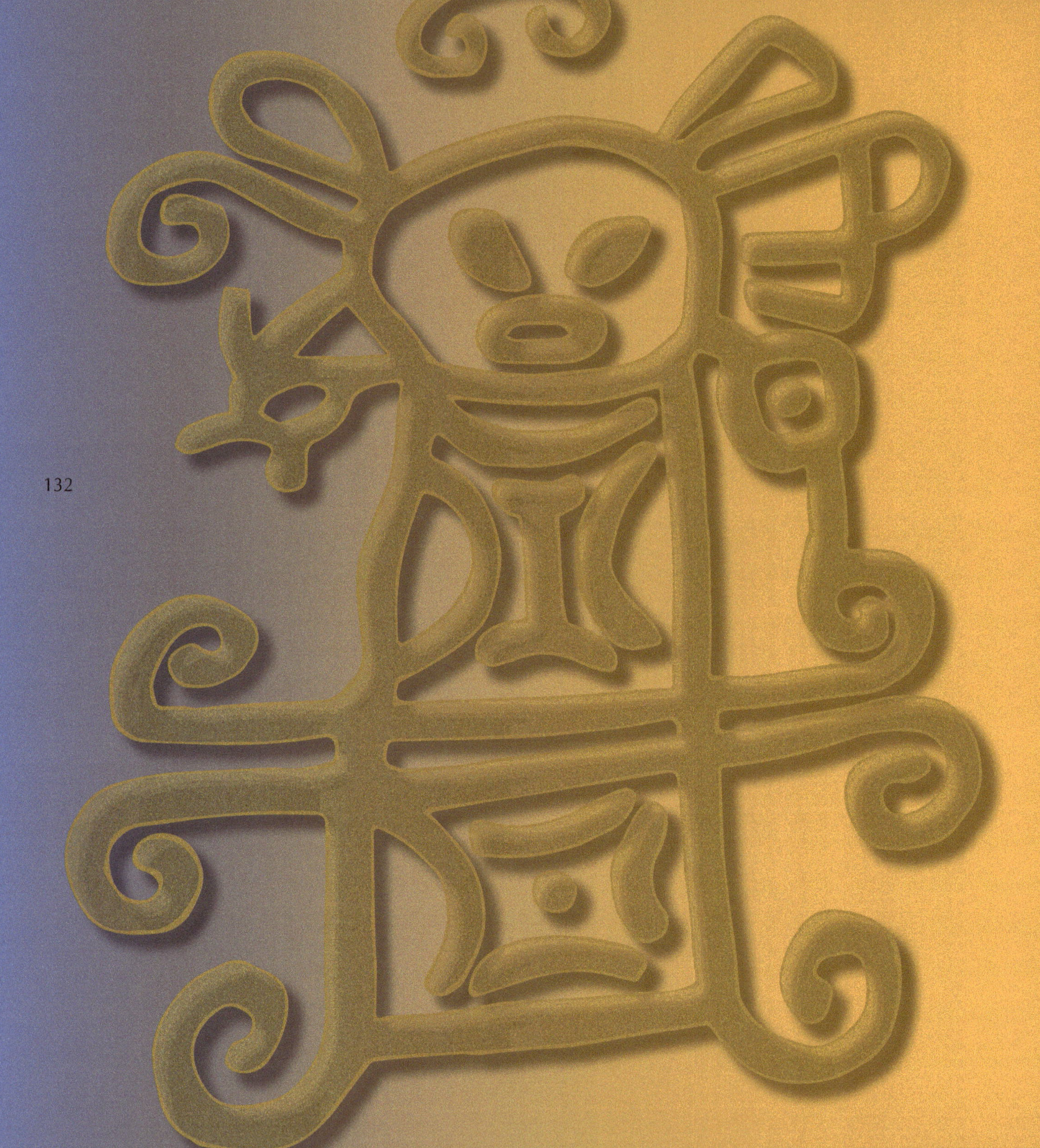

Evidence, in the form of tools such as chopping and scraping implements, shows human habitation in the area now known as Venezuela from about 15,000 years ago. Venezuela has high biodiversity, with habitats ranging from the Andes Mountains in the west to the Amazon Basin rainforest, extensive plains, the Caribbean coast and the Orinoco River basin. Archaeological evidence shows the occupation of the territory by agro-pottery communities in successive waves from the Amazon basin, using the Orinoco River as a means of communication and settlement. Humans migrated to the Venezuelan coast and from there to the West Indies and Florida. The first groups to take root and spread were primarily the Arawaks around 100 CE, a millennium before the Caribbean groups.

South America | Venezuela

The Arawak language may have emerged in the Orinoco River valley. By the time of European contact, it had become the most widely used language family in South America. At some point, the Arawakan-speaking Taíno culture emerged in the Caribbean. The Taíno were the first American people to encounter Europeans when Christopher Columbus visited multiple islands on his first voyage. As noted earlier, the Taíno population declined rapidly after European colonization; by the end of the century, they had disappeared as a distinct ethnic group.

The Arawak and the Caribbean developed symbols and reproduced them on objects of everyday life, in basketry, clay, stone and rock art. One of the largest petroglyph sites in Venezuela is the Parque Arqueológico Piedra Pintada at Vigirma in Carabobo State near Lake Valencia. The site has more than 165 clusters of petroglyphs and two megalith constructions, possibly created for religious and ceremonial reasons. The symbolic language of Venezuela rock art is related to natural phenomena, animals, plants, sky, agricultural practices, all connected with the magical-mythical world and trying to establish a balance between the material and immaterial. Piedra Pintada is regarded by archaeologists as a ceremonial site due to the absence of burials, pottery and other remains that typically characterize an indigenous settlement.

Most representations correspond to the surrounding fauna and to daily life, both cultural and spiritual. The petroglyphs represent pyramidal, square and snake-like shapes, displayed on, over and around the rocks at the site. Some show images of childbirth, pregnancy or menstruation. The images are accompanied in most cases with other figures forming a unique thread or story. One, called the Piedra de la Fertilidad, or "stone of fertility," shows a pregnant figure with spirals in her abdomen surrounded with vulvas. An adjoining rock is covered with star shapes. The act of giving birth was a magical, mysterious event. Water is essential for all the natural world and human life to continue. Diosa Lluvia is a rain goddess who is still considered to have strong energy today.

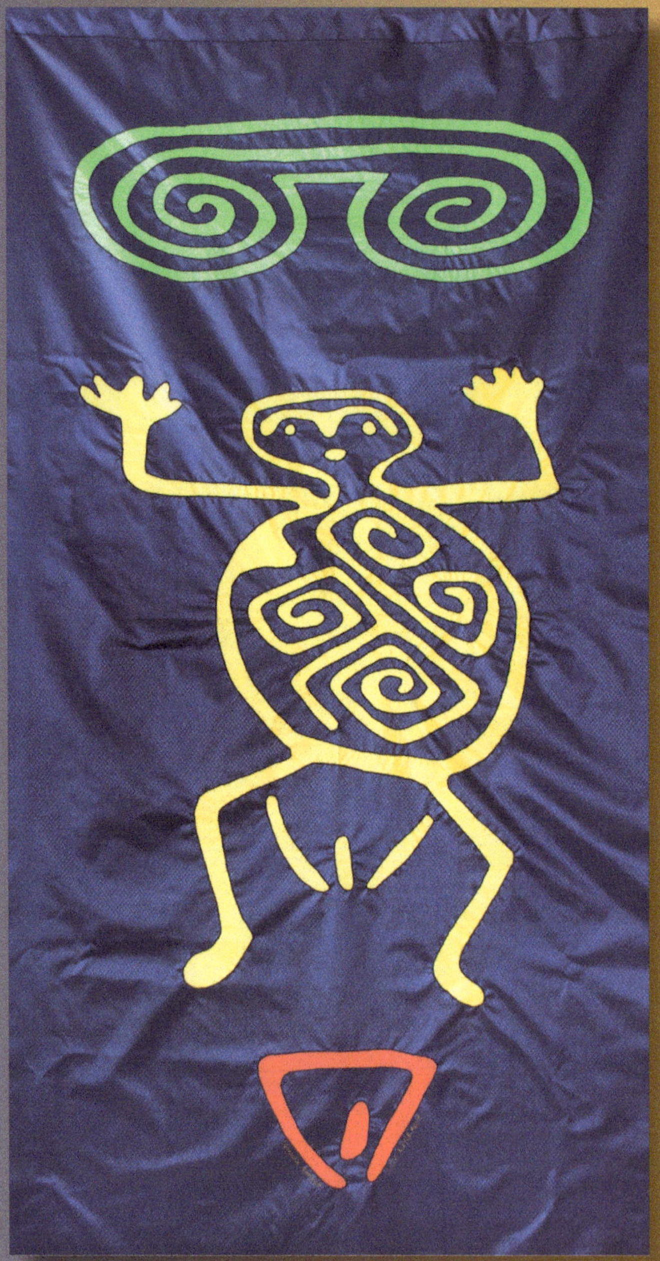

Venezuelan matriglyph rock art is from the magical world of the indigenous inhabitants of the northwest Amazon region. Vulvas are prominent in the rock art, as are spirals representing both the human and spiritual journeys. I see the Piedra de la Fertilidad matriglyph telling the human story of survival through the great mother.

Venezuela Matriglyph

Source: Rock art, n.d. Piedra de la fertilidad Municipio Puerto Cabello, Estado Carabobo

Diosa Lluvia, Goddess of Rain, is the best known petroglyph in the Vigirima River valley of Venezuela. She is bundled up and represents winter rains. Stylized snails on both sides symbolize winter moisture. Piedra Pintado, which means "painted rock," may have served as a religious and ceremonial center for the pre-Hispanic indigenous people. The petroglyph style has been linked to the Taíno and Arawak cultures of the Caribbean.

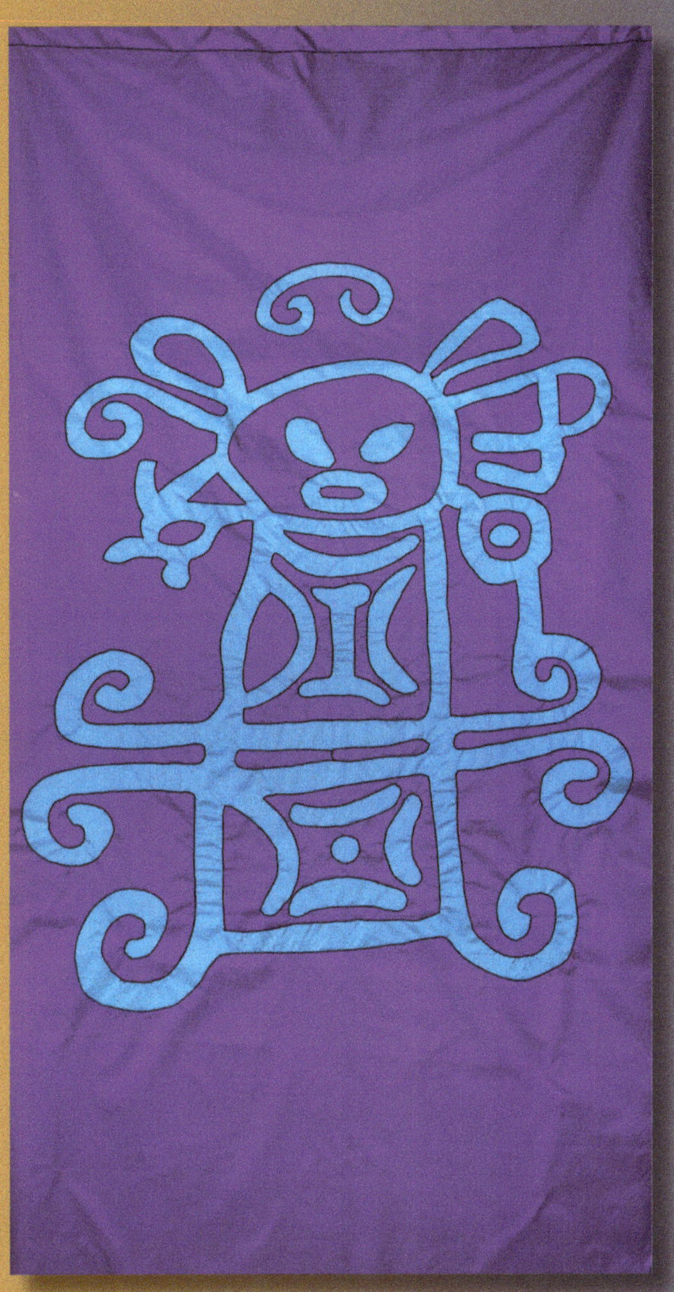

Diosa Lluvia

Source: Rock art, n.d.
Painted Rock Archaeological Park
Vigirima, Carabobo, Venezuela

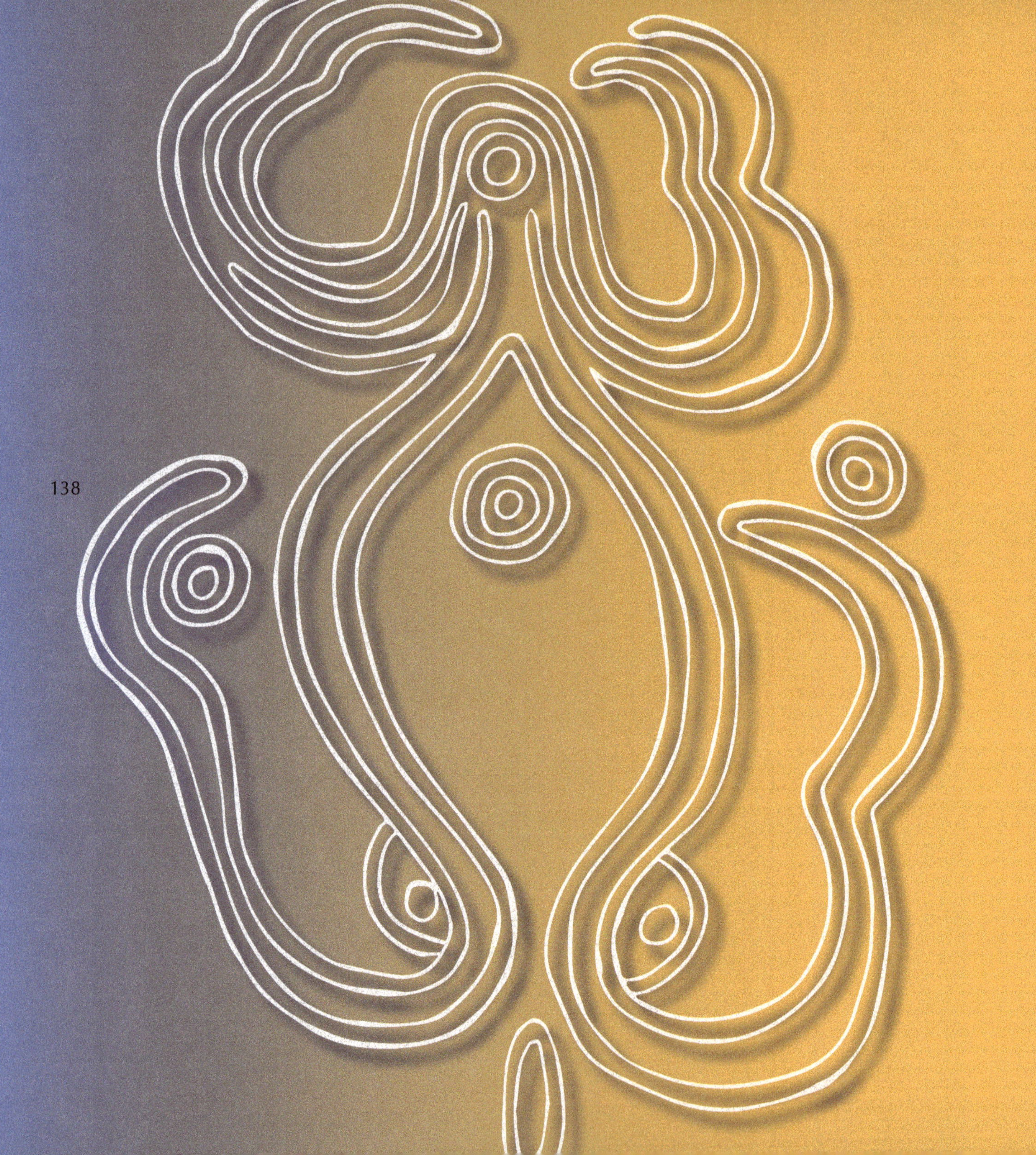

Rapa Nui, also known as Easter Island, lies thousands of miles west off the coast of Chile in the middle of the southern Pacific Ocean. Famous for its Maori large standing stone statues, it became a special territory of Chile in 1888.

Easter Island rock art was overlooked until 1981, when an intensive documentation project began. It soon became apparent that the rock carvings and paintings represented a body of work that was both sophisticated and unique.

Over 4000 petroglyphs have been documented on Rapa Nui, with a variety of motifs. There are also several thousand *cupules,* or small carved hollows usually three to five centimeters in diameter, which usually act as decorative elements around petroglyph panels. Most of the petroglyphs are carved in bas relief and, in some instances, painted, particularly with pigments of red and white. Paintings can be found in several caves as well as in stone dwellings.

South America | Chile | Easter Island

Easter Island's cupules may relate to fertility, as they appear to be closely associated with *komari,* or "vulvas." An example of this is found at the sacred ceremonial village of Orongo, where the two elements are on a carved house post, which features a group of *komari* and cupules in association with faces and birdmen. There are hundreds of *komari* carved into the rocks as well as on portable objects from pillows and skulls. Next to cupules, vulva signs comprise the largest design category on Easter Island. I was excited to find a rock art image combining vulva, cupules and bird-like wings, which I see as bird woman.

Baile Pájaro Dancing Bird Goddess Matriglyph is a rock art image from Easter Island. There are many vulva symbols on the famous Maori giant standing figures on the island and on its rock art. In a fragile environment, new life was essential for survival.

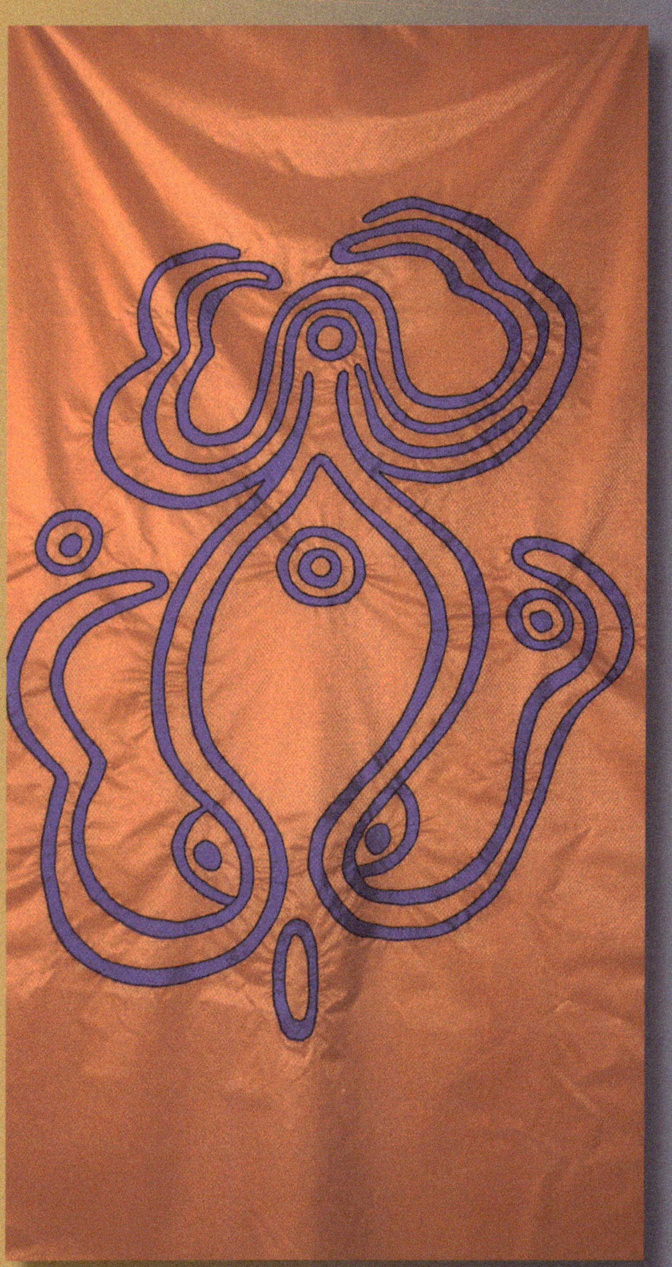

Baile Pájaro Dancing Bird Goddess Matriglyph

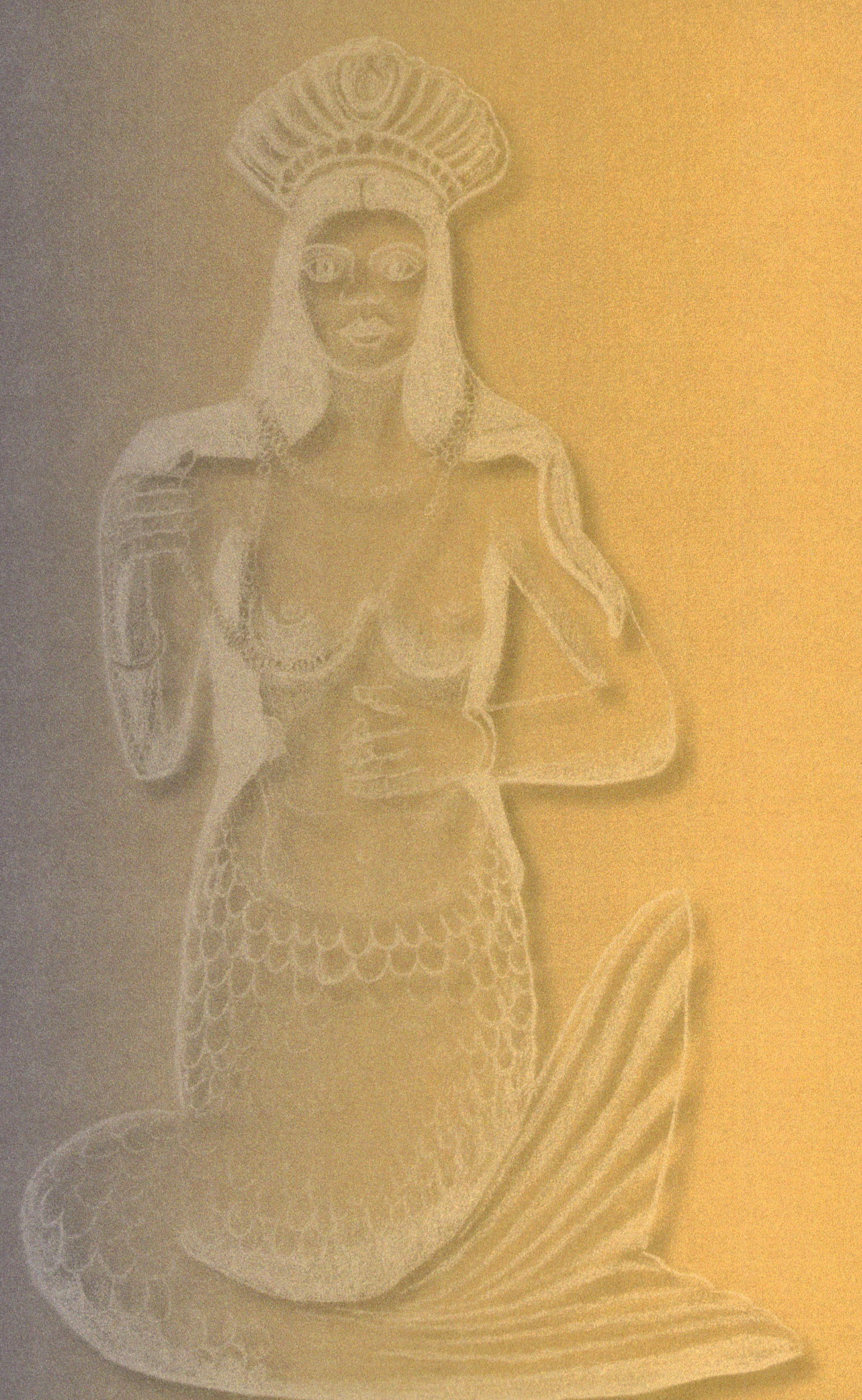

Some time ago, I met Edemir Rossi, a Brazilian shaman healer. After using some of my Black Madonna Goddess banners in a workshop, he asked if they could take them to Brazil. I created Nossa Senhora de Aparecida for the journey. Edemir continues to do healing journeys to Brazil and México and my goddess banners hang for them.

Syncretism refers to the coming together of cultures and sharing of traditions evident in Brazil, such as the way West Africans and Portuguese melded their traditions with those of the indigenous people. Afro-Brazilian Candomblé religious communities are led by older priestesses, contemporary examples of ancestral matriarchal organization. Older women are considered to be protective progenitors, healers and guardians of morality and social order. Candomblé practitioners focus on the life force that infuses all beings with divine energy. This is achieved through ritual, drumming, dance, sacred foods and trance structured around a physical space, the *terreiro*, which symbolically recreates a mythical African village community.[xviii]

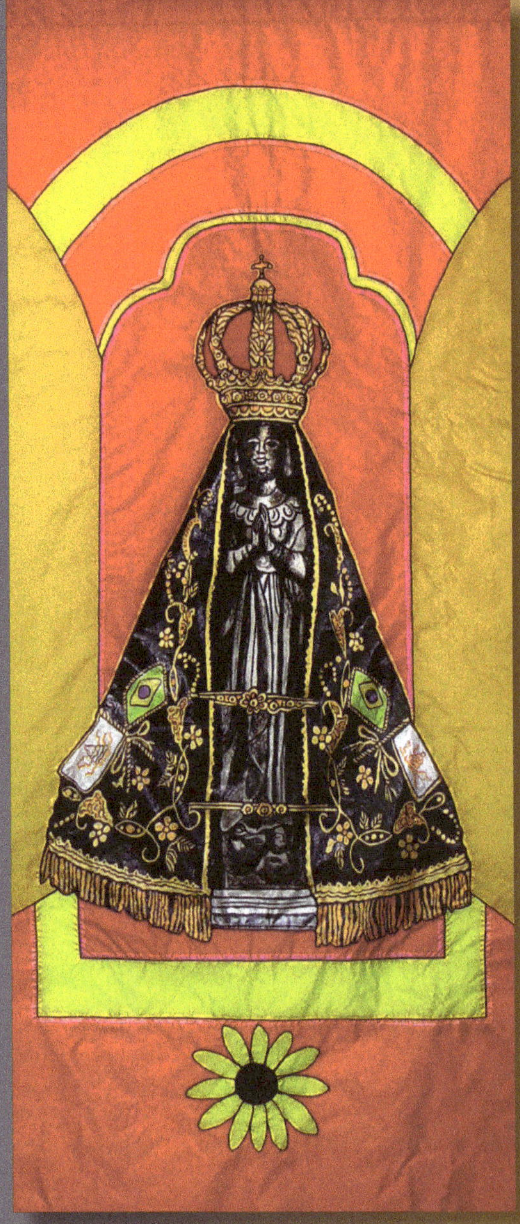

Nossa Senhora, who is the mother of the excluded and patroness of the poor, is also called Our Lady Aparecida. She is a beautiful, petite, black figure standing on a crescent moon. The Aparecida, who is also patroness of Brazil, was found by a fisherman in the Paraíba River in the state of Sao Paulo. She is enshrined in a basilica and is carried in processions and celebrations on her feast day, which is October 12. In the Afro-Brazilian tradition, the Black Madonna Aparecida is connected to Orixá Oxum, the Great Mother of Africa, who is the patroness of pregnancy, children, rivers, seas, gold, honey, laughter, beauty, seduction, shrewdness and wisdom. She is our supreme ancestral mother.

Nossa Senhora, Nuestro Senora Aparecida

Source: Dark wood sculpture, 1717 CE
Aparecida Basilica
Sao Paulo, Brazil

Photo by Malgorzata Oleszkiewicz-Peralba.

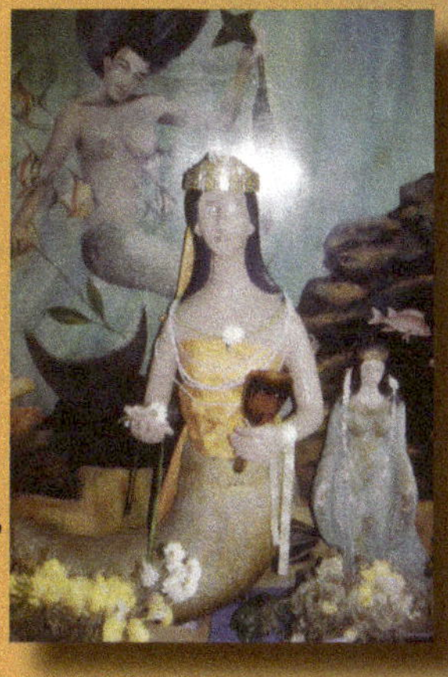

Oshun is the Yoruba Goddess of sweet waters. In Brazilian Candomblé, she is called Oxum and is depicted as a mermaid with flowing black hair. Figureheads on European trading ships possibly influenced her image. She is omnipresent and omnipotent.[xvix]

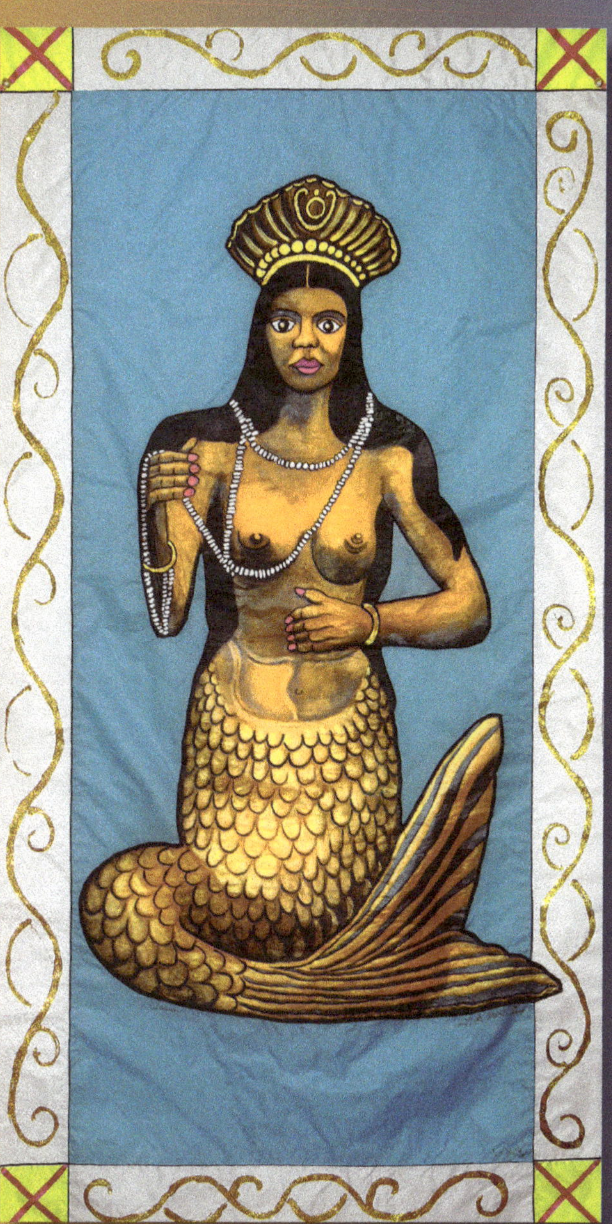

Oshun

Source: Malgorzata Oleszkiewicz-Peralba's photo of Oxum's sculpture, 1996 Casa Branca Terreiro Salvador, Bahia, Brazil

Endnotes

[i] Moyers, Bill. *Joseph Campbell and The Power of Myth*. Retrieved September 24, 2015 from www.billmoyers.com/spotlight/download-joseph-campbell-and-the-power-of-myth-audio.

[ii] Allen, Paula Gunn. *The Sacred Hoop*, (Boston: Beacon Press, 1986), 13.

[iii] See more about Susan Elizabeth Hale in her book *Song and Silence: Voicing the Soul* (Albuquerque, NM: La Alameda Press,1995).

[iv] Randolph, Carol Patterson. "The 'Yellow Women' Prehistoric Kachina Mask Paintings of the Keres," Utah Rock Art Research, XIV (1995). Accessed September 24, 2015 at http://www.utahrockart.org/pubs/proceedings/papers/14-08_Patterson_Rudolph_-_The_Yellow_Women_Prehistoric_Kachina_Mask_Paintings_Of_The_Keres.pdf.

[v] Grant, Campbell. *The Rock Paintings of the Chumash: A Study of California Indian Culture* (San Luis Obispo, CA: Santa Barbara Museum of Natural History,1993).

[vi] Getty, Adele. *Goddess of Living Nature*, (London: Thames and Hudson,1990), 94.

Endnotes

[vii] To find out more about Laura Kealoha Yardley, see her book *The Heart of Huna* (Honolulu, HI: Advanced Neuro Dynamics Inc., 1982).

[viii] See more about the Kihawahine at http://waihili.blogspot.com/2006/04/hidden-meaning-of-moo-goddesses.html and http://www.hawaiialive.org/realms.php?sub=Wao+Lani&treasure=555&offset=0.

[ix] Foundation for the Advancement of Mesoamerican Studies (FAMSI). *John Pohl's Mesoamerica*. September 24, 2015 http://www.famsi.org/research/pohl/chronology.html#PRECLASSIC.

[x] American anthropologist and archaeologist Zelia Nuttall reportedly translated Cuicuilco into Spanish as "lugar donde se hacen cantos y danzas," which in turn translates into English as "the place where songs and dances are made."

[xi] Cortés, Noemi Cruz. *Las señoras de la Luna*, (México: UNAM, 2005), 15.

[xii] Ibid.

[xiii] Tedlock, Dennis. *Popol Vuh: The Mayan Book of the Dawn of Life*. (New York: Simon & Schuster, 1996), 103.

Endnotes

[xiv] Cosentino, Donald J., ed. *Sacred Arts of Haitian Vodou.* (Los Angeles: UCLA Fowler Museum, 1995).

[xv] For more information, visit the Bradshaw Foundation at www.bradshawfoundation.com.

[xvi] See more about Kathy Doore at www.labyrinthina.com.

[xvii] See more about Heide Göttner-Abendroth at www.hagia.de/de/international-academy-hagia.html.

[xviii] This section is based on the Chapter 3 of Malgorzata Oleszkiewicz-Peralba's book, *The Black Madonna in Latin America and Europe: Tradition and Transformation* (Albuquerque, NM: New Mexico University Press, 2007).

[xvix] For more on Oxum, see Malgorzata Oleszkiewicz-Peralba's book, *The Black Madonna in Latin America and Europe: Tradition and Transformation* (Albuquerque, NM: New Mexico University Press, 2007).

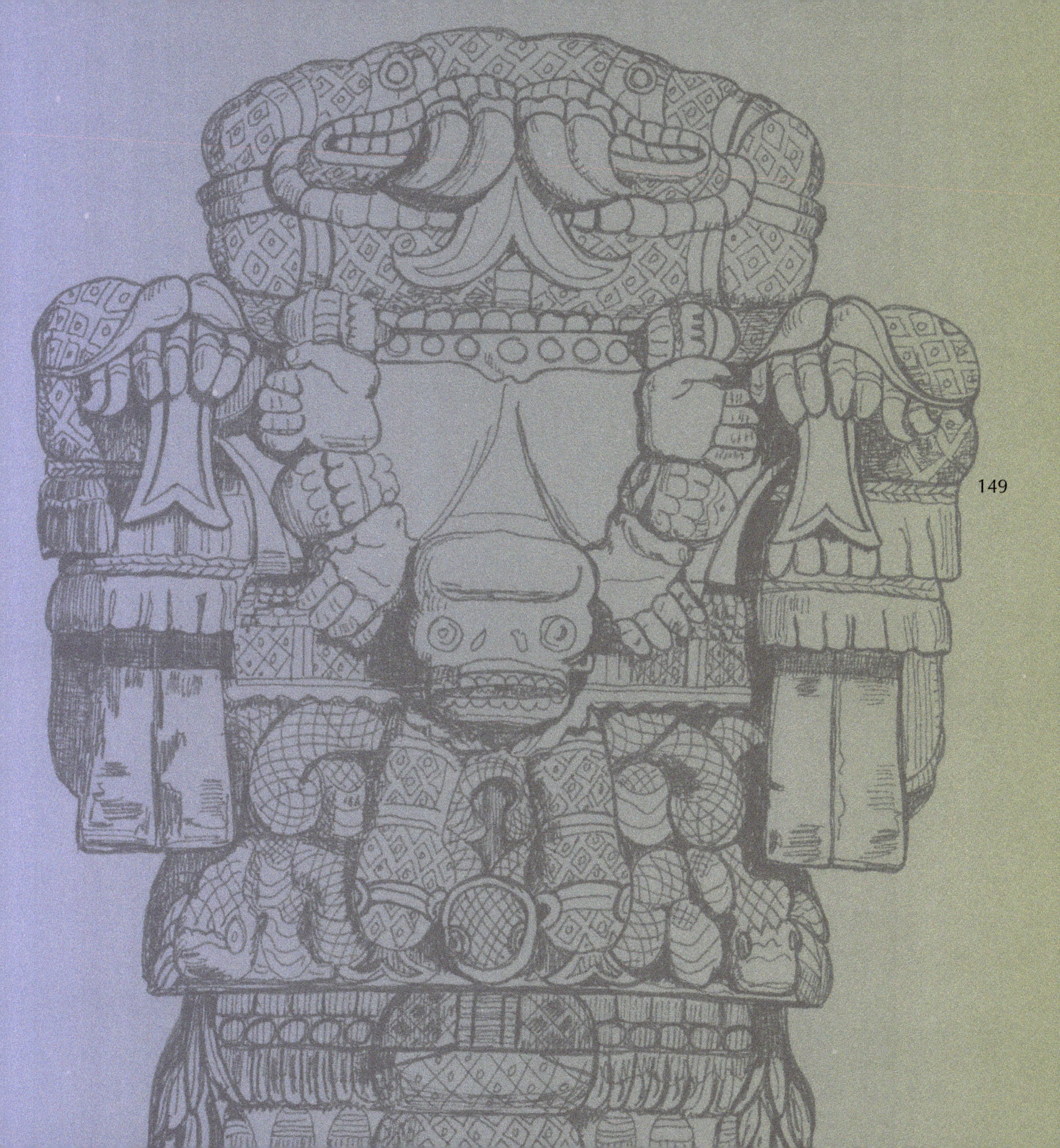

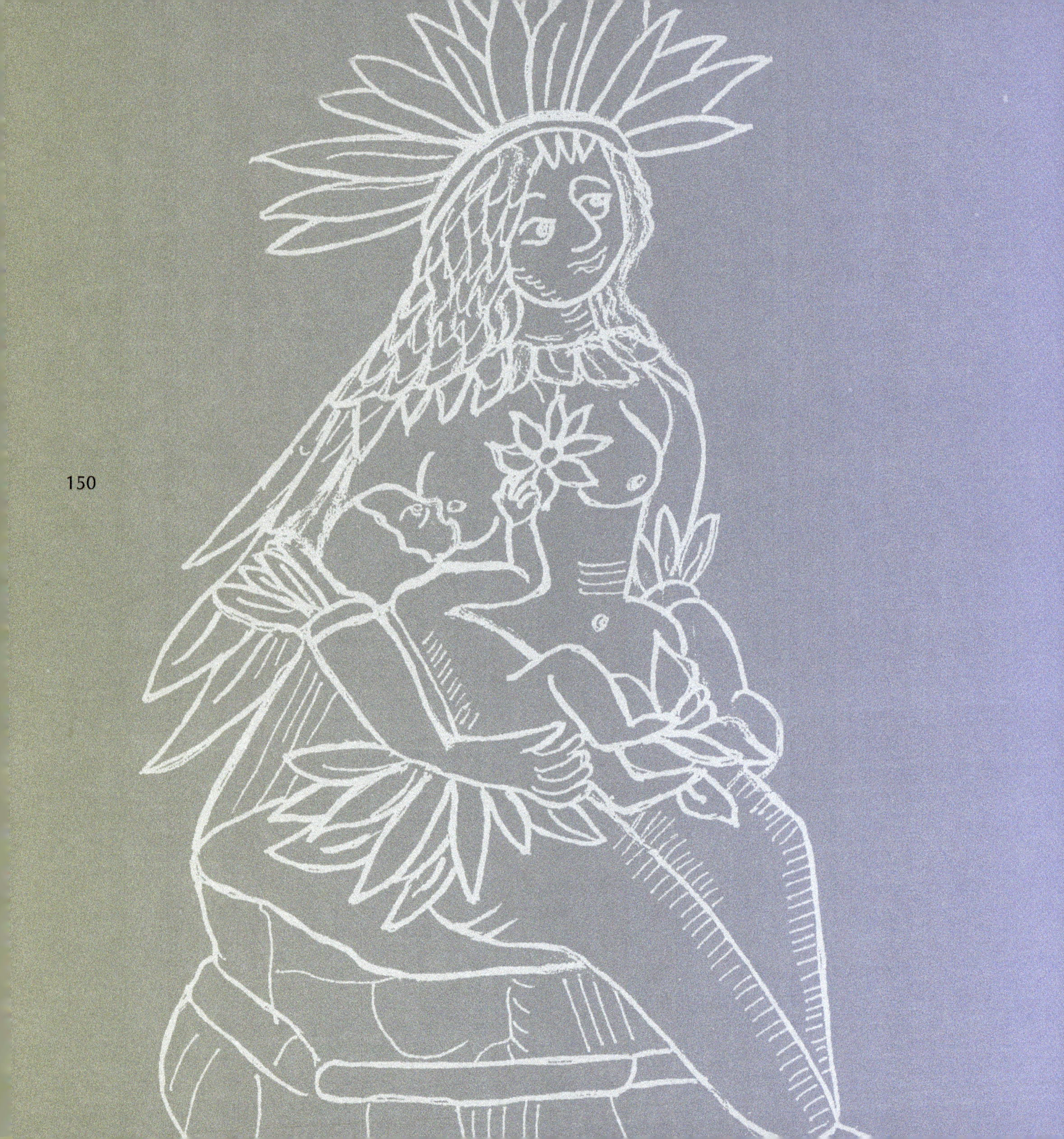

150

Acknowledgements

I am deeply grateful for my publisher, Goddess Ink, and to Anne Key, my editor and interpreter. My gratitude to all those who brought their expertise to bear on the interpretation of these powerful images: Dr. Carolyn Tate, Veronica Iglesias, Dr. Malgorzata Oleszkiewicz-Peralba, Dr. Candace Kant, and Dr. Ann Filemyr. Thanks to Lynne Melcombe for careful editing and to Louise Keirnes, a superb vyxillographer, and to Pat Alles who helped create a beautiful book.

Muchas Gracias to Cecilia Corcoran and Goddess GATE, Apela Colorado, Sandra Dayton, Angela Dolmetsch, Kathy Doore, Kathy Pasley, Robert Rocheleau, Edemir Rossi, Sandra Roman, Maria Suarez Toro, Jose R. Altamirana Vallenas, and my niece Katie Hoffner for helping me find the Goddesses in the Americas. For the women and men who traveled with and helped me on my many journeys in the Americas.

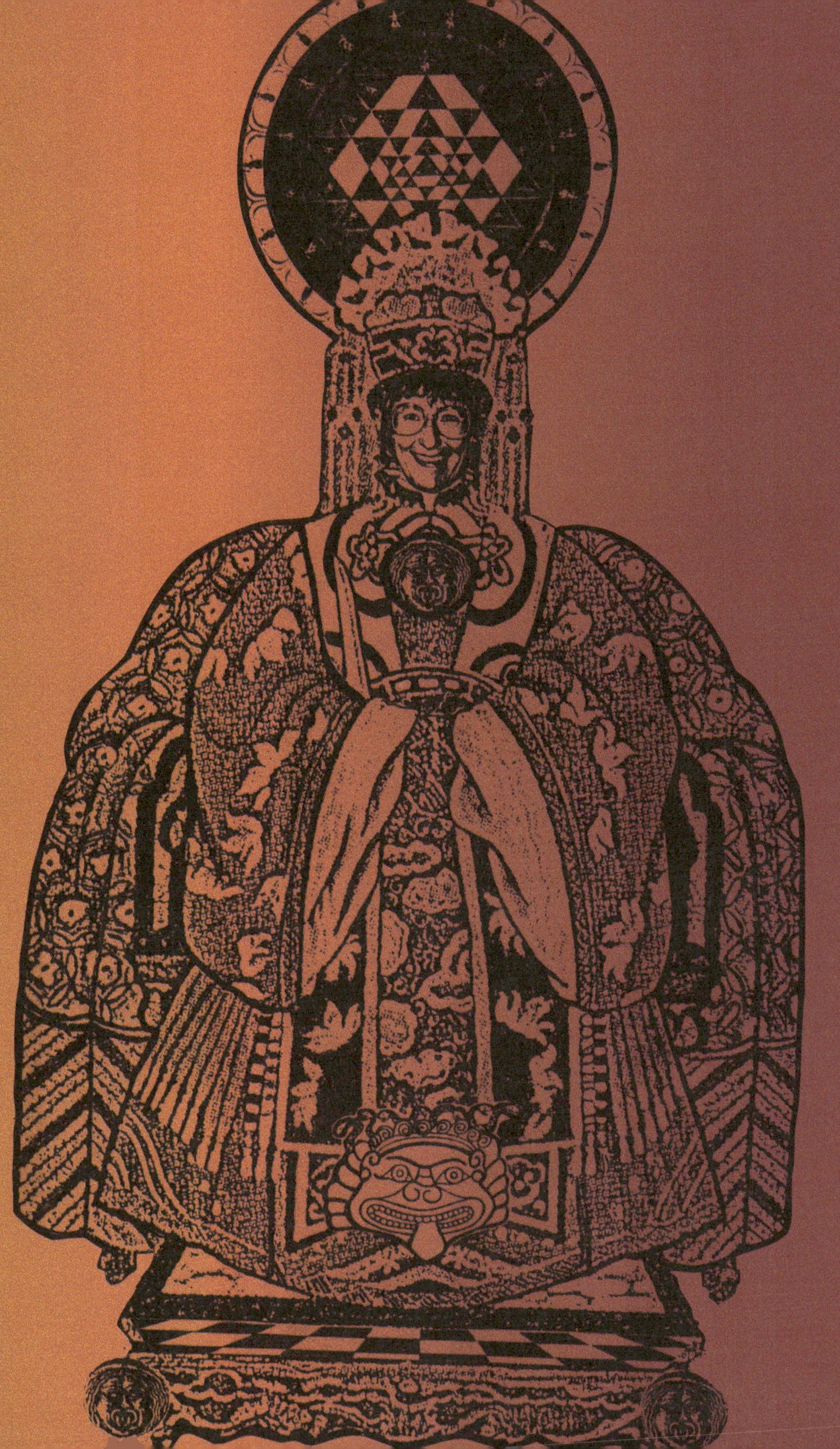

About the Author

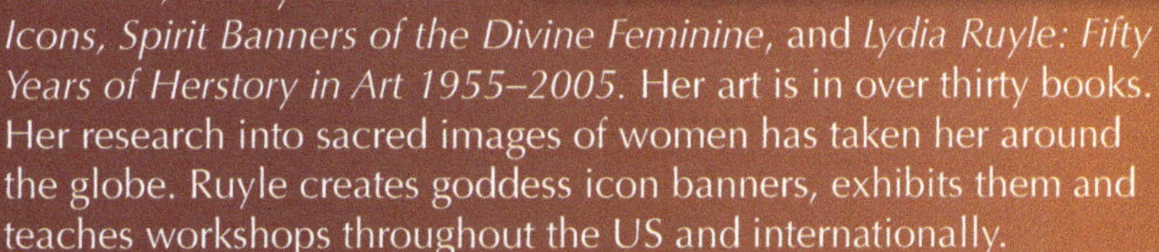

Lydia Ruyle is an artist, scholar, and author of *Goddess Icons: Spirit Banners of the Divine Feminine*, *Turkey: Goddess Icons, Spirit Banners of the Divine Feminine*, and *Lydia Ruyle: Fifty Years of Herstory in Art 1955–2005*. Her art is in over thirty books. Her research into sacred images of women has taken her around the globe. Ruyle creates goddess icon banners, exhibits them and teaches workshops throughout the US and internationally.

Ruyle began making the banners based on research and study which began in Ephesus, Turkey in 1995, where she was on the trail of the Mother Goddess in Anatolia. She has now produced over 300 banners, which have flown in Australia, New Zealand, Canada, Britain, France, Luxembourg, Italy, Spain, Iceland, Switzerland, Greece, Serbia, Bulgaria, Romania, Germany, Austria, Czech Republic, Hungary, Poland, Russia, Turkey, Ghana, Kenya, South Africa, Brazil, México, Peru, Argentina, Costa Rica, Japan, Nepal, Bhutan, Tibet, China, Cambodia, South Korea and more than half of the United States

The banners fly at sacred sites to empower and teach, and to share their stories around the world. They hang in museums, colleges, kindergartens, temples, universities, conference halls, studios, palapas, galleries, monasteries, festivals, graduations, art centers and a women's prison.

To see Ruyle's work visit: www.lydiaruyle.com

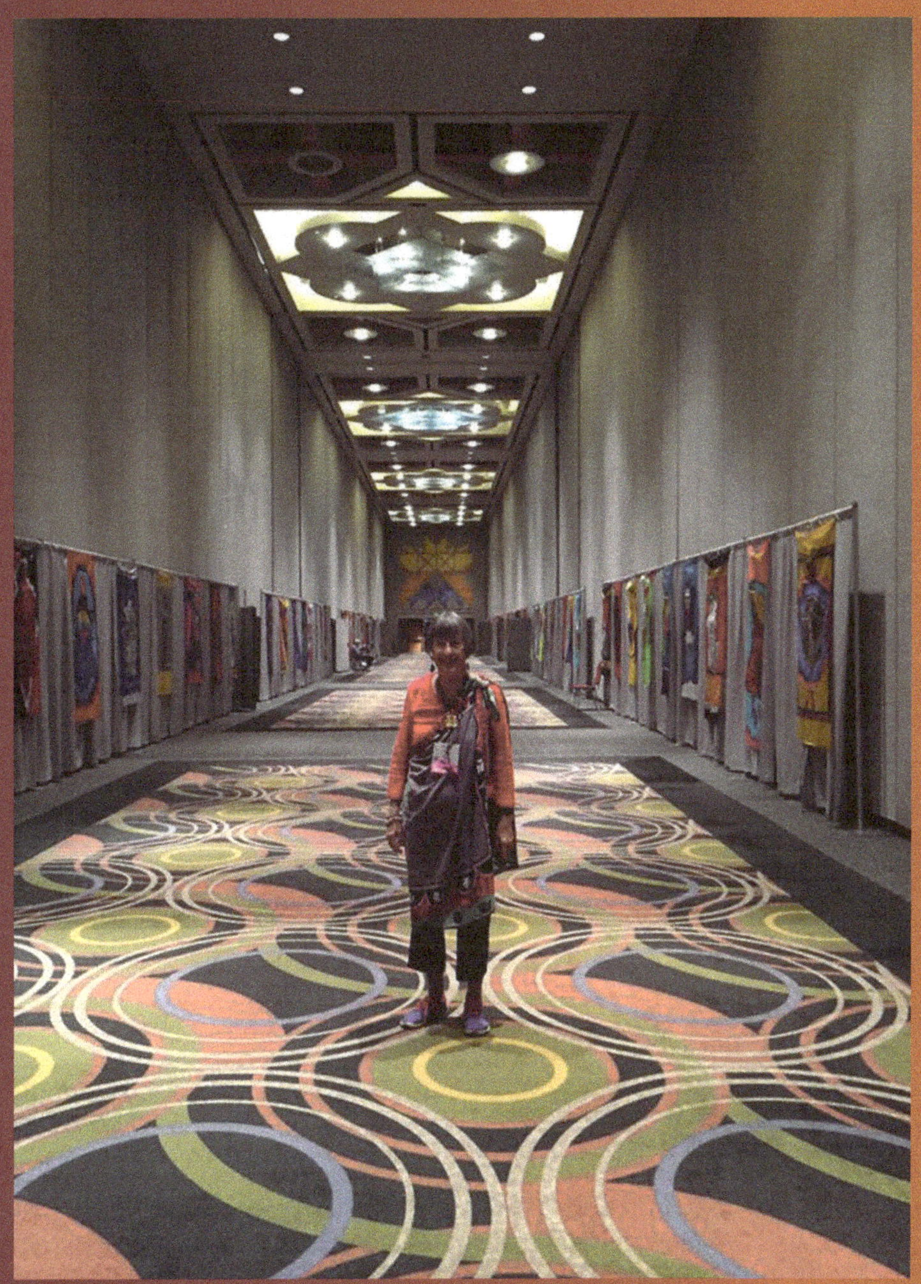

Lydia and banners at World Parliament of Religions

www.ingramcontent.com/pod-product-compliance
Lightning Source LLC
LaVergne TN
LVHW060639110826
845147LV00018B/1010

* 9 7 8 0 9 9 6 9 6 1 7 1 4 *